The Local Magistrates of Roman Spain

Local aristocracies were crucial to the administrative and social assimilation of provincial communities in the Roman world. Leonard Curchin focuses on local political élites in the Iberian Peninsula, providing the first comprehensive and up-to-date prosopographical catalogue of all known local magistrates in Roman Spain.

Curchin makes full use of the latest epigraphic discoveries, including not only the recorded careers of local magistrates but also the new Lex Irnitana. In his introduction he examines both the political role of the magistrates and the social mechanics of élite romanization. Among the traditional assumptions he challenges are the standard size of the local senates, the fixed order of offices, and the nature of the 'quattuorvirate.' He also discusses magistrates' origins, career progression, duties, social status, personal nomenclature, and private wealth.

Entries in the catalogue are arranged alphabetically by city within each province. Indexes of names and magistracies facilitate cross-referencing. The volume includes statistical tables as well as maps.

LEONARD A. CURCHIN is an Associate Professor in the Department of Classics, University of Waterloo.

PHOENIX

Journal of the Classical Association of Canada
Revue de la Société canadienne des études classiques
Supplementary Volume XXVIII
Tome supplémentaire XXVIII

LEONARD A. CURCHIN

The Local Magistrates
of Roman Spain

UNIVERSITY OF TORONTO PRESS
Toronto Buffalo London

Canadian Cataloguing in Publication Data

Curchin, Leonard A.
The local magistrates of Roman Spain

(Phoenix. Supplementary volume ; 28 = Phoenix.
Tome supplémentaire, ISSN 0079-1784 ; 28)
Includes bibliographical references.
ISBN 0-8020-5841-8

1. Spain – Officials and employees – History.
2. Spain – History – Roman period, 218 BC-41 AD
3. Magistrates, Roman. I. Title. II. Series: Phoenix.
Supplementary volume (Toronto, Ont.) ; 28.

DP9-.C87 1990   936.6'03   C89-090743-9

CONTENTS

MAPS

PREFACE

Of this I am convinced: that it is better, braver and more helpful for us to believe we should investigate what we do not know, than to assume we cannot or should not.

Plato *Meno* 86 b

While we shall never possess a thorough understanding of the social history of the Hispano-Roman upper classes, the Iberian Peninsula offers a wealth of information on local, romanized élites which has never been dealt with in any systematic or comprehensive fashion. In preparing my doctoral thesis, 'The Creation of a Romanized Elite in Spain' (University of Ottawa 1981), I was able to utilize the prosopographical studies of Spanish priests by Etienne and Alföldy, and of Spanish senators and knights by Wiegels; the catalogues and discussion provided by these scholars represent an essential research tool for the provincial historian. But while the careers of these officials have been exhaustively studied, those of municipal magistrates (by far the most numerous of the attested members of the Spanish élite) have been almost entirely neglected, despite the recognized importance of local élites in the romanization of provincial society and the fact that the holders of provincial priesthoods and junior equestrian posts were frequently recruited from the urban aristocracy. Given the lack of an up-to-date epigraphic corpus (the last attempt was published in 1892) or of an authoritative treatise on Spanish coins (whose chronology remains uncomfortably haphazard), it is hardly surprising that no one has until now undertaken the labour-intensive task of cataloguing all known magistrates. One area where considerable work has been done is the study of Spanish colonial and municipal laws (those of Urso, Malaca, and Salpensa), though little effort has been made to correlate their provisions with the recorded careers of real officials.

However, the recent publication of the new and important *Lex Irnitana* has compelled abandonment or modification of many previous assumptions, and its full implications have yet to be realized.

These remarks should serve to explain the origin and rationale of the present monograph. Its purpose is twofold: first, the presentation of a catalogue which compiles, for the first time, all known local magistrates of Roman Spain, who now number nearly a thousand; and second, a study of the social dynamics of the Roman magisterial system in Spain. If the scope of the work seems limited, it is precisely because local magistrates are the one element of the elite which has hitherto lacked the attention it merits. By filling this gap I hope to have paved the way for further study of the social history of the provincial upper classes in the Iberian Peninsula, and ultimately throughout the Empire.

I have the pleasant task of thanking the many friends and colleagues who have assisted at various stages of my research, as well as the Calgary Institute for the Humanities which funded the initial preparation of the manuscript. Professor Colin Wells first interested me in the romanization of provincial elites and directed my attention to Spain. Professors Robert Etienne and Robert Knapp read an early version of the draft and offered valuable comments, as did the late Professor Edith Wightman for chapter 6. Professor Wightman's work on the romanization of Gallia Belgica also inspired several of the graphs presented in that chapter. Finally I wish to thank the readers of the Canadian Federation for the Humanities and of the *Phoenix* Editorial Board for a number of helpful suggestions.

This book has been published with the help of a grant from the Canadian Federation for the Humanities, using funds provided by the Social Sciences and Humanities Research Council of Canada.

L.A.C.
Waterloo, Ontario
May 1988

Postscript As this volume goes to press, I have been unable to obtain *AE* 1986 or P. Palol and J. Vilella, *Clunia II: Epigrafía* (Madrid 1987), which may contain new magistrates. Also, Dr A. Stylow kindly informs me of a new inscription from Regina (Baetica) naming Iustus Modesti f., *decemvir maximus*.

ABBREVIATIONS

Ancient and modern works are normally cited according to the system employed in *The Oxford Classical Dictionary* 2nd ed (Oxford 1971) or other standard reference works, especially *L'Année philologique* for periodicals.

In addition, the following abbreviations of Latin terms should be noted: conv. for *conventus*, f. for *filius* in naming by filiation, i.d. for *iure dicundo*, p.H.c. for *provinciae Hispaniae citerioris*, and r.p. for *rei publicae*. Inv. stands for the inventory number at the Archaeological Museum of Mérida.

Abbott and Johnson MARE   F.F. Abbott and A.C. Johnson *Municipal Administration in the Roman Empire* Princeton 1926
AEA   *Archivo Español de Arqueología*
AHAM   *Anales de Historia Antigua y Medieval*
Albertos OPP   M.L. Albertos Firmat *La onomástica personal primitiva de Hispania Tarraconensis y Bética.* Salamanca 1966
Alföldy *Fasti*   G. Alföldy *Fasti Hispanienses* Wiesbaden 1969
Alföldy *Flamines*   G. Alföldy *Flamines provinciae Hispaniae Citerioris* Madrid 1973
Arnold *Roman System³*   W.T. Arnold *The Roman System of Provincial Administration* 3rd ed Oxford 1914 (repr Freeport 1971)
Bol. Aur.   Boletín Auriense
BRAH   *Boletín de la Real Academia de la Historia*
Callender *Roman Amphorae*   M.H. Callender *Roman Amphorae* London 1965
CIC   J. Gómez-Pantoja *El conventus iuridicus Caesaraugustanus: Personas y ciudades* (a. 45-a.D. 192) diss, Universidad de Navarra 1983

x Abbreviations

CIP 'Corpus Inscriptionum Palentinorum [sic]' in L. Sagredo San Eustaquio and S. Crespo Ortiz de Zárate Epigrafía romana de la provincia de Palencia Palencia 1978

Clavel and Lévêque Villes et structures M. Clavel and P. Lévêque Villes et structures urbaines dans l'Occident romain Paris 1971

CPIL R. Hurtado de San Antonio Corpus provincial de inscripciones latinas (Cáceres) Cáceres 1977

EJER A. d'Ors Epigrafía jurídica de la España romana Madrid 1953

ELSaguntum F. Beltrán Lloris Epigrafía latina de Saguntum y su territorium Valencia 1980

ERAE L. García Iglesias Epigrafía romana de Augusta Emerita diss, Madrid 1973

EREsp. Pflaum in Les empereurs romains d'Espagne Paris 1965

ERLérida F. Lara Peinado Epigrafía romana de Lérida Lérida 1973

ERZaragoza G. Fatás and M.A. Martín Bueno Epigrafía romana de Zaragoza y su provincia Zaragoza 1977

Estructuras sociales Francisco Martín in Estructuras sociales durante la Antigüedad: Actas del I Coloquio de Historia Antigua Oviedo 1978

Etienne Culte R. Etienne Le culte impérial dans la Péninsule Ibérique Paris 1958

FC J. Alarcão and R. Etienne ed Fouilles de Conimbriga 7 vols Paris 1974-9

Galsterer Untersuchungen H. Galsterer Untersuchungen zum römischen Städtewesen auf der iberischen Halbinsel Berlin 1971

Gil O. Gil Farrés La moneda hispánica en la edad antigua Madrid 1966

Gorges Villas J.-G. Gorges Les villas hispano-romaines Paris 1979

Grant FITA M. Grant From Imperium to Auctoritas Cambridge 1946

HAEp. Hispania Antiqua Epigraphica

Hardy Charters E.G. Hardy Three Spanish Charters and Other Documents Oxford 1912

Hardy Laws E.G. Hardy Six Roman Laws Oxford 1911

Heiss Monnaies A. Heiss Description générale des monnaies antiques d'Espagne Paris 1870

Hisp. Ant. Hispania Antiqua

ILER J. Vives Inscripciones latinas de la España romana 2 vols Barcelona 1971-2

ILGranada M. Pastor Muñoz and A. Mendoza Eguaras Inscripciones latinas de la provincia de Granada Granada 1987

IRB S. Mariner Bigorra Inscripciones romanas de Barcelona 1973

IRC   G. Fabre et al. Inscriptions romaines de Catalogne 2 vols Paris 1984–5

Irn.   Lex municipii Irnitani (=) J. González 'The Lex Irnitana: A New Copy of the Flavian Municipal Law' JRS 76 [1986] 147–243)

IRPac.   J. d'Encarnação Inscrições romanas do conventus Pacensis Coimbra 1984

IRPC   J. González Inscripciones romanas de la provincia de Cádiz Cádiz 1982

Jacques Liberté   F. Jacques Le privilège de liberté: Politique impériale et autonomie municipale dans les cités de l'Occident Paris 1984

Kajanto Cognomina   I. Kajanto The Latin Cognomina Helsinki 1965

Knapp Roman Experience   R.C. Knapp Aspects of the Roman Experience in Iberia 206–100 BC Vitoria and Valladolid 1977

Langhammer Magistratus   W. Langhammer Die rechtliche und soziale Stellung der magistratus municipales und der decuriones Wiesbaden 1973

Lex Mun. Tarent.   Lex municipii Tarentini (ILS 6086 = FIRA i² 18)

Liebenam Städteverwaltung   W. Liebenam Städteverwaltung im römischen Kaiserreiche Leipzig 1900 (repr Amsterdam 1967)

Mackie Administration   N. Mackie Local Administration in Roman Spain AD 14–212 Oxford 1983

Mal.   Lex municipii Malacitani (ILS 6089 = FIRA i² 24)

MCV   Mélanges de la Casa de Velázquez

MM   Madrider Mitteilungen

NAH   Noticiario Arqueológico Hispánico

Palomar Lapesa Onomástica   M. Palomar Lapesa La onomástica personal pre-latina de la antigua Lusitania Salamanca 1957

Pastor Los Astures   M. Pastor Muñoz Los Astures durante el imperio romano Oviedo 1977

PB   C. Castillo García Prosopographia Baetica Pamplona 1965

Pflaum Carrières   H.-G. Pflaum Les carrières procuratoriennes équestres sous le Haut-Empire romain Paris 1960–1

PME   H. Devijver Prosopographia militiarum equestrium quae fuerunt ab Augusto ad Gallienum Louvain 1976–80

RIT   G. Alföldy Die römischen Inschriften von Tarraco Berlin 1975

Salp.   Lex municipii Salpensani (ILS 6088 = FIRA i² 23)

Schulze Eigennamen   W. Schulze Zur Geschichte lateinischer Eigennamen Berlin 1904 (repr Berlin 1966)

Stevenson Administration   G.H. Stevenson Roman Provincial Administration till the Age of the Antonines New York 1939

Syme RP   R. Syme Roman Papers ed E. Badian and A.R. Birley 5 vols Oxford 1979–87

Tab. Her.   *Tabula Heracleensis* (*ILS* 6085 = *FIRA* I² 13)

Thouvenot *Essai*²   R. Thouvenot *Essai sur la province romaine de Bétique* 2nd ed Paris 1973

Urs.   *Lex coloniae Genetivae Iuliae sive Ursonensis* (*ILS* 6087 = *FIRA* I² 21)

Veny *Corpus*   C. Veny *Corpus de las inscripciones baleáricas hasta la dominación árabe* Madrid 1965

Villaronga *Aes Coinage*   L. Villaronga Garriga *The Aes Coinage of Emporion* Oxford 1977

VM   A. Vives *La moneda hispánica* 4 vols Madrid 1926–8

Wiegels   R. Wiegels *Die römischen Senatoren und Ritter aus den hispanischen Provinzen* diss, Freiburg 1971

Wiseman *New Men*   T.P. Wiseman *New Men in the Roman Senate 139 BC–14 AD* Oxford 1971

Note Boldface numbers in the text, tables, notes, and indexes refer to the Catalogue entries found on pp 137–242.

Introduction

1

The Evolution of the Magisterial System

The study of local élites in the Roman Empire could hardly find a more appropriate starting-point than the Spanish provinces. Apart from being Rome's earliest provincial acquisition on the European mainland, Spain – or at any rate her civilized southern and eastern sectors – achieved a level of romanization unexcelled anywhere else in the Empire (albeit matched, eventually, by neighbouring Narbonensis). This conjunction of precedence and progress allows us to trace the complete development of the municipal system in Spain from pre-Roman times to the Late Roman period, thereby providing a model or case-study with instructive implications for the Empire as a whole. As a leading provincial specialist has rightly counselled, 'any account of Roman municipalization must turn to the Iberian peninsula.'[1]

One cannot over-emphasize the role of the local unit, the city, as a focal point of romanization. Within this urban context, the municipal élite – the local magistrates and town council – were instrumental in making provincial romanization feasible. It was in the cities that the mechanics of romanization, the interaction and assimilation of natives with Romans, were worked out.[2] Magistracies, in both the Roman and pre-Roman periods, were the status symbols, and indeed the political power bases, of the local aristocracy. Participation in local government was the preserve, duty, and hallmark of civilized, upper-class provincials under the Early Empire,[3] though later, as we shall discuss, it threatened to become their bane.

The existence of local magistrates in Spain is not demonstrably earlier than the third century BC. Prior to the introduction of magistracies, the political institutions in Spain – so far as we are informed by classical sources – consisted essentially of two types, monarchical and tribal, each with its own geographic affinities. The monarchical system was confined to the southern and eastern coasts, precisely those regions which had been colonized and influenced by the Phoenicians and Greeks; hence there exists a strong possibility that it was imported from the eastern Mediterranean. In the west, north, and centre of the peninsula we find no kings, but rather a clan system dominated by tribal war-lords (*principes*). The so-called princes (*reguli*) of the Ebro river valley appear to have been little more than tribal chieftains.[4]

The transformation from regional monarchies and tribal chiefdoms to a system of local magistrates marks a decisive change in the political structure of pre-Roman Spain. The introduction of local magistracies heralds a new concept, that of the city as a political unit, with its own internal government and appointees. Unlike the king or chief, whose power is permanent, personal, and absolute, the magistrate exercises a temporary mandate entrusted to him by the city, to which he remains responsible and accountable.[5] (This need for accountability, it may be recalled, was instrumental in replacing kingship at Rome with a system of annually elected magistrates.) The institution of magistracies is an important, though not obligatory, concomitant of urbanization and represents a genuine advance in civilized government.

The first known Spanish magistrates make their appearance in 206 BC, in the context of the Second Punic War. In that year the Roman commander P. Cornelius Scipio captured Castax (Castulo) in southeastern Spain and appointed one of its leading citizens, a man of high repute, as a *de facto* magistrate. Later in the same year we hear of *sufetes* at Gades (Cádiz). *Sufetes* is the Phoenician word for 'judges' (cf Hebrew *shophetim*) and clearly indicates magistrates with juridical power.[6] The first brief experiment with *sufetes* in place of kings had been made at Phoenician Tyre, between 564 and 557 BC. By the third century BC, *sufetes* had become the chief magistrates of the Punic settlement at Carthage in North Africa, and the institution was subsequently implanted in the Carthaginian territories of Sardinia and Malta.[7]

The status of Gades at the time of the Punic conquest of Spain is open to some question. The fabled land of Tartessos (which several of the ancients identified, rightly or wrongly, with Gades)[8] had once been ruled by such legendary kings as Gargoris, Habis, and Arganthonius; yet when the Tartessians were attacked and defeated by Hasdrubal Barca in 216 BC, their ruler was a mere chieftain (*dux*) named Chalbus (Livy 23.26.6). This apparent decline notwithstanding, it seems likely that it was the Carthaginians who introduced to Gades the typically Punic office of *sufes*. This assumption goes far towards explaining the fury of the Carthaginian general Mago in 206 when the *sufetes* of Gades refused to permit him entry to the city: they were probably his own government's appointees. It should hardly surprise us, therefore, that he subsequently had them crucified as traitors (Livy 28.37). And although there is no explicit evidence, it would be reasonable to suppose that the Carthaginians installed *sufetes* in other Spanish cities (Carthago Nova, for example) under their control.

The conclusion of the Second Punic War brought under Rome's dominion the southern and eastern coasts of Spain, areas which had already changed hands several times in preceding centuries. There was, at first, no wholesale reform of urban institutions. On the contrary, the wide variety of local offices attested on coins and inscriptions suggests that the pre-Roman towns were permitted to maintain their own systems of internal government during the early days of Roman rule. But the Romans were already establishing new towns in Spain – Italica in 206, Carteia in 171, Corduba in 152, Palma and Pollentia ca 122, Valentia ca 120 – which presumably had magistrates on the Italian model.[9] Since this model came eventually to dominate all cities in Spain, it is necessary to examine briefly its origin and character.

The ordinary magistrates in most Italian towns in the classical period were of three types: duovirs, aediles, and quaestors. Since these offices appear to have corresponded in nature and duties to the consuls, curule aediles, and quaestors at Rome, it has been suggested that town councils were modelled on a relatively early form of government at Rome which antedated the creation of additional magistracies (praetors, censors, plebeian aediles) in that city.[10] To validate this claim, however, one would need to demonstrate not only that the 'additional' magistracies were, in fact, of later date than the others, but also that the first local governments outside Rome were established before the extra magistracies were created. Neither endeavour admits of success. The plebeian aediles are first mentioned in 449 BC, while the curule aediles were apparently not created until 367. The title of praetor is actually older than that of consul,[11] although the praetorship did not assume its familiar judicial function until 366. Censors are already attested in 443 BC (Livy 4.8.7).

On the other hand there is no early evidence for the existence of local magistrates on the Roman model outside of Rome. Abbott and Johnson allege that these first occur in the colony at Antium, since Livy records that when the Antiates complained (ca 317 BC) that they had no regular statutes or magistrates, the Roman Senate authorized the drafting of laws (presumably some form of charter) by the colony's patrons. Such a charter, according to Abbott and Johnson, included elected magistrates in place of the prefects hitherto dispatched from Rome.[12] This assumption concerning the contents of the Antiate laws is, however, pure speculation based on the surviving charter fragments of the first century BC, and moreover is almost certainly erroneous. The context of the Antiates' complaint, according to the same passage in Livy, was that word had just reached them that Capua had been given laws at her own request. These laws provided that prefects would be sent annually from Rome to administer the hitherto chaotic affairs of Capua; and it is reasonable to suppose that the new regulations for Antium, issued under similar motivation, would likewise have provided for such prefects.

In short, we have no certain idea when and where the system of local government by duovirs, aediles, and quaestors was first introduced; but there is at least no evidence to support the claim that it was based on some early Roman political system involving only consuls, aediles, and quaestors. Furthermore there is no cogent proof that the local post of duovir was inspired by, or closely modelled upon, the consulship at Rome. Similarities between these two offices are superficial: both operated in pairs (but so did most Roman magistracies), and both were executive appointments whose holders presided over a senate or council (but this is a normal function of civic leaders in many cultures, ancient and modern). If duovirs really emulated the consuls, it is curious that they did not adopt their titulary. One could argue that the Romans would not allow them to do so, but any consistent policy on this rationale would similarly have banned the use of 'aedile' and 'quaestor' outside of Rome. Moreover, the powers of duovirs were comparatively restricted, yet much of their attention seems to have been devoted to jurisdiction (civil suits, fines, legacies), in which consuls (who were often busy commanding armies) rarely involved themselves. An alternative model presents itself. Duovirs had already existed as judicial magistrates at Rome in the early Republican period,[13] and it is at least possible that they, rather than the consuls, may have been the inspiration, in name as well as function, for the judicial magistrates in Italian (and ultimately provincial) towns. Nonetheless, it must be admitted that any reconstruction of magisterial origins is speculative and reposes on the slimmest of grounds.

While Rome's earliest satellites had no local magistrates,[14] her absorption of major Italian towns, whose traditional right of internal self-government could not easily or prudently be suppressed, and her foundation of Roman colonies, whose loyalty and motives were in any event beyond question, eventually obliged her to cede autonomy in internal matters to local senates and local magistrates. These local governments in fact proved to be far more effective than the prefects imposed by Rome in earlier days, for the local magistrates were both familiar with and responsive to local conditions and problems, had a real pride in their community, and took an active interest in its welfare.

The nature of the magistracies in these towns depended very much on local custom and practice. The older Italian communities had possessed, and under Roman toleration continued to possess, a wide variety of magistrates – archons and *stratēgoi*, consuls and praetors, aediles (as chief magistrates), even dictators and *interreges*. Younger communities, however, and in particular the new colonies founded by Rome, were generally willing to accept the Roman system of duovirs, aediles, and quaestors. Thus we find duovirs and quattuorvirs (a collective term for the duovirs and aediles) specified in the *Lex Rubria de Gallia Cisalpina* of 49 BC as the authorized local magistrates.[15] Julius Caesar attempted to impose uniformity of municipal organization in all parts of Italy, a policy apparently continued, at least briefly, after his death.[16] This move may not have eliminated all the old magistracies, but clearly there was encouragement to conform to the system of duovirs and aediles.

Duovirs and aediles were also stipulated in Caesar's charter for the colony of Urso in Hispania Ulterior, which dates to 44 BC. Captured by Caesar's forces in April of 45, and having lost its own *principes* through treachery a short time before,[17] Urso was reorganized as a colony with Roman magistrates. One of the earliest of these, C. Vettius, had been a centurion in the Thirtieth Legion, which was patently (as its high number indicates) created during the Civil War. It may well be that Vettius was nominated or appointed by Caesar to be one of the initial duovirs at Urso. The charters granted to other colonies and *municipia* by Caesar and his successor Augustus effectively eliminated the *reguli, principes, duces*, and other anomalous leaders and replaced them with local magistrates on the Roman model.[18] In some cases the transition to 'new' magistrates was not particularly shocking. Obulco in Baetica, which became a *municipium* (perhaps under Augustus) and adopted duovirs, already had pairs of magistrates in the mid-second century BC, as her coins attest.[19]

The creation of numerous colonies and *municipia* in Spain by Caesar and Augustus[20] was symptomatic of an emerging imperial emphasis on urbanization and romanization: creating new towns, transplanting hill-fort dwellers into settlements on the plains, granting Latin rights to sufficiently assimilated communities. The process of municipalization was initially concentrated in Baetica (Ulterior) and on the east coast, where cities were already numerous. Out of 175 Baetican communities listed by the elder Pliny (*NH* 3.7, referring to the period before AD 6), just under a third (fifty-five) were of Roman or Latin status. While Augustus' immediate successors pursued a more cautious policy in extending the franchise, Vespasian granted *ius Latii* to 'all' of Spain, or at any rate to a great many communities.[21]

More by incentive than by force, the towns of Spain grew and flourished.

Members of the local élite, emulating the Italian model, competed for municipal honours and the coveted Roman citizenship. Roman municipal institutions were adopted, the Roman system of government imitated, until many Spanish cities had become, of their own volition, microcosms of Rome herself. In return, Rome interfered as little as possible in the internal management of these cities, permitting local self-determination within the parameters of Roman law.

Local government was vested in a local council known officially as the *ordo decurionum* but popularly as the *senatus*. Most forms of pre-Roman government in Spain – whether indigenous, Greek, or Punic – probably included a council of elders, as advisers to the local king, chieftain, or magistrates. Their presence would hardly be astounding, since such councils were a very widespread institution throughout the ancient world. The literary sources record councils of elders at several Celtiberian towns.[22] The obvious Latin translation for such local councils was *senatus* (derived from *senex* 'elder'), and it makes its appearance early. Saguntum had a *senatus* in 219 BC, and Cato summoned together all the *senatores* of the east coast in 195 (Livy 21.14.1, 34.17.7; Sil. *Pun.* 1.564–5). These local senates were recognized by Rome, and although the use of the term *senatus* by them was perhaps considered an impertinence,[23] we find it employed rather often, mostly in the early period but also under the Empire.[24] Nonetheless, in incorporated communities the local senate is regularly called the *ordo decurionum*.

Important and influential as local senates may have been, it was the magistrates who exercised the executive, judicial, and financial powers of government in each community. In subsequent chapters we shall examine the nature and duties of their offices, as well as their social and economic backgrounds and the means and success of their romanization. Before we embark on such specifics, however, it is crucial to appreciate the nature of our evidence, which on one hand furnishes a flurry of data for the periods of the Late Republic and Early Empire, and on the other, imposes certain limitations on their usefulness.

Notes

1 C.B. Rüger *JRS* 63 (1973) 256. Cf M.I. Rostovtzeff *Social and Economic History of the Roman Empire* 2nd ed (Oxford 1957) 593 n 4 on the need for more monographs on the municipal history of the Empire. For the tardiness of romanization in Narbonensis see Th. Mommsen *The Provinces of the Roman Empire* 1 tr W.P. Dickson (London 1909, repr Chicago 1974) 86.

2 On cities as the focus for romanization, see Clavel and Lévêque *Villes et structures* 52, 56; L.A. Curchin *Classical Views* 5 (1986) 282; T.R.S. Broughton *Cahiers d'histoire mondiale* 9 (1965) 127.

3 Cf J.J. Wilkes *Dalmatia* (London 1969) 192.

4 On monarchy, see J. Caro Baroja in *Estudios sobre la España antigua* (Madrid 1971) 156–7; A. Arribas *The Iberians* (London and New York 1964) 116–19; on tribal chieftains, see Livy 22.21, 26.49, 27.19, 34.11–12; cf M. Guallar Pérez *Indibil y Mandonio* (Lérida 1956) 56–8.

5 J. Gaudemet *Institutions de l'Antiquité*, 2nd ed (Paris 1982) 151

6 For *sufetes* at Castax and Gades, see, respectively, App. *Iber.* 32 and Livy 28.37; and on *sufetes* generally, cf PW s.v. 'Sufeten,' col 643, and J. Dus *Archív Orientalní* 31 (1963) 444–69.

7 For *sufetes* at Tyre, see Joseph. *Ap.* 1.157; and at Carthage, G. Charles Picard and C. Picard *The Life and Death of Carthage* (New York 1968) 210; B.H. Warmington *Carthage*, 2nd ed (New York 1969) 140. For the territories, see IG XIV 608, 953; Y. Debbasch *Rev. Hist. Dr. Fr.* 31 (1953) 35–8. Cf M. Christol and J. Gascou *Mélanges d'arch.* 92 (1980) 329–45. Two *sufetes*, both named Halasbaal, are mentioned as eponymous magistrates in the Punic 'sacrificial tariff' inscription from Massalia (*Corpus inscriptionum Semiticarum* I [Paris 1881] 165); but they are surely *sufetes* at Carthage, not Massalia (*contra* E.S. Bouchier *Spain under the Roman Empire* [Oxford 1914] 12), since the inscription concerns sacrifices for the temple of Baal Saphon at Carthage.

8 On the identification of Tartessos as Gades, see Sall. *H.* 2.5 M; Cic. *Att.* 7.3.11; Avienus *Ora marit.* 269–70.

9 On these early settlements, see the treatment by Knapp *Roman Experience* 111–39.

10 Hardy *Charters* 69

11 For plebeian and curule aediles, see Livy 3.55.7, 6.42.14. Livy's veracity on many details is open to question and he probably overemphasizes the 'struggle of the orders,' but he does seem reliably informed on the major events of each year. For the title of praetor, see Livy 3.55.12, 7.3.4ff; and for discussion see W. Kunkel *An Introduction to Roman Legal and Constitutional History* 2nd ed (Oxford 1973) 15; M. Cary and H.H. Scullard *A History of Rome* 3rd ed (London 1975) 586 n 4.

12 Livy 9.20.10; Abbott and Johnson MARE 3–4

13 They appear only once after 287 BC; cf R.A. Bauman *The Duumviri in the Roman Criminal Law and in the Horatius Legend* (Wiesbaden 1969) 7–9.

14 Abbott and Johnson MARE 3

15 On the magisterial system in older Italian communities, see Hardy *Laws* 33, 138–9; Abbott and Johnson MARE 56. Regarding the Roman magisterial

system in younger Italian communities, several points are worthy of note.
The *quattuorviri* originally consisted of *duoviri iure dicundo* and *duoviri aedilicia potestate*. These titles came to be abbreviated as *duoviri* and *aediles* respectively: cf Hardy *Laws* 147. The singular form *duovir* is a back-formation from the nominative plural *duoviri*, while the alternate form *duumvir* is a doublet derived from the old genitive plural *duumvirum* (A. Ernout and A. Meillet *Dictionnaire étymologique de la langue latine* 4th ed [Paris 1967] 188; cf D.R. Shackleton Bailey's commentary on Cic. *Att.* 2.6.1). The Flavian municipal charters use the genitive plural *duumvirorum* (e.g., *Irn.* 19, 60), which is also cited by Cicero (*Orat.* 46.156). On the *Lex Rubria*, see FIRA I² 19; Hardy *Laws* 125–35. See further chap. 3, n 72.

16 A.N. Sherwin White *The Roman Citizenship* 2nd ed (Oxford 1973) 170–1

17 On duovirs and aediles at Urso, see FIRA I² 21; Hardy *Charters* 22–60, and for Urso's loss of its own *principes*, see *BHisp.* 22. As part of the aftermath of Ategua, the massacre of the *principes* is probably to be dated to late February.

18 This is a far cry from the situation in Africa, where *sufetes* continued to appear at many towns well into the Imperial period; undoubtedly such magistrates were more compatible with the Roman municipal system than were *reguli*. Lepcis Magna compromised by having both duovirs and *sufetes* simultaneously; cf J. Gascou *La politique municipale de l'Empire Romain en Afrique Proconsulaire* (Rome 1972) 76.

19 F. Vittinghoff *Römische Kolonisation und Bürgerrechtspolitik unter Caesar und Augustus* (Mainz 1952) 1321

20 Vittinghoff *Römische Kolonisation* 1288–97. On the foundation dates of the various colonies and *municipia* in Spain cf Galsterer *Untersuchungen, passim.*

21 Claudius granted municipal status to Baelo, and allegedly wanted to see all Spaniards, Gauls, Greeks, and Britons in togas (Sen. *Apocol.* 3.3). On Vespasian and the *ius Latii*, see Pliny NH 3.30; and my discussion in chap. 5.

22 On councils of elders, see L.A. Curchin *Florilegium* 2 (1980) 69 n 33. On a presumably Punic senate at Carthago Nova in 210 BC cf Polyb. 10.18. For *presbyteroi* at Segeda (153 BC), Cauca (151), Lutia (133), Belgeda (92), see Diod. 31.39; App. *Iber.* 52–4, 94, 100.

23 So Arnold *Roman System*³ 256; Abbott and Johnson MARE 64–5. I am not entirely convinced; indeed, the Romans may even have been flattered by such emulation. Cf the possible use of the term *senator* to designate members of northern Italian town councils: G. Alföldy *Noricum* (London and Boston 1974) 44.

24 *Tab. Her.* 86–8 and *passim*; Galsterer *Untersuchungen* 51–3. On the term

senatus used by ancient sources, see *BRAH* 167 (1979) 424 (Contrebia, 87 BC); Cic. *Balb.* 41 (Gades, 56 BC); *CIL* II 3695 = *ILS* 6098 = *ILER* 5828 (Pollentia, AD 6); *CIL* II 5346 (Augustobriga, perhaps during principate of Augustus); *AE* 1967, 239 = *ILER* 5823–4 (Maggava, AD 14); *ILER* 5831 (Munigua, under Augustus or Tiberius); *HAEp.* 547 (Iptuci, AD 31); *HAEp.* 549 = *AE* 1953, 267 (Termes, second century AD). In the early first century BC, Toletum issued coins stamped 'ex s[enatus] c[onsultu]' (VM 134:1, 4–5 = Gil 819, 932–4); the senate in question is presumably the local *ordo*. A parallel occurs among the Tiberian coin issues of Carteia (VM 128–9 = Gil 1806–15), where several types bear the legend 'ex d[ecreto] d[ecurionum]' but one reads 'ex s[enatus] c[onsultu].'

2

Evidence for Local Magistrates in Roman Spain

Examination of the evidence from the Spanish provinces is essential to an understanding of local government in the Roman Empire. The Iberian Peninsula has yielded not only a wealth of lapidary inscriptions naming individual magistrates – welcome grist for the prosopographer's mill – but also a series of miraculously preserved bronze tablets from southern Spain, containing substantial portions of colonial and municipal charters of the first centuries BC and AD.

These charters are of tremendous importance for the municipal history of Roman Spain and indeed of the Roman West as a whole, for without the Spanish evidence, our knowledge of municipal regulations would depend almost entirely on surviving charter fragments from Italy; and the extent to which these might apply in the provinces would remain a matter of conjecture. Not surprisingly, even a casual comparison of the Italian and Spanish charters reveals both similarities and differences, and the reasons for the latter are not always apparent. Thus, while information missing from the Spanish fragments can be surmised to some extent from the Italian documents, the exercise demands caution.

The longest of the Italian charter fragments is the *Tabula Heracleensis*, discovered near the ancient city of Heraclea in Lucania (*ILS* 6085 = *FIRA* I² 13). This document, dating to 44 BC, curiously prescribes regulations applicable both 'in, and within one mile of, the city of Rome' and 'in a *municipium*, colony, prefecture, forum, or *conciliabulum* of Roman citizens.' It thus purports to be a charter for the various towns of Italy, and is sometimes dubbed the *Lex Iulia Municipalis* in consequence. We also have a fragment of the municipal charter of Tarentum, apparently issued between 88 and 61 BC (*ILS* 6086 = *FIRA* I² 18); the so-called *Lex Rubria* of 48–41 BC discovered in the ruins of ancient Veleia and providing regulations for the towns of

Cisalpine Gaul, to which Julius Caesar extended the citizenship (*CIL* I.2²
592 = *FIRA* I² 19); and a short fragment from Ateste in Transpadane Gaul,
dated to 48 BC (*CIL* I.2² 600 = *FIRA* I² 20). All of these charters provide some
information on the roles of local magistrates in Late Republican Italy,
though in none of the surviving texts are these listed systematically under
each of the several offices. For more detailed information we are compelled
to consult the Spanish charters.

The Colonial Charter of Urso

The *Lex Coloniae Genetivae Iuliae* is preserved on four bronze tablets
discovered near Osuna (ancient Urso), two in 1870 and two in 1874. An
additional twelve fragments found at El Rubio (near Osuna) in 1925 are
believed to pertain to the same charter. Having supported the Pompeian
faction during the Civil War, the town of Urso had its lands confiscated by
Julius Caesar in 45 BC for the implantation of a Roman colony (*BHisp.* 26,
28, 41; *Urs.* 106). The charter itself dates to 44 BC, as shown by mention
of *Lex Antonia* (a decree authorizing the colony) in chapter 104. Marc
Antony was consul in 44; whether the *Lex Antonia* and the charter were
issued before or after Caesar's death in March of that year remains a moot
question. The surviving copy of the charter is not, however, the original,
but can be dated palaeographically to the Flavian age. One fragment, indeed,
appears to be post-Flavian and contains interpolations, including the anach-
ronistic mention of 'Baetica' in chapter 127.

The fragments of the Urso charter represent little more than a third of
the original document. Especially lamentable is the loss of the first sixty
chapters, which presumably dealt with the organization and composition of
the colony, and the election and principal duties of the magistrates. The
extant portion treats of various legal, financial, and religious matters, in
which reference is frequently made to the role of local magistrates in
administering or enforcing the regulations.

The most obvious difference between this charter and the *Tabula Heracleensis* is that the latter, though issued in the same year, is a 'blanket'
charter for every type of Italian city, from Rome itself down to the humblest
market town, whereas the Urso law was specially issued for a particular
colony. The question naturally arises, to what extent the Urso charter was
unique. The Spanish municipal charters of the Flavian period, discussed
below, are (where they overlap) virtually identical in wording, differing
only in the name of the town. Whether the Urso charter is similarly a
carbon copy of a 'standard' colonial constitution can only be determined
with certainty if the charter of another Caesarian colony with identical

wording should be unearthed. Nonetheless, it seems unlikely that a special charter with radically different provisions would be drawn up for each colony, and we may therefore reasonably suppose that the charters of the various Caesarian colonies in Spain (and perhaps elsewhere) were of similar content. By this argument the Urso charter would not be *sui generis* but rather typical of colonial charters of its age, and the provisions concerning its magistrates would likewise apply in other colonies.[1]

The Flavian Municipal Law

Substantial fragments survive of the town charters of three Flavian *municipia* in the province of Baetica, inscribed upon bronze tablets. Those of Malaca and Salpensa (towns attested in Pliny and other sources) have been known since the nineteenth century, while that of the *municipium Flavium Irnitanum* (a hitherto unattested town) came to light only in 1981 through a chance discovery, and its surviving chapters conveniently overlap those of the other two fragments.[2] In addition, we have smaller fragments from the Flavian charters of Basilipo, 'Italica,' Ostippo, and an unknown town near Seville (the so-called *Fragmenta Villonensia*).[3]

The 'Italica' fragment was originally reported as found at Cortegana near Huelva at the beginning of this century, whence it passed into the Lebrija collection. The difficulty with the subsequent claim (started by antiquities dealers) of an Italican provenance is that Italica became a *municipium* under Augustus, ca 15 BC, as both coins and inscriptions attest (see Catalogue, **139–41**). It makes little sense that an Augustan *municipium* should have a charter whose only extant fragment contains chapter 90 of the Flavian municipal law. Moreover, the fragment is a copy dating to the second or early third century AD, whereas Italica is known to have changed its status from *municipium* to *colonia* under Hadrian.[4] Wherever the fragment was 'found,' it should belong, not to Italica, but to a town which was granted municipal status under the Flavians, and which was still a *municipium* a century or so later when it ordered a fresh copy of its charter to be engraved. The attribution to Italica should therefore be abandoned. If the provenance as originally reported is accurate, the *municipium* in question must lie near Cortegana. Alicia Canto has lately revived the possibility of identifying Cortegana with Ptolemy's Corticata; on this basis the fragments may be evidence for a *municipium Flavium Corticatense* (which, like Irni and Basilipo, escapes mention in Pliny's survey of Baetica).[5]

The fact that these several town charters contain virtually identical wording in the numerous chapters which overlap in the surviving fragments[6] leaves no doubt that they are copies of a single prototype, a *lex municipalis* of Flavian date. This law, presumably issued at Rome, was reproduced *verbatim* (apart from minor orthographic variants) at each town, with only the toponym and perhaps a few minor details (e.g., the number of decurions) changed to give the appearance of an 'individualized' town charter. This 'carbon-copying,' no doubt a bureaucratic convenience at the time, is of the greatest benefit to modern investigators. We know that Vespasian granted *ius Latii* to 'all' of Spain, almost certainly during his censorship with Titus in AD 73–4.[7] Since municipal status was thereby handed out *en masse* to deserving Spanish cities at this time, and since (as is clear from the surviving charters) a copy of a common municipal law was issued to each, it seems safe to postulate that all Flavian *municipia* in Spain operated under these same regulations. *Ceteris paribus*, there is no reason why any Flavian *municipium* should *not* be subject to the same terms of reference as another. The regulations in the charters should therefore be regarded, not as unique to a particular town, but rather as the standard provisions of the Flavian municipal law.[8]

Whether the same law was used throughout the entire Empire cannot be demonstrated, since evidence is lacking; but since nothing in the existing text is specifically applicable to Spain (other than the town's name inserted in each copy), there seems no reason to suppose that Spanish *municipia* required regulations different from those elsewhere. Indeed, the fragmentary charter of Lauriacum in Noricum, dating to the period AD 212–17, contains an only slightly altered version of chapter 25 of the Flavian municipal law,[9] a coincidence which might suggest not only that this law applied in the eastern as well as the western provinces, but that parts of it continued in use with minor modifications into the Late Empire. If this reasoning is accepted, the Spanish charters are primary documents for the municipal history of the Empire; at the very least they are crucial to an understanding of privileged towns in Baetica.

To judge from the ending of the *Lex Irnitana*, the Flavian municipal law contained ninety-six chapters. The majority of these (about 70 per cent) are preserved in one or more copies of the law.[10] Apart from seven chapters missing somewhere between chapters 31 and 51 (the chapters in *Irnitana* are not numbered) the only significant gap is the loss of the first eighteen chapters. We can infer with confidence that chapter 18 dealt with the rights and powers of the duovirs, since chapters 19–20 detail the rights and powers of the aediles and quaestors, respectively. The preceding seventeen chapters presumably dealt with such matters as the grant of *ius Latii*, the composition of the citizen body, and the religious obligations of the *municipium*. Regrettable as this loss may be – and it may yet be recouped through subsequent discoveries – the surviving chapters are full of information on the status and duties of local magistrates.

Discrepancies between Charters

A comparison of the Urso charter with the Flavian municipal law reveals numerous resemblances and differences in the regulations concerning magistrates. The reasons for the discrepancies include the earlier date of the Urso charter (though the existing copy is of Flavian date), but also, and more importantly, the essential dissimilarities between colonies and *municipia*. Granted that the municipal charters are copies of a standard municipal law, and that the provisions of the Urso charter are unlikely to have been custom-made for a single colony, the surviving documents enable us to consider the functions of magistrates, not only in a few specific communities, but in colonies and *municipia* generally. The extant charter fragments may thus be seen as representative of colonial and municipal regulations throughout Spain (and probably elsewhere).

In fact, the dissimilarities between *coloniae* and *municipia*, already blurred in the *Tabula Heracleensis*, became less striking with the passage of time. There is, to be sure, an extensive literature on the differences between these two species of privileged town, the essential distinction being that, while colonies were originally new settlements of Roman citizens, *municipia* were pre-existing towns which had been granted Roman or Latin citizenship.[11] In practice, however, colonies were also formed in native settlements like Urso, and in the second century AD numerous titular colonies were created, among them former *municipia* such as Italica. As a result, the difference between colonies and *municipia* almost disappeared, and the functions of their magistrates became practically identical.[12]

Career Inscriptions

The charters explain what local magistrates did; to discover who they were requires intensive sifting through Hispano-Roman epigraphy. Such a venture is by no means easy, not because of difficulties inherent in deciphering the stones (though the correct reading of some inscriptions is in question) but simply through scholarly neglect. The Catalogue appended to this study collects data from hundreds of texts, many of which are not readily available in a standard compendium. Volume II of the *Corpus Inscriptionum Latinarum*, dealing with the inscriptions of Roman Spain, was published in 1869, with a supplement in 1892. Since that time, a myriad of new inscriptions, and corrections to old ones, have appeared in a frustrating variety of periodicals, often 'journals of short life and little circulation.'[13] Some of these have been collected in provincial *corpora* (again, local publications often difficult to find outside the Iberian Peninsula), but others remain obscure. Moreover, many of these addenda have not appeared in *L'Année Epigraphique*, the standard reference work for new Latin inscriptions. A Spanish corpus of sixty-eight hundred texts was published in 1971, but is so full of mistakes as to be almost wholly unreliable.[14] Antonio Beltrán's *Hispania Antiqua Epigraphica* has collected (uncritically) most of the inscriptions published between 1950 and 1969, but has not been updated. A supplement to *CIL* II has been in preparation for some years but is still far from publication. Our Catalogue, then, not only collects relevant information on Spanish magistrates, but does so from a multitude of sources, many of them unfamiliar to the average Roman historian.

These inscriptions nearly all date to the so-called Early Empire, roughly the first two centuries AD, a period of prosperity in which the 'epigraphic habit' (to borrow a felicitous phrase from Ramsay MacMullen) was at its greatest intensity. The texts include honorific monuments erected by a grateful town in honour of a local dignitary; epitaphs of deceased magistrates, erected either by the town or by the family; and dedications of statues, altars and buildings by the magistrates themselves. Typically these inscriptions provide us with the full name of the magistrate, a list of his titles, either in order of importance or in chronological sequence, and information on his family or his special achievements. Admittedly, some of these inscriptions do not seem outstandingly informative; but even the humblest ones can be of value. For instance, mention of the office of quattuorvir may suggest (for reasons to be discussed in the next chapter) that the magistrate's town was a *municipium*. If his voting tribe is given as Quirina, he almost certainly received the Roman citizenship through holding office in a town granted *ius Latii* under the Flavians. Moreover the magistrate's *nomen* (and Spanish magistrates sometimes have unusual ones) may allow us to find relatives among the nomenclature of his own and neighbouring towns, thus enriching our prosopographical knowledge and perhaps allowing us to trace social connections. For although magistrates were elected by the people, prominent families tended to dominate local government, and we often find several members of the same family holding office in their home town. Information about a magistrate's nomenclature and title can also be used statistically to determine, e.g., preference for the *tria nomina* or for the quattuorviral title in a particular region or historical period. Thus any mention of a magistrate is a minute contribution to our understanding of the social history of Roman Spain; and while the collection of such 'microinformation' from the provinces may seem unimportant to the student of mainstream political history, it is a procedure fundamental to social history, ancient or modern. Quantitative analysis of epigraphic data has yielded impressive results for Spain and other provinces;[15] the fruits of its application to Spanish magistrates will be evident in the course of this study. And while the number of careers attested in inscriptions must be only a fraction of the actual number of office holders over the years, there is no reason to doubt that the sample, preserved by chance, is representative of the group as a whole.

Coins

Local coinage issues are our chief source for the names and titles of magistrates during the Late Republic. These issues continue into the Julio-Claudian period, thereby overlapping the rise of the 'epigraphic habit.' The coin legends are necessarily much shorter than career inscriptions, sometimes giving only an abbreviated name or even initials, and only occasionally naming the magistrate's office. Moreover, scholars are in disagreement as to the dating of many of these coins. For our purposes, however, a difference of a decade or two does not substantially affect the overall picture, and many inscriptions on stone cannot be dated with even this much precision.[16] Though the legends are sometimes overly succinct, coins are an important reminder of the monetal function of magistrates in many towns. Additionally, the earlier examples reveal a wealth of unromanized names which contrast sharply with the largely romanized nomenclature in the career inscriptions and help us to trace the progress of romanization.

Other Sources

Literary sources are of little assistance in this study, although some ancient authors (e.g., Cicero) comment on aspects of magistrates, while the elder Pliny informs us about the status of many privileged towns in Flavian Spain. The legal sources (particularly the Theodosian Code and the *Digest*) are much more helpful, though susceptible to interpolations. While rarely mentioning Spain specifically, the jurists (mostly dating to the late second and early third centuries AD) have a great deal to say about the legal position of magistrates, thus providing a valuable supplement to the charters; and for the Late Empire, the legal texts are a major source. Finally, architectural evidence is occasionally pertinent to magistrates, e.g., the size of local senate houses or the excavation of a villa known to belong to a magistrate.

We thus have several different types of information on Spanish magistrates. Unlike so much of Roman history, which is dependent on relatively late literary versions (e.g., Livy on the early history of Rome, or Dio Cassius on the Julio-Claudians), the bulk of the evidence for Spanish magistrates (charters, career inscriptions, coins) consists of primary sources – contemporary documents providing first-hand attestation of some important facts.[17] The value of these witnesses will be evident in the discussions which follow.

Notes

1 H. Galsterer *JRS* 78 (1988) 83 supposes the Urso charter to be a special, *ad hoc* composition. The alleged colonial law of Ilici in eastern Spain (*Eph. Epigr.* IX 349 = *EJER* 2 = *AE* 1952, 80) is in fact a duplicate of the Tiberian *rogatio* from Magliano (*AE* 1949, 215).

2 Malaca: *CIL* II 1964 = *ILS* 6089 = *FIRA* I² 24 = *EJER* 9; Salpensa: *CIL* II 1963 = *ILS* 6088 = *FIRA* I² 23 = *EJER* 8. Irni (the name is conjectural): J. González *JRS* 76 (1986) 147–243

3 Basilipo: J. González *Stud. Doc. Hist. Iur.* 49 (1983) 395–9 = *AE* 1984, 510; A. d'Ors *Emerita* 73 (1985) 31–41; 'Italica' (Cortegana): *FIRA* I² 25 = *EJER* 11 = *HAEp.* 544; Villonensia: *Eph. Epigr.* IX 261 = *EJER* 10; *HAEp.* 2014 = *AE* 1964, 80. The Ostippo fragment is to be published by A. Marcos Pous. A fragment from Emporiae (A. d'Ors *Ampurias* 29 [1967] 293 = *AE* 1969–70, 287) and two fragments from Clunia (P. de Palol and J.A. Arias Bonet *Boletín del Seminario de Arte y Arqueología* 34–5 [1969] 313–19 = d'Ors *Emerita* 40 [1972] 59–60 = *AE* 1971, 204) have been suspected of belonging to municipal charters, but without adequate evidence.

4 On the status of Italica, see A. García y Bellido *Colonia Aelia Augusta Italica* (Madrid 1960) 33–7 and 69; J. González *MCV* 20 (1984) 17–21.

5 A.M. Canto *ZPE* 63 (1986) 217–20

6 *Irn.* duplicates the nine extant chapters of *Salp.* and ten of the chapters of *Mal.* The Ostippo fragment contains part of chap. 62, the 'Italica' fragment part of chap. 90.

7 'Universae Hispaniae Vespasianus imperator Augustus ... Latium tribuit,' Pliny *NH* 3.3.30. On the date, see Galsterer *Untersuchungen* 37; R. Wiegels *Hermes* 106 (1978) 196–213; Mackie *Administration* 215–16.

8 We do not speak of a 'Vespasianic' municipal law because, although that emperor granted the municipal status, there was apparently a delay of several years before the 'standard' municipal law was compiled and promulgated. The delay was possibly due to the number of charters needed: cf T.R.S. Broughton *Cahiers d'histoire mondiale* 9 (1965) 136. The three major charters date to the reign of Vespasian's son Domitian. What type of docu-

ment the town originally received from Vespasian to notify it of the grant is unknown. Vespasian's letter to the town of Sabora in 77, granting it the use of the Flavian name, makes no mention of *ius Latii* or municipal status (*CIL* II 1423 = *ILS* 6092 = *FIRA* I² 74 = *EJER* 4). Possibly there was an imperial decree listing the towns to receive the *ius Latii*; cf the *Lex Antonia* for Urso.

9 *FIRA* I² 26 = M.H. Crawford *JRS* 76 (1986) 242

10 For a convenient table showing the preserved chapters of the various copies see C. Castillo *Stud. Doc. Hist. Iur.* 52 (1986) 392.

11 See, e.g., J. Toutain *Mélanges d'arch.* 16 (1896) 315–29; Liebenam *Städteverwaltung* 459–61; L. Tanfani *Contributo alla storia del municipio romano* (Taranto 1906) 12–33; Abbott and Johnson *MARE* chap. 1; E. Schonbauer *Municipia und Coloniae in der Prinzipatzeit* (Wien 1954); Langhammer *Magistratus* 7–22; F. Millar *The Emperor in the Roman World* (London 1977) 398–409.

12 Cf Galsterer *Untersuchungen* 2; J.F. Rodríguez Neila *Hisp. Ant.* 6 (1976) 165–6; E.T. Salmon *The Making of Roman Italy* (Ithaca 1982) 138–9, 180; G. Alföldy *Gerión* 2 (1984) 224; P.D. Garnsey and R.P. Saller *The Roman Empire: Economy, Society and Culture* (Berkeley and Los Angeles 1987) 27.

13 T.R.S. Broughton *Proceedings of the American Philosophical Society* 103 (1959) 650

14 J. Vives *Inscripciones latinas de la España romana* (Barcelona 1971–2, published posthumously)

15 E.g., A. Mócsy *Gesellschaft und Romanisation in der römischen Provinz Moesia Superior* (Amsterdam and Bucharest 1970); R.C. Knapp *Ancient Society* 9 (1978) 187–222; R. MacMullen *AJPhil* 103 (1982) 233–46; E.M. Wightman *Gallia Belgica* (London 1985); L.A. Curchin in *Studien zu den Militärgrenzen Roms* III (Stuttgart 1986) 692–5 (on Central Spain); Curchin *AEA* 60 (1987) 159–71 (on Tarraco)

16 In general I follow the dating of O. Gil Farrés *La moneda hispánica en la edad antigua* (Madrid 1966). While not always convincing, his treatment is far more up-to-date than the old standard, A. Vives *La moneda hispánica* (Madrid 1926–8), which is, however, still useful for its plates.

17 On the distinction between primary and secondary literary sources, see now M.I. Finley *Ancient History: Evidence and Models* (New York 1986) 10–11, which challenges the widespread assumption that anything ancient is primary.

3

Career Progression:
The *Cursus Honorum*

Careers at Rome traditionally followed a more or less fixed order of offices (*cursus honorum*). The applicability of such a rigid *cursus* to local magistrates in the provinces is a rather more complex question. The purpose of the present chapter is to examine the career structure of magistrates in Roman Spain, including the requirements for entry to various offices, the types of magistracy available, and career progression both within the local system and beyond. The evidence for this presentation consists principally of the surviving Spanish charters, which (as explained in chapter 2) are probably typical of the regulations in all privileged communities. Frequent reference will also be made to the career records of individuals from the Catalogue, illustrating the extent to which these laws were followed in actual practice.

Decurions

Since magistrates necessarily belonged to, and in essence composed, the *ordo decurionum*, it is necessary to begin by considering the nature of decurions in general and the prerequisites for admission to their order. The term 'decurion' originally signified a member of a *decuria* (**decem-viria*, board of ten men). How this decadal structure relates to municipal senates is far from clear. The *Oxford Latin Dictionary*, under 'decurio,' assumes that the senates comprised ten panels of ten men each; but the ancients did not share this view. Pomponius (second century AD) believed that when a colony was founded, a tenth of the colonists were formed into a council. Isidore of Seville (seventh century) thought decurions were named after the *curia* or senate; but *curia* is derived from *co-viria*, and *decurio* is not a compound of it. Whatever the origin of their title, the fact remains that decurions were local senators, and their presence indicates the existence of a self-governing town, of whatever type.[1] Like the senators of Rome, decurions in Spain (and in the West generally) were also known as *conscripti*.[2]

The number of decurions in Italian cities was sometimes one hundred, and this figure is accepted by modern handbooks as the norm for the Roman Empire.[3] In fact the number was variable. In Italy and Africa, *ordines* of fifty to sixty members are common, and in both regions there is at least one instance of an *ordo* of thirty. At the opposite end of the scale, we find senates of three hundred to six hundred in the East, and of six hundred at Massalia under Tiberius and at Thuburbo Maius in Africa under Commodus. These large *ordines* seem to have emulated the Senate at Rome, whose membership under the Principate numbered about six hundred.[4] In Spain, the large cities could undoubtedly have supported a local senate of one hundred or more, but in smaller towns this number would be neither feasible nor desirable. The Urso charter sometimes specifies a fixed quorum of twenty, thirty, forty, or (in one case) fifty decurions for various types of business; elsewhere it prescribes that two-thirds or a majority must be present. Discounting for the moment the lone mention of fifty, one could plausibly conjecture an *ordo* of, say, fifty-nine members, with thirty as a simple majority and forty as two-thirds. The business requiring fifty members is approval of applications to demolish buildings (*Urs.* 75). Granted that town planning may have been extremely important to local senates, it remains unclear why such a large quorum was needed in a town like Urso, when the Flavian *municipia* required only a simple majority of decurions for the same business (*Mal.* 62). Could the number 'L' in the Urso document represent an epigraphic error (e.g., for 'XL'), or a passage transcribed too literally from a prototype charter, or an interpolation reflecting later conditions? The surviving copy of the Urso charter dates to the Flavian period, by which time the *ordo* might have been considerably larger than at the colony's foundation a good century earlier.

More explicit evidence for the size of an *ordo* comes from the new *Lex Irnitana*. Chapter 31 of this charter provides that the duovirs shall arrange for the election of replacements if the number of decurions has fallen below sixty-three, 'which there were, by law and custom of that *municipium*, before this charter was passed.'[5] The clear implication is that the town was to retain its traditional *ordo* of sixty-three senators; the phrase 'iure more' probably refers to conditions prior to the grant of *ius Latii* and not simply those between the date of the grant and the issuing of the charter.

To what extent does this figure apply to other *municipia*? As explained in the previous chapter, the existing municipal charters with their identical provisions are patently copies of a master municipal law, with a few blanks, such as the name of the town, to be filled in locally. Since it is most unlikely that unprivileged towns were obliged to have the same size of local council – and the number sixty-three certainly seems peculiar – I would submit that chapter 31 contained such a blank, in which each *municipium* was to insert the number of senators to which it was accustomed. It may seem strange that the granting of municipal status was not accompanied by a regularization of the number of decurions, to the axiomatic one hundred, for example. But the varying sizes of towns receiving privileges (whether municipal or colonial) would have made rigid application of such an arbitrary number impractical. In a large town the competition for the decurionate would have been fierce, whereas in smaller *municipia* there might have been real difficulties in finding one hundred suitably qualified persons. The drafters of the Flavian municipal law may thus have found it expedient to respect the existing size of local *ordines*, an allowance not inconsistent with the principle of local self-government.

Archaeological evidence may also throw some light on the problem. Six cities in Africa have senate houses (*curiae*) with an internal area of ca 120 square metres, which by modern calculations would have just accommodated an *ordo* of one hundred. (The Curia at Rome, by comparison, had an interior space of ca 455 square metres to accommodate a senatorial attendance which seems rarely to have exceeded four hundred.) But the Flavian *curia* excavated at Conimbriga in Lusitania has an internal area of only 74.25 square metres, and indeed is one of the smallest in the Roman world.[6] This suggests that Conimbriga had an *ordo* considerably smaller than one hundred in this period.[7] The Conimbrigan *curia* could perhaps have accommodated fifty or sixty elders, a size consonant with those proposed for Urso and attested in the *municipium Irnitanum*.

At the other extreme we seem to have persuasive evidence from which a senate considerably larger than one hundred at Barcino can be calculated. An inscription from this city, datable to ca 160, records a legacy of one hundred thousand sesterces from L. Minicius Natalis Quadronius Verus: this was to be invested at an interest of five per cent, and the resulting annual earnings of five thousand sesterces were to be distributed at the rate of four denarii (sixteen sesterces) to each decurion and three denarii (twelve sesterces) to each of the Augustales (*CIL* II 4511 = *EJER* 34 = *IRB* 32). Provision is made for an increased distribution per capita in the event of absentees, the clear implication being that if all the decurions and Augustales were present for the donative, the entire five thousand sesterces would be expended at the specified rate. The number of Augustales serving at one time was limited to six in this period, though former members of the college could continue to use that title.[8] But even if we assume an improbably high figure of one hundred former and current Augustales, as well as the 'standard' one hundred decurions, the amount of the largesse would only be twenty-eight hundred sesterces – little more than half the allotted sum. Therefore the number of decurions must have been considerably higher than one hundred. The donative of five thousand sesterces would be compatible with a decurion:Augustalis ratio of 250:83, 275:50 or 300:16. Thus, in the absence of an adequate sample of precise figures from Spanish cities, caution should be exercised in positing assumptions about the 'standard' size of local senates.

There is some evidence to suggest that certain towns had a dual *ordo*, paralleling a situation occasionally found in Italy and Africa. A series of inscriptions from Valentia, in the late second or early third century AD, mentions the 'Valentini veterani et veteres' as well as 'uterque ordo' ('both senates') and 'universus ordo' (the latter expression presumably denoting both *ordines* combined).[9] 'Universus [ordo?]' is also attested at Dertosa, and 'utrique sen[atui]' (if the reading is correct) at Pax Iulia (*CIL* II 4060, 52 = *ILER* 1383, 1516). A better-preserved inscription includes the phrase, 'to this man the Old Senate (*ordo vetus*) of Singilia also decreed in its own name the same honours that it had decreed previously in the Combined Senate (*in universum*)' (*CIL* II 2026 = *ILER* 1485) The rationale for a double senate, meeting separately on some matters and collectively on others, is not at all apparent; and for the same measure to be passed *both* separately and collectively seems redundant.

The recently published *Lex Irnitana* rules that the decurions are to vote 'each in his own *ordo*' ('quisque in suo ordine'), beginning with those who have the most children and ending with those who have none. Where several decurions have the same number of children or equivalent privileges (*ius liberorum*), the vote goes first to ex-duovirs, in order of seniority, then to other decurions in order of seniority (*Irn.* B). Clearly there is a pecking order here, similar to that at Rome, where opinion was sought first from the *princeps*, then from the consulars, then from other senators in order of seniority. However, neither at Rome nor in the *municipium Irnitanum* does this procedure show that there was more than one *ordo* (though the editor of the new law interprets it to mean that there were two *ordines*, one of duovirs and one of non-duovirs);[10] the phrase 'quisque in suo ordine' really means 'each in his own turn,' and has nothing to do with a multiple senate.

The term *ordo* designated both the local senate and the decurial 'class,' a privileged élite whose membership was by no means accessible to the general public. Candidates for admission to the decurionate were required to meet several basic qualifications. One of these was citizenship or residence in the local community.[11] Although decurions were normally natives of the town in which they held office, resident aliens (*incolae*) were also eligible. Hence in Spain we not infrequently find citizens of one town belonging to the *ordo* of another, and sometimes pursuing the *cursus* at both, though not simultaneously. A native of Corduba, L. Lucretius Severus (**24**), specifically informs us that he rose 'ex incolatu decurioni' in the town of Axati; it is not necessary to suppose, with Hübner, that he actually acquired local citizenship. But the residence requirement was strictly enforced, and we know from the Urso charter that a decurion who did not maintain a domicile within one mile of the town could be expelled from the *ordo* (*Urs.* 91).

A further and hardly surprising requirement was free birth. Although Julius Caesar had allowed freedmen to hold office at Urso and other colonies, the free-birth requirement was strictly enforced under the Empire. Illegitimate children, on the other hand, were not debarred from the local senate, though Roman law required that preference be given to legitimate candidates.[12] However, there was also an age restriction. Those under age twenty-five – thirty during the Republic, though allowance was made for military service – or over fifty-five (gradually extended to seventy in the Late Empire when there was a shortage of decurions) were not normally admissible.[13] This requirement ensured that incoming decurions were mature but not decrepit.

A property qualification was also demanded, paralleling the senatorial census at Rome. At Comum in northern Italy during the time of Trajan, this was one hundred thousand sesterces. While the existence of a similar property qualification is assumed for cities in Spain, as a means of restricting senate entry to the local élite, we have no figures on its value. It may have been less in the provinces than in Italy, and it may have varied from city to city.[14] Jacques suggests that one hundred thousand sesterces was appropriate to a medium-sized city: in smaller towns the local élite was probably less affluent and the property requirement proportionately reduced.[15] We do know from *Irn.* 86 that there were free men with property worth at least five thousand sesterces who did not qualify as decurions, whence it follows that the property qualification for admission to the *ordo* exceeded that figure.

The final prerequisite was freedom from any type of moral or legal stain which might reflect adversely on the dignity of the *ordo*. Persons barred under this provision included those convicted of theft or other criminal offence, whether at Rome or locally; those condemned in an action for trust, partnership, guardianship, or fraud; those who made a false accusation; those who abandoned a public prosecution without permission; debtors, bankrupts, and insolvent persons; army officers or soldiers who had been dishonourably discharged; and those employed in disreputable trades (auctioneers, undertakers, sailors, gladiators, keepers of brothels or gladiatorial schools). These five prerequisites (residence, birth, age, wealth, respectability) ensured that the *ordo* was restricted to an affluent, and socially acceptable, local élite.[16]

It was the responsibility of the local magistrates to ensure that unqualified persons did not enter the *ordo*; they were also forbidden to increase the number of decurions, which might today be termed 'stacking' the house (*Tab. Her.* 83–8, 126–34). In cases where a candidate's eligibility for admission to the senate was disputed, the question could be referred to the provincial governor (Pliny *Ep.* 10. 79–80, 112–13). It is clear from these provisions that the holding of a magistracy was not a prerequisite for admission to the *ordo*, whereas the holding of a magistracy would confer *de facto* membership. Obviously, when a new town was founded there would be no former magistrates to compose the *ordo*, and a local senate would have to be created *ex nihilo*. Also, there are numerous attestations of Spanish decurions who died without ever having held any magistracy.[17]

Admission to the *ordo* was effected either through election (*creatio*) or extraordinary means (*adlectio*). Election of qualified persons to vacant seats in the *ordo* was held annually, on a date agreed upon by the duovirs and decurions. Nominations were approved by vote of the decurions; but the exact procedure for nomination and election is not preserved. Under the Early Empire at any rate, the consent of the candidates was required.[18] Adlection of unqualified persons (e.g. non-residents) could be made either by vote of the decurions – a process also known as *cooptatio* – or by the intervention of the emperor (presumably through patronage). Several examples of both types of adlection are attested in Spain.[19] The list of decurions was revised every fifth year by the *quinquennales* and the names of new members entered into the official register (*album*); those decurions elected in the interval were known as *pedan[e]i*.[20]

The number of decurions required in attendance at any senate meeting depended initially upon the type of business to be conducted. Thus in chapter 69 of the Urso charter we see that for routine matters as few as twenty members sufficed; in other cases the number required is stated as thirty, forty, or fifty. Alternatively, in both the Urso and Flavian charters, we find the quorum expressed as a fraction of the total membership, e.g., two-thirds, three-quarters, or a majority. In later times, a quorum of two-thirds of the decurions was required for a local senate to be legally convened.[21]

At Urso, a decurion could be expelled from the *ordo* upon being convicted by a *quaestio* of conduct unbecoming a decurion (*Urs.* 105, cf 124). Such expulsions (as well as other penalties, such as exile) presumably applied in all towns, to judge from their repeated mention in legal sources and the insistence (already mentioned) that decurions be men of untainted character. On this matter, unfortunately, the relevant section of the Flavian charters does not survive. In the case of temporary exile (*relegatio ad tempus*), the ex-decurion might subsequently be readmitted to the *ordo* (if, of course, there was a vacancy), although by the reign of Marcus Aurelius such reinstatement required the emperor's permission.[22] Membership in the *ordo* was thus a revocable privilege, and it was in the interest of the local élite to ensure that any 'undesirable' members were removed from their prestigious circle.

Magistrates – Qualifications for Office

Since magistrates were members of the *ordo decurionum*, it followed that those who did not meet the qualifications for admission to the decurionate could not normally compete for municipal office either. Existing decurions could become magistrates if they met all necessary qualifications.[23] In addition to being a citizen or resident of the town and having attained the requisite age, a candidate for office had to be solvent and owe no public debts. Since most magistrates (even aediles, as we now know from the Irni charter) handled public funds, the rationale for this restriction is apparent. Though minors were occasionally elected (e.g., **442** and **446**, aediles of Barcino at age seventeen and eighteen respectively), boys under the age of puberty could not be admitted even if there were a shortage of candidates. Alföldy suggests that the minimum age for office at Barcino was lower than elsewhere, but this is difficult to prove from only two examples.[24] Free birth was normally a requirement, and although freedmen were theoretically allowed to hold office at Urso, none is attested. Criminals were of course excluded, although the son of a criminal, like the son of a freedman, was not necessarily debarred; and persons accused of a crime could not hold office until their case had been decided (with, we must assume, an acquittal).[25] Women, not surprisingly, could not hold political office;[26] but a man's religious beliefs were apparently not a barrier.[27]

Candidates for the duovirate, and probably for other magistracies as well, could not have held office within the previous five years (*Mal.* 54). This provision was presumably intended to allow more decurions an opportunity to exercise these offices. It was also understood that a magistrate, once elected, would be required to perform certain public services out of his own pocket (see below, chapters 4 and 7). This expectation was consonant with the timocratic nature of the Roman ruling classes, which gave privileges to the rich but at the same time imposed obligations; a parallel is offered by the ancient Greek system of liturgies.

Election of Magistrates

Since a magistrate's term of office coincided with the calendar year, as shown in the Urso charter (*Urs.* 63), elections would be held the previous year (as was also the case at Rome, and in many modern systems). It is clear from the Flavian municipal law that the election of magistrates, unlike that of decurions, was the prerogative of the entire citizen body voting in *comitia*, not an intramural decision of the *ordo decurionum*. The magistrates to be elected normally comprised two duovirs, two aediles and two quaestors – a collegial system whose roots can be traced to the early days of the Republic, when the Senate refused to entrust power to one man.

The procedure for nomination of candidates was presumably spelled out in chapter 50 of the Flavian regulations, which is unfortunately lost. Chapters 51–2 provide that in the absence of any or sufficient candidates, a list of all persons qualified for office shall be posted by the presiding magistrate, i.e., the senior duovir. Each person on this list is allowed to present himself before this magistrate and to nominate candidates from the list. Whether resort was actually had to this procedure during the Early Empire is a doubtful question; it appears to have been merely a provision to cover a remote possibility. As has recently been suggested, the drafters of the Flavian regulations may have inserted this provision because they doubted the willingness of the provincials to undertake the required duties.[28]

The senior duovir (the elder by birth) presided over the *comitia* for the election, and where necessary, by-election, of duovirs, aediles, and quaestors. The duovirs were elected first, followed by the other offices. Citizens voted in polling booths or compartments (*consaepta*), casting secretly marked ballots (*tabellae*) according to *curiae*, corresponding to the voting tribes at Rome; the new charter fragments show that the number of *curiae* was limited. Election was determined by a plurality of ballots in each *curia*; the two candidates receiving the largest number of votes in each *curia* were returned, and the pair who carried the greatest number of *curiae* were declared elected.[29] In the case of a tied vote in any *curia*, preference was given to married men and those with children (an apparent reflection of Augustan marriage legislation, which awarded privileges to those who perpetuated their families). If the tied candidates had equal claims in this regard, the decision was made by drawing lots. Candidates winning a majority of the *curiae* were obliged to swear an oath that they would perform all duties of the office, and that they had not committed nor would commit any wrongful deed, including unlawful summoning of the decurions (*Mal.* 56, 59; *Salp.* 26). They were also required to provide sureties (bondsmen) and securities (property) as a pledge that they would not mishandle any public moneys. This requirement applied even in the case of magistrates nominated compulsorily. The requirement for securities ensured against both embezzlement of municipal funds and insolvency of city officials. It was once thought that aediles would be exempt from providing securities, since their duties did not require them to handle public funds; however, the *Lex Irnitana* makes it clear that aediles not only handled such funds but had to submit accounts at the end of their aedileship.[30]

Magistrates could run again for the same office after waiting the requisite five years; this repetition of the same magistracy was termed *iteratio*. Examples of magistrates holding the same office twice (*bis, iterum*) or even three times occur fairly frequently in Spain. There is no compelling evidence that this 'waiting period' could be waived or legally bypassed, allowing a magistrate to hold the same office two years in succession. The younger Balbus (**96**) had himself re-elected to the quattuorvirate, but illegally. Also, the phrase 'designatus iterum' (**140–1**) implies re-election for a second, but not necessarily consecutive, term. Although one scholar has suggested that the phenomenon of re-electing the same magistrates points to a shortage of candidates,[31] a likelier explanation may be personal ambition and individual popularity. The 'election fever' evident in the Flavian graffiti from Pompeii certainly points to voluntary candidature and enthusiastic campaigning, not to political apathy.

Order of Offices

It was once believed – and the myth still has adherents – that there was a fixed progression of municipal offices in the Roman West, namely from quaestor to aedile to duovir.[32] However, the number of municipal *cursus* which deviate from this supposed norm is so substantial as to cast doubt on the whole scheme. An examination of these three 'standard' offices is therefore in order.

Of all the links in the chain, the most vulnerable is the quaestorship. Since this office was a personal *munus* rather than an *honor* (in some towns at any rate), it could be held at any point in the *cursus*, if held at all. In the inscriptions it occurs sometimes after the aedileship, sometimes after the duovirate, sometimes after a post-duoviral flaminate – in short, it seems, anywhere except the beginning of the *cursus*. Nor is this syndrome confined to Spain: we find similar irregularity of order in the inscriptions of Italy, Gallia Narbonensis and Africa.[33] Moreover, Spanish quaestors occur almost exclusively in the *conventus Tarraconensis* (fifty-nine total). There are only seven attested in Baetica, four in Lusitania, and none at all in the rest of Hispania Citerior. Clearly the quaestorship did not exist in all towns, and the quaestors' financial duties must have been undertaken by the other magistrates.[34] From the fact that the quaestorship is mentioned in the charter of Salpensa (a *municipium*) but not that at Urso (a colony), Stevenson conjectured that colonies did not have quaestors.[35] This theory is however disproved by the inscriptions, which attest numerous quaestors at the colonies of Tarraco and Valentia, plus one from either Emerita or Norba (**890–4, 896–7, 899, 903, 907, 909–10, 950–5, 393**); it is nonetheless disturbing to find none at Barcino. There may be some validity to Mackie's theory, that the odium attaching to quaestors in their role as tax collectors may have discouraged them from advertising this office on their inscriptions. Alternatively, if we accept that the quaestorship was a junior post and not an *honor*, it may have seemed too unimportant for an ex-duovir to bother mentioning. On the other hand, at Saguntum, the small number of quaestors (compared with aediles and duovirs) and the fact that, in career inscriptions, this office is cited after the duovirate and sometimes after the high-priesthood of the Salii have prompted Alföldy to conclude that there was only one quaestor per year and that the quaestorship was the highest honour in that city.[36] Though the dearth of quaestorial mentions could have other interpretations, the curious placement of the title at the climax of the *cursus* seems to support Alföldy's view.

A particularly enigmatic problem is the interpretation of the designation 'q.' on certain coins. In inscriptions on stone, 'q.' usually stands for 'quaestor,' rarely 'quinquennalis.' Many of the coins of Emporiae are stamped 'q.,' and this apparently stands for 'quaestor' since some of the coins give an alternative and fuller form, 'QVAIC.'[37] At Carthago Nova, on the other hand, we have monetal magistrates called 'IIvir q.,' and here the 'q.' in at least three cases can be demonstrated to mean 'quinquennalis': Helvius Pollio (**541**) is called 'IIvir q.' on some coins but 'IIvir quin.' on others; King Juba is called 'IIvir qu.' on coins but 'IIvir quinq.' in an inscription; Laetilius Apalus (**568**) is called 'IIvir q.' on coins but 'IIvir quinq.' in an inscription.[38] It therefore appears that 'IIvir q.' at Carthago Nova designates a *quinquennalis*.

What then of the 'IIviri q.' at Ilici? In the absence of evidence to the contrary, 'q.' should be 'quaestor'; 'quinquennalis' would be 'q.q..' But in view of the proximity of Ilici to Carthago Nova, where 'q.' is 'quinquennalis,' one has to admit uncertainty. Beltrán Lloris contends that the Ilici magistrates are *quinquennales*, but weakens his credibility by suggesting that 'q.' is 'quinquennalis' also at Emporiae, Valentia, Urso and Corduba.[39] It might be argued that 'q.' may have a different meaning when it follows 'IIvir,' especially since 'quaestor' is supposedly a lower office and should precede the higher. Such an argument is in fact very hazardous: Beltrán Lloris cites a magistrate of Emporiae (L. Rosius Rufus, 727) with the titulary 'aed. IIvir q.' as evidence that 'q.' is 'quinquennalis' there; he is seemingly unaware of another magistrate from the same city (L. Minicius Rufus, 723) whose inscription reads, unequivocally, 'aed. IIviro quaestori'. In short, it seems that the quaestorship could be held at even a late stage of the *cursus*. As for the 'q.' abbreviation on coins, its meaning doubtless varied from place to place.

A final aspect of the 'q.' problem is the possibility that the abbreviation designates a quaestor of Rome rather than a local magistrate. Grant observed that 'L. Ap. Dec. q.' is attested on coins of Baelo, Urso and Myrtilis (28, 288, 358) as well as at Lilybaeum in Sicily. He argued that all these coins refer to the same individual, who by virtue of the multiplicity of mints involved cannot be a local official. Grant concluded that L. Ap. Dec. must be a Roman quaestor, and that the only context for the same man issuing coins in both Spain and Sicily was the civil wars of the 40s BC. More recently, Crawford has argued that these coins might better be dated, for metrological reasons, during the Sertorian War of the 70s BC, and that L. Ap. Dec. would be an otherwise unattested son of C. Appuleius Decianus, who was tribune in 98 BC.[40] Unfortunately the coins themselves lend little support to the concept of multiple issues by a single individual. The Baelo example, formerly read as 'L. Ap. q.,' actually reads 'L. Apo.,' making an identification with Appuleius impossible. The Myrtilis coins display a bewildering variety of name-abbreviations which may or may not refer to a single magistrate, but none of them actually reads 'L. Ap. Dec.' and none of them includes 'q.' This inconsistent nomenclature and lack of titulary accord poorly with the hypothesis of an official issue by a Roman quaestor. Only the Urso coins read 'L. Ap. Dec. q.,' but with Baelo eliminated and Myrtilis doubtful, the 'q.' could be a local magistrate, whose *nomen* could be Aponius or Appius as easily as Appuleius; and the Sicilian example (whose connection with Spain neither Grant nor Crawford can explain convincingly) may be unrelated.

The aedileship tends to occur rather more regularly than the quaestorship, and normally precedes the duovirate. Its omission from many inscriptions leaves a *non liquet* as to whether the office had actually been skipped, or whether its mention was merely considered superfluous beside that of the duovirate. The irregularity in the sequence of priesthoods in the municipal *cursus* might suggest that there were alternate avenues of advancement: for instance, that one could bypass the aedileship by holding a *sacerdotium* or quaestorship. On the other hand, the flaminate and pontificate seem to have ranked even higher than the duovirate, and frequently follow it in the *cursus*; moreover, priesthoods are not proper magistracies. In any event, it seems unlikely that the aedileship was a necessary stepping stone to the duovirate, though it was often used as such. There were only two aediles and two duovirs per year; therefore, if one of the aediles died, retired from political life, or went on to other office (e.g., an equestrian career or a priesthood), there would be a shortage of qualified candidates for the duovirate (except by iteration of a previous duovir after a five-year interval).[41] In such a situation it might be necessary to elect a duovir who was not an ex-aedile. In fact, there are plenty of career inscriptions attesting aediles who never became duovirs, which would suggest that the aedileship was not merely an intermediate rung in a *cursus*, nor an automatic springboard to the duovirate, but could be a terminal post, either by the desire of the individual or by his failure to secure election to higher office. Thus the aedile-to-duovir transition was by no means a fixed step in one's career.

Additional light on the order of offices may be provided by chapter 54 of the Flavian municipal law. This chapter, which demonstrates that *duoviri iure dicundo* have superior *potestas* to aediles and quaestors, lumps together these last two offices as if to suggest that they had equal *potestas*. Aediles and quaestors have, moreover, the same minimum age requirement of twenty-five rather than a sliding scale. This requirement suggests that one could hold *either* the aedileship or the quaestorship as the first office, followed later by the duovirate. The quaestorship, of course, could also be held later, whereas the aedileship could only be a preliminary office. In towns where the quaestorship existed we sometimes find the *cursus* 'quaestor IIvir', which may suggest that the quaestorship was held instead of the aedileship.[42]

However, chapter 54 also gives the minimum age of the duovir as twenty-five. We know that in the Late Republic the minimum age for all magistracies was thirty. The theory that Augustus reduced it to twenty-five has never been proved;[43] however, if the age could be thirty across the board (rather than a sliding scale), there is no reason why it could not later be twenty-five across the board. If so, the basic age requirement of twenty-five for all three positions would mean, in effect, that there was no municipal *cursus*: one could run for the duovirate without holding any previous office. Against this solution there are two technical obstacles: first, chapter 54 is preserved only in the Malaca copy, and the mention of age twenty-five (xxv) for the duovir could be a transcription error for thirty (xxx) or thirty-five (xxxv); secondly, chapter 25 of the same law (preserved in two copies, as well as in one of the Lauriacum fragments: *Salp.* 25 = *Irn.* 25 = *FIRA* I² 26) stipulates that the minimum age for the prefect who replaces the duovir is thirty-five, and there is no evident reason why a twenty-five year old could only be replaced by a thirty-five year old. The minimum age for the duovir thus remains in doubt. If it was thirty-five, there is still no explicit requirement that he must first serve as aedile or quaestor. If, on the other hand, one could hold the duovirate without any preliminary office, it is curious that a large number of Spanish magistrates chose to begin with at least one of the junior posts. The third possibility is that there was an 'unwritten law' that one should hold a junior office first; needless to add, what was unwritten cannot be recovered now.

Duovirs versus Quattuorvirs

A further problem is the tendency of some cities to call their chief magistrates *duoviri* (or *duumviri*, the terms apparently being interchangeable),[44] and of others to call them *quattuorviri*. Various hypotheses have been advanced to account for this inconsistency. One is that colonies had duovirs, while *municipia* had quattuorvirs. A second is that communities which already had two chief magistrates retained duovirs, while the others adopted quattorvirs. A third hypothesis holds that communities which were Roman in origin had duovirs, while those that were Roman only by incorporation (i.e., hitherto autonomous) had quattuorvirs. And according to a fourth hypothesis, quattuorvirs are found only in places chartered before a certain date.[45] The first hypothesis, as Stevenson pointed out long ago, was applicable only to Italy, not the provinces; and even for Italy, both the first and second have now been superseded by the third.[46] This hypothesis is not, however, valid for Spain, since the vast majority of *municipia* (which were previously self-governing) have duovirs. Neither is the fourth hypothesis viable: Rudolph's contention that new *municipia* were quattuorviral until Julius Caesar and duoviral thereafter, and likewise Frere's statement that quattuorvirs were unfashionable in Spain by the Flavian period, are disproved by the appointment of quattuorvirs at the new Flavian *municipia* of Munigua and Sabora.[47] All four hypotheses must therefore be discarded and the problem examined afresh.

Nearly all incorporated communities in Spain, be they colonies or *municipia*, had duovirs. Six known *municipia* (Asido Caesarina, Sabora, Gades, Munigua, Carmo, Sigarra) had quattuorvirs, although the first four named also had duovirs. There is no apparent rationale for these anomalies. Gades, an Augustan *municipium* (and once the seat of two *sufetes*) had quattuorvirs both before and after Augustus (**96**, **98**, **102**, **104**). Both it and Munigua seem to have had duovirs and quattuorvirs simultaneously. Sabora, upon becoming a *municipium* in AD 77, converted its magistrates from duovirs to quattuorvirs.[48] The *civitas* of Liria had both types of magistracy (**782–4**), while L. Porcius Serenus of Aeso (a town of unknown status) was both a quattuorvir and duovir (**401**).

Roman colonies in Spain did not have quattuorvirs. Carteia had them, conceivably because it was a Latin colony, where quattuorvirs were the rule. But Knapp postulates, not unreasonably, that Carteia became a *municipium* ca 90 BC; and a recently discovered inscription from Carteia bearing the phrase 'in munic...' appears to confirm this status, if not the date.[49] The quattuorvirs at Clunia apparently antedate the granting of colonial status under Galba: all but one of them appear on coins of Tiberius, and the other also belongs to the first century (**634–49, 659**). Perhaps Clunia was formerly a *municipium*.[50] A possible quattuorvir at Emerita (**334**) is doubtful and unlikely, for there is no other quattuorvir in Lusitania. The sole remaining exception is a 'IIIvir IIIIvir' at the Augustan colony of Ilici (**761**), neither of whose titles is explicable. Ilici otherwise has duovirs and aediles, not quattuorvirs.

The likeliest explanation for the quattuorvirate in the *municipia* is that it was simply an alternate title. As explained above (chapter 1, n 15), the quattuorvirs were a joint board comprising two duovirs and two aediles. Thus a duovir could legitimately call himself a quattuorvir, in addition to or instead of his title of duovir, since he belonged to both the board of two and the board of four. This is the only feasible way to account for the simultaneous presence of duovirs and quattuorvirs in the same town, and for the apparent tenure of both offices by the same individual. Moreover, the use of the title quattuorvir in certain *municipia* and unincorporated towns seems to have been a matter of local preference, rather than in accordance with the dictate of Rome. In other towns the title was apparently unfashionable: among this group the Roman colonies figure prominently. Being more closely controlled by Rome, they had little or no choice in the matter.

Prefects

The prefects (*praefecti*) attested in Spanish communities were not ordinary magistrates, but rather promagistrates appointed to assume the functions of duovirs who for one reason or another (death, illness, absence, impeachment) were unable to perform them. The institution stems originally from the *praefecti iure dicundo* sent out by the praetor to govern Rome's early settlements in Italy. In the Imperial period we still find prefects being appointed in peregrine *civitates* and in some of the less romanized provinces (e.g., the Danubian provinces and the Three Gauls); these were not sent from Rome, but were selected from among the local aristocracy.[51]

There is very little evidence for this type of prefect in Spain. Hyginus mentions prefectures at Emerita,[52] and one such prefect is possibly attested in an inscription (**334**). In Baetica, inscriptions of the Imperial period attesting *praefecti iure dicundo* at the *conventus* capitals of Corduba, Astigi, and Gades, led Knapp to assume that such prefects were a legacy of Roman prefects who had originally dispensed justice at these towns under the Republic. This ingenious theory fails to explain why the *praefectus i.d.* at Gades was *ab decurionibus creatus* (97); nor does it account for juridical prefects in cities which were not *conventus* capitals, such as Urso and Salpensa.[53] The charter of the latter town informs us (in chapter 25) that the prefect was appointed, not by the decurions, but by whichever of the duovirs was last to leave town; he must be a decurion, not less than thirty-five years of age, and must take an oath of office. Moreover, it appears that most of the prefects attested in career inscriptions from Spain had already held the duovirate.[54]

A special type of prefect, the *praefectus Caesaris*, was appointed by the emperor when a town offered the office of honorary duovir to a member of the Imperial family. This prefect exercised the same rights as a sole duovir. If however (as occurs until the reign of Tiberius) the emperor or another dignitary was offered the honorary duovirate jointly with a local decurion, there was no requirement for the appointment of a prefect, for the local duovir would discharge the duties of the honorary one. Conversely, when both duovirates were held by Imperial appointees in the same year (as sometimes occurs in Spain under Tiberius) a prefect was presumably required. Apart from members of the Imperial family, we find King Juba of Mauretania and his son Ptolemy holding honorary duovirates at Carthago Nova; Juba was also honorary duovir at Gades.[55]

Curators

While any local magistrate might be called a *curator*, i.e., person in charge of a certain portfolio (*cura*), the *curator rei publicae* was a special and powerful official in a category by himself. *Curatores r.p.* were appointed to assist with local finances and administration. They first make their appearance under the Flavians (or possibly under Nero), and under Trajan and Hadrian the office becomes widespread in most of the Empire, although none is attested in Africa until the Severan period.[56] In the senatorial province of Baetica we have a tantalizingly truncated mention of a ' ... curato[r]' in an inscription dated by Hübner to the reign of Trajan (interestingly enough, from Trajan's home town of Italica). There is no guarantee that this supposed magistrate (143) is a *curator r.p.*, rather than some locally appointed official or even a '[pro]curato[r].' Nor is the approximate dating to Trajan necessarily accurate: we could have here a *curator r.p.* from a later period. It may be relevant that Italica was granted colonial status by

Hadrian; the emperor expressed surprise at the town's request, since colonies were less autonomous than *municipia* and more liable to financial interference by Rome (Gell. *NA* 16.13). Also in Baetica we find two curators under the Antonines (**295, 298**), one in 196 (**267**), five in the third century (**110, 151, 152, 153, 262**), and one undated (**91**). Lusitania has one in the third century (**349**) and one undated (**320**); a lone curator appears at Tarraco in the fourth century (**921**).

There has been much debate among scholars as to whether the curator was a magistrate or a professional civil servant. A recent re-examination of the problem makes it clear that the curatorship was neither a magistracy nor a required stage in an Imperial career.[57] The position of *curator r.p.* was, however, prestigious for the individual, as well as having a decided impact on the management of the city.

Curators were normally appointed by the emperor, held senatorial or equestrian status, and were non-natives of the city where they held office.[58] However, two of the Baetican curators were apparently locals, for both held the duovirate: Q. Vibius Laetus of Corduba (**91**) and C. Aufidius Vegetus of Villafranca (**298**). Moreover, the latter of these two curators dates to the mid- or late second century. If the man was really a *curator r.p.*, the date of this example would contradict Burton's contention that curators did not become local officials until the late third century.[59]

Unusual Magistracies

Previous scholars have remarked upon the 'bewildering variety' of municipal offices in the provinces. Spain in particular provides a number of offices other than the normal duovirs, aediles and quaestors. In most cases these are remnants of a pre-romanized local government. In particular, the vague title *magistratus* (of which twenty-four are attested) could mask a variety of indigenous officials.[60] The fact that four or more so-called *magistratus* can occur simultaneously (**351–4, 666–70**) suggests that the term denotes all members of the board of local magistrates, not just the chief magistrate or pair of magistrates.

Praetors With the exception of two examples at Bocchoris in the Baleares in 6 BC (whose title may be the Latin translation of a Punic magistracy),[61] praetors are found only in the Ebro Valley. The earliest magistrates attested at Contrebia Belaisca (87 BC) are a praetor and five *magistratus*, all with indigenous nomenclature (**665–70**). The office of praetor is very strange in such a context: Roman colonies often had a pair of praetors in charge, both in Italy and outside,[62] but here we have a single praetor in what is patently not a Roman town. The board of five magistrates is equally suspicious (cf below on *quinqueviri*). It would appear that we are dealing with an intermediate stage in the romanization of Contrebia: the *princeps* and his council have adopted equivalent Latin titles for their appointments, but have not actually adopted the Roman magisterial system. The same inscription shows that Contrebia had a *senatus* and *iudices*; the names of these bodies clearly imitate those at Rome (perhaps too closely), but one suspects that they are romanized in name only and are basically pre-Roman institutions.[63]

During the third quarter of the first century BC we find pairs of magistrates styled 'pr. IIvir' on coins of Celsa and Calagurris. One of the pairs from the former city is 'pr. quin.' 'Pr.' is probably again *praetor*, imitating the pre-duoviral title of the chief magistrates of Roman colonies, and numerous parallels may be adduced epigraphically. The other possible interpretation, 'pr[aefecti pro] IIvir[is]' and 'pr[aefecti pro] quin[quennalibus]' is more complex but cannot be entirely ruled out, since a *praefectus pro IIviro* would enjoy all the powers of a duovir, including coinage.[64]

Principes While *principes* (chieftains, leaders) were common enough in the pre-Roman period, only a few survive in inscriptions, all from the north: **819** (Palantia), **790, 791**, and **967** (all *conventus Lucensis*). These inscriptions cannot be closely dated, but perhaps belong to the first century AD. *Principes* are still found in other provinces in the second century.[65]

Censors Three censors are attested on the coinage of Carteia in the second half of the first century BC (**55–7**). The appearance of this office at Carteia is perhaps explained as a remnant of this town's earlier status as a *colonia Latina*, for censors are often found in Latin towns. The office recurs sporadically throughout the Empire, and it is interesting to note that local censors are still found in Bithynia in the second century AD. It is clear that the appointment of censors in Italy and the provinces was part of a gradual process of decentralization of the tasks of the censors at Rome.[66] However, the dearth of attestations of this office in Spain makes it equally clear that local censorial duties were in most towns performed not by censors but by the duovirs.

Strange Numbers of Magistrates Inscriptions record the office of *decemvir* at Cartima in Baetica (**71**), and possibly at Lara de los Infantes (ancient name unknown) in Tarraconensis (**776**), as well as *decemvir maximus* at the Baetican cities of Ostippo (**234**) and Ulia (**271**). The three Baetican examples range in date from 49 BC to AD 54. The adjective *maximus* presumably designates the senior *decemvir*, like *praetor maximus* or *pontifex maximus* at Rome. The office of *decemvir* is probably based on the Italian municipal system, where the decemvirate antedates the granting of *ius Latii* to a town, although there remains a possibility that in Baetica it represents the continuity of a Punic institution.[67] Mackie has suggested that *decemvir* at Ostippo is a title contrived to mark the town's special status as an *oppidum liberum*. This hypothesis hardly explains the appearance of this magistracy at Cartima, unless we assume without evidence (as Mackie does) that the latter town also held free or federate status.[68] Few will be deluded by the circular nature of this reasoning, and the new inscription from Ulia should lay Mackie's hypothesis to rest.

In the Augustan period we find an *octovir* in Lusitania (**393**). This odd title is possibly the remnant of a pre-Roman local government, although parallels from Italy can be adduced.[69] Since the findspot of the inscription, Alburquerque, is equidistant from Norba and Emerita, Galsterer suggests that the *octovir* may have belonged to the latter city and have somehow been involved with the prefectures. However, Norba, as the earlier foundation, may have a stronger claim to this archaic title.[70]

An inscription from Lacippo in Baetica possibly mentions a *quinquevir* (**167**), and an intriguing if unrelated parallel is provided by the board of five *magistratus* at Contrebia, already cited. *Quinqueviri* did exist as commissioners at Rome, but they were hardly *magistratus*.[71] Another odd number is evident in the *triumvir* attested at Ilici, if the reading is sound (**761**). There is also some indirect evidence for the possible existence of triumvirs at Castulo around the end of the second century BC (three names on each coin: **585–7**) and at Maggava in AD 14 (three magistrates named on a *tessera hospitalis*: **793–5**). One is reminded of the odd numbers of magistrates in semi-romanized towns of Africa: triumvirs at Cirta, three *sufetes* at Mactar, and *undecemprimi* elsewhere.[72]

Interreges Chapter 130 of the Urso charter stipulates that persons proposing or publishing a decree illegally may be prosecuted by a duovir or *interrex* or prefect. The mention of *interrex* has been interpreted either as an interpolation, or as a perpetuation of the Italian practice (also copied in Narbonensis) of appointing an *interrex* in times of emergency, or when no duovirs were elected.[73] The latter view now seems likelier, in view of the recent discovery of an inscription from the territory of the *municipium Siarense* naming an actual *interrex* (**248**). The man in question had already served as duovir, and one may doubt whether there was in fact much difference in function between an *interrex* and a *praefectus*. The editor dates this text to 'probably the end of the Republic' (has he been influenced by the Urso charter?). At any rate the fact that the magistrate's tribe is Galeria strongly suggests that Siarum received municipal status under Julius or Augustus Caesar.

Omnibus honoribus functus In the two Imperial provinces, and particularly in Tarraconensis, members of the local élite are sometimes said to have discharged *omnes honores*. As Alföldy has rightly pointed out, this catch-all title does not make its appearance before AD 120 (*RIT* 253). But what is meant by *omnes honores*? Although Ladage would have us believe that it refers to magistrates only, *omnes honores* seems rather a lofty title for only three posts (or two, since the quaestorship is a *munus*, not an *honor*).[74] Apparent proof that priesthoods could be included in this designation is provided by a text describing a woman of Mago as *omnibus honoribus functa*.[75] Since women could not be magistrates, this can only refer to the holding of religious offices. Moreover, there is some indication in legal sources that *honores* and magistracies were not synonymous: Gaius mentions Roman citizenship being granted to those who held 'vel magistratum vel honorem' (Gaius *Inst.* 1.96).

But although priesthoods were not necessarily excluded from *omnes honores*, it should be noted that the title became commonplace, a synonym for having progressed to the top of the local ladder. Thus *omnes* need not always be taken literally, nor does it imply the same offices in different towns. Thus at Tarraco (as Alföldy has again discerned) it regularly means 'aedile, quaestor, IIvir,' but not priesthood, while at Barcino at least one example shows *omnes honores* as equivalent to 'IIvir, flamen' (**438**, referring to an outsider who apparently skipped the aedileship by 'purchasing' the top magistracy).[76]

Legates The position of municipal envoy was somewhat anomalous, in that it did not figure in the formal *cursus honorum*, nor was it a publicly elected office. Ambassadors were not even chosen at regular intervals or for a standard term of office, but rather on an 'as-required' basis for a specific mission. The procedure for approving the dispatch of an embassy is detailed in chapter 92 of the Urso charter and chapter G of the *Lex Irnitana*. The duovir proposes the embassy to the decurions, who decide by majority vote of those present. The actual selection of legates is arranged annually by dividing all decurions under the age of sixty into three *decuriae* of equal size. Lots are then drawn to decide the order in which the *decuriae* will provide embassies, as well as the order of names of potential legates in each *decuria*. This is certainly a more complicated method than the seniority system recommended in the *Digest*.[77] A person chosen to perform such an embassy must either do so, or provide a substitute; failure to comply with this law would incur a fine (ten thousand sesterces at Urso, twenty thousand at Irni). According to Ulpian, the delinquent legate would also be expelled from the *ordo*. Serving magistrates, ex-magistrates whose accounts had not yet been approved, persons in charge of public funds or who lacked the right to prosecute, and former gladiators were all ineligible to serve as legates.[78]

Distribution of Offices

The distribution of attested magistracies and quasi-magistracies in Roman Spain (Table 1) reflects regional and historical disparities amongst the three provinces, as well as illustrating the wide range of magisterial titles. Baetica retains such oddities as censors, quinquevirs, and *interreges*, which are lacking in the other provinces. Also of interest are the paucity of quaestors outside of Tarraconensis and the complete absence in Baetica of the *omnibus honoribus functus* formula. It may also be noted that there are well over sixty quattuorvirs – far fewer, certainly, than the duovirs, but sufficient to undermine a recent contention that the quattuorviral title was 'very rare in Spain.'[79] Despite the conformity which romanization endeavoured to impose, there was clearly great variety in magisterial titulary.

The Local *Cursus:* An End in Itself?

Whereas at Rome there is no question that the apex of the *cursus honorum* was the consulship, the situation in the provinces was more ambiguous. True, one could advance to the duovirate and perhaps to a priesthood, the highest positions available in the community; but it was also possible to leave one's home town and enter the Imperial civil service or the army, to become a knight or a senator or even (as in the case of Trajan) emperor. Yet, given the influence of local aristocratic families within their own communities, we may reasonably ask how many magistrates were content with local honours.

Certainly there was an attraction to being *domi nobilis*, a large fish in a small pond, rather than a 'new man' in the capital. In 59 BC Cicero laments to Atticus that he would rather be one of the duovirs in the town of Antium than consul at Rome. In recent studies, Syme and Drinkwater have documented the continuing control of local offices in the Three Gauls by aristocrats 'averse from ambition or display,' while Finley and Garnsey have shown how members of the Sicilian and African élites spurned Imperial service for local careers. Hopkins claims to discern a chronological pattern: in the early period, rich provincials were content with local offices, whereas

TABLE 1
Distribution of Attested Magistrates

	Baetica	Lusitania	Tarraconensis
decurio	10	3	13
decurialis			1
decurionatus ornamenta	5		
decurionatus honor	1		1
quaestor	7	4	59
aedilis	48	17	120
aedilis designatus	1	1	
aedilicius			3
aedilicia potestas	3		
aedilicii honores			9
aedilicia ornamenta			1
duovir (duumvir)	136	49	271
duovir q. (?)			5
duovir quinquennalis			34
quinquennalis			3
duovir designatus	4		1
duovir iure dicundo	1		
duoviralis		2	3
duoviralis potestas	3		
duovirales honores			2
duoviralia ornamenta	1		
quattuorvir	36	1	29
quattuorviralis potestas	2		
praefectus	9	4	4
praefectus Caesaris (Imperatoris)	3	1	4
praefectus iure dicundo	4		
praefectus pro duoviro		1	
praefectus quinquennalis			2
curator (rei publicae)	9	2	1
praetor	1		3
pr.	1		6
pr. quin.			2
princeps	2		4
principalis			2
censor	3		
decemvir	3		1
octovir		1	
quinquevir	1		

TABLE 1 – continued

	Baetica	Lusitania	Tarraconensis
triumvir			1
omnibus honoribus functus		2	45
legatus	19		22
legatus perpetuus	1		
interrex	1		
magistratus (so called)		6	17
apparent magistrate (no title given)	59	12	41

in the course of the Empire they expanded their horizons and, having acquired Roman citizenship, began competing for Roman honours.[80] While perhaps valid on general lines, Hopkins' theory fails to take into account the whims of individuals – for after all, the decision to leave home and pursue a career abroad is a personal one. Far from being only a function of time, this 'career decision' is largely a function of ambition and individual preference. Members of the same family, even brothers, made widely different choices, as two Spanish examples will illustrate.

L. Cornelius Balbus Maior was born into a noble family of Gades. After a distinguished military career with the Roman army in Spain, he became Caesar's lieutenant, was one of the most powerful men in Rome, and in 40 BC became the first provincial consul.[81] Lucius' brother Publius, on the other hand, is an unknown. Probably the elder of the two (his son was consul only eight years after Lucius), Publius presumably remained in Gades looking after the family business (his father was dead by 72 BC). Publius' son followed in his uncle's footsteps rather than his father's, and became the first provincial ever to win a triumph (19 BC). A more familiar example is provided by the sons of the elder Seneca, a Roman knight from Corduba. The two eldest sons (L. Iunius Gallio, the governor of Achaea who tried St Paul; and the younger Seneca, the Stoic philosopher and Nero's chief minister) attained the highest offices of state. The third son, M. Annaeus Mela, scrupulously avoided the Roman forum and preferred to remain a knight, much to the disappointment of his family.[82] Yet the son of this black sheep was the celebrated poet Lucan.

The local magistrates of Spain have left no opinion of life in their home towns, but some instructive testimony is provided by the Spanish poet Martial (ca 40–104). Like Cicero he developed a distaste for Rome and longed for the small-town life, so he packed his bags and returned to his native Bilbilis. But boredom soon set in and he regretted his decision; he was depressed by the lack of intellectual and recreational outlets in this *provincialis solitudo* (Mart. 12 pr.). No doubt many Spaniards felt a similar dissatisfaction with a small-town existence and desperately sought external career progression; others were apparently content to remain in a familiar, unhurried environment and to boast about their exclusively local achievements in inscriptions.

Of course, the failure of a career inscription to mention honours beyond the community level does not necessarily mean that the individual never held such higher posts. In some cases the erection of the inscription may have preceded the attainment of further offices. Moreover, persons who did proceed to a loftier *cursus* may not have bothered to mention in their career inscriptions the junior posts which would enable us to trace their local roots. Senators in particular are notorious for omitting reference to their early careers. Nonetheless, there appear to have been many Spanish magistrates who lacked either the will or the ability to achieve offices outside their home town. A case in point is the magistrates of Saguntum, a seemingly closed élite which neither admitted newcomers nor sought (with rare exceptions) rewards beyond the municipal level – a far cry from the upwardly mobile élite of Tarraco.[83]

The Religious *Cursus*

When discussing Roman priesthoods we must bear in mind that Roman religion had political overtones, and especially so under the Empire when the Imperial Cult was flourishing. The Imperial Cult served indeed as a legitimation and glorification of the reigning emperor in that it showed his descent from (or succession to) a divine predecessor. Religious office was accordingly an important and prestigious reward for those of proven loyalty to the emperor. The lowest priesthood, the sevirate, was normally allotted to a handful of deserving freedmen, who of course could not hold magistracies, although free-born sevirs are also known, and at least one (**39**) seems to have reached the local senate.[84] The pontificate or flaminate within a town often went to a local magistrate, while the provincial priesthood was, in origin, an equestrian post. The Imperial Cult in Spain has been the subject of extensive work by Etienne and Alföldy, and it would be redundant to iterate their conclusions here.[85] However, a few remarks are in order concerning the relationship of magistracies to priesthoods.

The exalted status of the local priesthood is indicated by its position in the *cursus honorum*. Although there are exceptions and variants, the priesthood was commonly held after the duovirate; in other words it was considered a higher honour than the top magistracy. We may draw a parallel with the city of Rome, where the office of *pontifex maximus* was usually held by an ex-consul in Republican times and by the emperor under the Principate. The office of augur also tends to fall at the end of the municipal *cursus*; the augurate clearly held the same prestige as the pontificate or flaminate. Priesthoods were important for another reason as well: while Rome had no political representative in local governments, it did have a religious representative, the priest of the Imperial Cult.[86]

The local priest is called *flamen* in Tarraconensis and Lusitania, whereas in Baetica he is more often designated *pontifex*. Etienne is probably correct in suggesting that in the two Imperial provinces the new Imperial Cult with its distinctive priestly title (*flamen*) would be received much more readily than in a senatorial province like Baetica, where conservatism favoured retention of the older, traditional title (*pontifex*) even when used to designate priests of the Imperial Cult.[87] In all three provinces, however, the provincial high priest is called *flamen*.

Just as the secular *cursus* varied from town to town and from individual to individual, so the holding of local religious office claimed no fixed place in the career. So far as is known, priesthoods were not a prerequisite for local magistracies, nor vice versa. Strictly speaking, the priestly *cursus* was an independent mechanism, with advancement based on service to the cult or temple in question. Since in actual practice, however, both magistracies and priesthoods tended to be held by members of a small local élite, individuals are frequently attested holding offices in both spheres. The homogeneity of the two groups is indeed illustrated at Urso, where the residence requirement and expulsion procedures for decurions and priests are identical, and where priests are elected in the same manner as duovirs (*Urs.* 68, 101). And although the order of offices was flexible, the top-ranking priesthoods tended to be held by the top-ranking magistrates. To complicate the picture further, career inscriptions occasionally list offices in reverse chronological order (e.g., **881**), or in order of prestige and importance to the individual; thus, for instance, M. Valerius Propinquus (**780**) lists the provincial flaminate before his earlier offices. Nonetheless, the overwhelming preference was to list offices in the order held; and it is therefore not surprising to find the prestigious municipal priesthood listed after a municipal magistracy or even after an equestrian post, while a provincial priesthood, the culmination of a successful career, is regularly the last appointment named.[88]

A priesthood peculiar to Saguntum is that of the Salii. At Rome the Salii or dancing priests of Mars were a priesthood restricted to patricians. At Saguntum this priesthood was similarly the preserve of the local aristocracy, and its distinctive Italian title perhaps recalls the close relationship and *fides* which existed between Saguntum and Rome in Republican times. While Saguntum also had *pontifices* and *flamines* to look after the Imperial Cult, the Salii (to judge from their position later in the *cursus*) held even higher status, and their leader, the *magister Saliorum*, was regularly an ex-duovir.[89]

In Baetica, the evidence for magistrates entering the provincial priesthood is disappointing: only three instances, all second century or later (**93, 145, 247**). The provincial priests of Lusitania, on the other hand, include both first and second century examples; three of the six known priests come from Emerita. Only Tarraconensis gives us a large body of evidence – the so-called *flamines provinciae Hispaniae citerioris*. The previous careers of the provincial priests in that province follow four patterns, already identified by Alföldy.[90] The first of these involves equestrian army officers who were not magistrates. The second is for local magistrates who became equestrian army officers before attaining the provincial flaminate; these two groups date mostly to the Flavian period and the early second century. The third model involves local magistrates who held the position of *iudex* at Rome as a stepping-stone to the provincial flaminate; these examples span the entire second century. The fourth and most frequent pattern, chiefly confined to the second century, is for local magistrates to proceed to the provincial priesthood without holding intermediate offices. Many of these examples date to the second half of the century, when few Spaniards were receiving equestrian positions in either the army or the civil service. Many provincial priests simply sum up their early careers with the comprehensive phrase, 'omnibus honoribus in re publica sua functus.'

In its early phases the provincial flaminate was undoubtedly a position of prestige and importance. Its easier accessibility in the second century suggests that it had become less prestigious and open to men of humbler background (and in some demonstrable instances, of obscure *origo*). There is, of course, no proof that these latter-day priests were not *equites*; but the lack of equestrian offices in their *cursus* is suspicious.

The Military *Cursus*

Military service was important not only as a means for provincials to acquire Roman citizenship (an alternative to local office-holding), but as the stepping-stone to an equestrian career. A substantial number of Spanish magistrates undertook military service either before or after their magistracy. The varying sequence in which they held their military and civilian posts reinforces what was stated earlier in this chapter about the irregularity of the *cursus honorum*.[91] The principal military posts (in descending order of rank) which were actually held by Spanish magistrates are discussed separately in what follows.

Military Tribunate Six magistrates (three from Baetica, three from Tarraconensis) held the tribunate before their magistracy; twelve (one from Lusitania, eleven from Tarraconensis) held it after. In both cases the inscriptions span rather evenly the first and second centuries, so there is apparently no question of a shift in trend between one period and another. Geographically there seems to have been a tendency in Baetica to hold the tribunate before, and in Tarraconensis to hold it after the magistracy, but the samples are fairly small. What is remarkable is the flexibility in the order of posts.

Prefecture of an Auxiliary Cohort Here again we find a military appointment which could be held either before or after a local civic career, although there is still a tendency for the magistracy to occur first. Again, the examples are well spread over the first two centuries AD. Ten men (two from Baetica, eight from Tarraconensis) held their magistracy before their prefecture. One magistrate and one decurion from Tarraconensis, and one possible magistrate from Baetica (**109**) held the prefecture first. Of three magistrates recorded as holding both the prefecture and military tribunate, one held both offices before his magistracies while two held them after. Of course, nearly all tribunes will have held the prefecture as a requisite preliminary office, even if they do not bother to record it. Since there is no example of a split military career (e.g., prefect to IIvir to tribune), we can probably conclude that in two-thirds of the cases (twelve out of eighteen) both the prefecture and the tribunate were held after the magistracy.

Centurionate Five centurions subsequently became magistrates or decurions – two in Baetica, three in Tarraconensis. There is no example of a magistrate subsequently becoming a centurion. In one instance (**445**) a retired centurion held the duovirate three times and left a legacy to the city.

Legionaries The only example of a ranker becoming magistrate occurs in the remote (though epigraphically rich) region of Lara de los Infantes, where a 'veteranus legionis VII Geminae Felicis' (the only legion in Spain) became duovir (**770**). The rural provenance of his epitaph, the naming upon it of an heir (which implies an estate), and the presumed property qualification for the duovirate combine to suggest that this man may have compensated for his undistinguished military career by subsequent success as a farmer.

The available evidence suggests that a minority of the equestrian officers, and all of the centurions, who entered municipal politics did so at the conclusion of their military service. After the compulsory tour (twenty years minimum for legionaries, twenty-five for auxiliaries) behind the colours, most of these will not have been young men; indeed the equestrian officers would include some who had risen from the ranks.[92] But the majority of prefects and tribunes had held their municipal offices (including the duovirate or equivalent) first. This sequence is not at all surprising, since a large proportion of the equestrian officers of the Roman army were in fact ex-duovirs, who were granted equestrian rank on the basis of their proven ability, administrative experience, and maturity.[93] Magistracy also conferred the Roman citizenship necessary for entry to these offices. The evidence from Spain conforms with the pattern in the Empire as a whole. What is disappointing is the failure of these ex-duovirs to complete the *tres militiae*: eighteen were legionary tribunes but only one (**780**) became *praefectus alae*.

Magistrates in the Civil Service and Judiciary

The period from Vespasian to Hadrian, inclusive, is marked by a surge of Spanish ex-magistrates into the administrative hierarchy of the Empire. The timing of this phenomenon can hardly be coincidental: this same era witnessed the admission into the Roman Senate of dozens of Spanish notables (often of Italian stock), culminating with the Spanish emperors Trajan and Hadrian. Vespasian, who granted Latin rights to Spain, also apparently instituted the policy of admitting members of the Spanish élite into the equestrian and senatorial ranks of the Roman state.

Nonetheless, the top posts seem to have been the preserve of Italian candidates, for not a single Spanish magistrate (excluding curators) is known to have advanced beyond the lowest grade of procurator (*sexagenarius*). Just as only one out of eighteen tribunes reached the next military rank, so too we find but a single *procurator Augusti ab alimentis* (**505**); another *procurator Augusti* (**892**) holds an unspecified portfolio. A possible *procurator Baetis* (**218**) is obviously a minor official, for he apparently held this office before the prefecture of a cohort; he was subsequently a *comes et adsessor legati*.

No known Spanish magistrate held an important prefecture, but several exercised minor ones. Specifically, there are five prefects of the seacoast (*praefecti orae maritimae*), two prefects of the Balearic Islands, and one prefect of Asturia. All of these local prefectures precede, coincide with, or replace the prefecture of a cohort. It therefore appears that they were at least partly of a military nature, and perhaps involved guarding the Asturian mines and the ports along the Costa Dorada and in the Baleares. So far as is known, these prefectures were always held by Spaniards, who were presumably more familiar than outsiders with local conditions in the zones in question, and were terminal offices, not leading to further advancement.

The other administrative, or rather judicial, post available to Spanish ex-magistrates was that of judge (*iudex*) of the five *decuriae*. The elder Pliny notes that these *iudices* came to Rome from as far away as Gades (*NH* 29.18). Ten ex-magistrates, all from Tarraconensis, served in this capacity, having been adlected by the emperor. Many of them mention that they had received the *equus publicus*, entitling them to membership in the eighteen centuries of Roman knights. Three *iudices* specify that they belonged to a particular *decuria*, viz. the first (**907**), the third (**899**), and the fourth (**910**). The last of these would not have been an equestrian, since the fourth and fifth *decuriae* consisted of *ducenarii*, those who met only half of the knights' census of four hundred thousand sesterces.[94]

Magistrates in the Roman Senate

Only one known Spanish magistrate was a Roman senator, and the circumstances were unusual. L. Cornelius Balbus Minor (**96**) was already a Roman senator, serving as quaestor in Hispania Ulterior, when he assumed the quattuorvirate of his native Gades (and secured an illegal re-election). According to the *Digest*, a Roman senator could still retain *honores* in his home town.[95] However, in the normal course of events one would presumably hold local offices at the beginning of the *cursus*, not after becoming a senator at Rome. It is frustrating that senators from Spain seldom give details of their early careers, for some of them may have been local magistrates in such prominent towns as Italica and Tarraco. After the mid-second century, however, very few Spaniards are attested as senators or even knights, and indeed in the fourth century it was made illegal for a municipal decurion to become a Roman senator.[96]

Syme has recently suggested that Roman senators from the western provinces tended to be recruited, not so much among Italian colonists (who were mostly discharged soldiers or impoverished civilians) but among the indigenous élite, who were already men of power and influence.[97] If these native aristocrats provided the majority of provincial senators at Rome, it would be perverse to suppose that they did not also dominate the local *ordines*, except perhaps in the colonies themselves – and even here there may have been a strong indigenous element, for many colonies were founded on or adjacent to the sites of pre-Roman towns (e.g., the joint Roman-indigenous colony at Corduba). But we cannot be certain that Syme's argument is valid for Spain. Thus, in Baetica for instance, while the Cornelii Balbi were presumably natives, the Annaei of Corduba and the Ulpii of Italica (Trajan and Hadrian) were apparently of Italian origin.[98] The most illustrious senatorial family on Spain's east coast, the Pedanii of Barcino, were immigrants from Rome, belonging to the urban tribe Palatina. In Lusitania, the Roscii of Emerita represent half the attested senators; their family seat is Brescia in Italy. And although we do find senators from the 'Spanish' tribes Galeria and Quirina, the vast majority of the approximately seventy-five known senators from Spain are of uncertain tribe and origin.

Whether of indigenous or Italian stock, both Roman senators and local magistrates came from prominent families in Spanish communities. However, the evidence suggests that they were not necessarily the same individuals. While a few senators may have begun their political careers as local officials, the majority probably abandoned their home towns at an early stage to pursue a loftier *cursus*. Wealthy scions of equestrian families, who displayed proficiency in military and administrative posts or in the courtroom, and who enjoyed the support of an influential patron, might eventually gain admission to the senatorial order at Rome without ever holding a local magistracy.

We have seen that the *cursus honorum* for local élites was not rigid. The order of civic offices, priesthoods, and the relationship of military service to a local career could vary considerably, even in a single town. Comparatively few local magistrates advanced to a higher career in the equestrian echelons, or as senators at Rome. On the other hand, the natural reluctance of local aristocrats to abandon privileged positions in their home towns may have made the local career an adequate and rewarding ambition. The holding of the same magistracy several times (which may strike a modern observer as career stagnation) was for local magnates the renewal of an honour and a reassertion of the family's claim to political influence.

Notes

1 Pompon. *De verb. signif.* 1239 = Dig. 50.16.239.5; 'quod sint de ordine curiae,' Isid. *Etym.* 9.4.23. On self-governance, see J. Gascou *La politique municipale de l'Empire romain en Afrique Proconsulaire* (Rome 1972) 166.

2 *Tab. Her.* 86–8, 96, 106, 109, 124, 127–8, 134–6, 138, 149–50; *Salp.* 24, 26; *Irn.* 30, 31; *Mal.* 54, 62–4, 66–8

3 *Centumviri:* CIL IX 4952, 4970–1, 4973, 4976. Cic. *Leg. Agr.* 2.35 suggests that one hundred was the normal number of decurions; so do Arnold *Roman System*[3] 255–7; Stevenson *Administration* 171; Langhammer

Magistratus 189–90 (though Langhammer admits exceptions). The album of Canusium (*CIL* IX 338 = *ILS* 6121) contains one hundred decurions if we deduct patrons and *praetextati*.

4 For the numbers of the *ordines* mentioned, see Liebenam *Städteverwaltung* 229; L. Tanfani *Contributo alla storia del municipio romano* (Taranto 1906) 211–12; Abbott and Johnson *MARE* 65; R.P. Duncan-Jones *PBSR* 39 (1962) 70, 115; Langhammer *Magistratus* 190; Mackie *Administration* 69–70; R. Lane Fox *Pagans and Christians* (New York 1987) 50; R.J.A. Talbert *The Senate of Imperial Rome* (Princeton 1984) 132–4. On the probability of an exceptionally large senate at Capua, see R.K. Sherk *The Municipal Decrees of the Roman West* (Buffalo 1970) 7.

5 'quod ante h[anc] l[egem] rogatam iure more eiius municipi fuerunt,' *Irn.* 31

6 For discussions of the respective dimensions, see Duncan-Jones *PBSR* 30 (1962) 72; Talbert *Senate of Imperial Rome* 121, 149–50; and J. Alarcão and R. Etienne *Fouilles de Conimbriga* I (Paris 1977) 37. A *curia* of unspecified size is attested at Peñarrubia, *CIL* II 3538 = *ILER* 2086.

7 The *curia* at Conimbriga was originally interpreted as an Augustan building, razed to make way for the Flavian forum. A new study by A. Roth Congès *Mélanges d'arch.* 99 (1987) 711–51 convincingly redates this *curia* to the Flavian period.

8 R. Duthoy *ANRW* II/16,2 (Berlin and New York 1978) 1266 and 1272, *contra* Etienne *Culte* 275

9 G. Pereira Menaut *Inscripciones romanas de Valentia* (Valencia 1979) pp 8–9 and nos. 12–17, 19–20, 22–5; Galsterer *Untersuchungen* 54. An inscription of the 'Arucitani veteres et iuvenes,' cited by J.M. Blázquez in *Studi in onore di Gaetano Scherillo* II (Milan 1972) 817, is in fact a fake (*CIL* II 100*, cf *CIL* II 269*, Arcobriga), as is a text cited by Galsterer (*Untersuchungen* 54 n 35) mentioning 'Turiason[enses] vet[eres] et iun[iores]' (*CIL* II 250*).

10 J. González *JRS* 76 (1986) 210

11 *Urs.* 91; G. Rupprecht *Untersuchungen zum Dekurionstand in den nordwestlichen Provinzen des römischen Reiches* (Kallmünz 1975) 63–5

12 For enforcement, *Mal.* 54; for children, *Dig.* 50.2.3.2 Ulp.; 50.2.6 Pap.

13 *Tab. Her.* 89–94; Cic. *Verr.* 2.2.49.122; *Mal.* 54; Pliny *Ep.* 10.79.1–2; *Dig.* 50.2.11 Call.; 50.4.3.10, 50.4.8 Ulp.; 50.5.8 pr. Pap. Minors, where elected, could not vote: *Dig.* 50.2.6.1 Pap. See chap. 5 below.

14 On Comum, see Pliny *Ep.* 1.19.2. Cf P.D.A. Garnsey *Social Status and Legal Privilege in the Roman Empire* (Oxford 1970) 243 and n 8. In the fourth century the property requirement was twenty-five *iugera* (about

$6^1/_4$ hectares) *Cod. Theod.* 12.1.33, which was perhaps only applicable
in remote eastern areas according to A.H.M. Jones *The Later Roman Empire*
(Oxford 1964) 738.

15 Jacques *Liberté* 535

16 *Tab. Her.* 94–6, 111–23; *Dig.* 50.2.6.3 Pap.; 50.2.9.1 Paul.; 50.2.12 Call.
Cf Mackie *Administration* 55, who sees the prerequisites as criteria of
responsibility and social prestige.

17 *Dig.* 50.4.6 pr. Ulp., which allows decurions to become magistrates, clearly
presumes that one could be a decurion first. For the Spanish decurions
who never were magistrates, see Catalogue **24**, **99**, **113**, **266**, **281** (Baetica);
347 (Lusitania); **436**, **440**, **447**, perhaps, **683**, **777**, **911** (Tarraconensis);
and probably also **328** and **337**, for the former was exempted from *munera*
and *onera* and the latter had the rank of decurion (rather than a magistracy) inscribed on his amphitheatre seat.

18 For the approval by vote of the decurions, see *Irn.* 31; *Dig.* 50.2.6.5 Pap.;
and cf. Langhammer *Magistratus* 196. An example from Gades appears
at Catalogue **97** 'ab decurionibus creatus'. For the candidates' consent, see
Dig. 50.2.2.8 Ulp. (early third century).

19 Tanfani *Contributo* 215–21; Mackie *Administration* 80–1. For those who
were adlected by the decurions, see Catalogue **328**, **436**, **445**; by the
emperor, **144**, **671**; and by unspecified means, **146**, **347**, **739**, **898**, **911**, **912**,
914.

20 On the *album*, see *Dig.* 50.3 Ulp.; Liebenam *Städteverwaltung* 230–2. For
pedanei as a barbarism for *pedarii*; see Gell. NA 3.18. For *pedani* listed
in an *album*, see CIL IX 338 = ILS 6121; cf Jacques *Liberté* 478–82. On *pedarii*
in the Roman Senate see Talbert *Senate of Imperial Rome* 516.

21 *Urs.* 64, 69, 75, 99, 100, 130 (cf Hardy *Charters* 15); *Salp.* 29; *Irn.* 31, D,
G, L, 61–2, etc.; *Dig.* 50.9.2–3

22 *Dig.* 50.2.2 Ulp.; 50.1.15 pr., 50.2.5 Pap.; 50.2.12 Papir. Iust.

23 *Tab. Her.* 135–41; *Urs.* 101; *Dig.* 50.2.7.2 Paul.; 50.4.6 pr. Ulp. The
wording of *Salp.* 21 implies that, under the Flavian municipal law,
magistrates were elected only from among the decurions. However, the
regulations on eligibility for election (*Mal.* 54), which specify that no
one can run for office who could not legally become a decurion, suggest that
it was possible (though perhaps unusual) for a man who was not yet a
decurion to seek a magistracy.

24 For solvency, see *Dig.* 50.4.6 pr., 1 Ulp. For the minimum age limit, see
Dig. 50.6.2; 50.16.239 pr.; 50.17.2.1; G. Alföldy *Gerión* 2 (1984)
209–10.

25 On free birth and freedman status, see *Urs.* 105; *Dig.* 50.1.37.1 Call.;

Abbott and Johnson *MARE* 87; Langhammer *Magistratus* 44. See further
in chap. 5. On the exclusion of criminals and the accused, see *Dig.* 50.4.3.9
Ulp.; 50.4.7 Marcian.

26 *Dig.* 50.4.3.3; 50.17.2 Ulp. Abbott and Johnson *MARE* 87 cite honorary
appointments of female magistrates in the Eastern provinces. See below on a
Spanish woman holding *omnes honores*.

27 Jews, at any rate, could hold office (*Dig.* 50.2.3.3 Ulp.). Christians were
presumably barred, though exceptions are known from the second century onward: M.L.W. Laistner *Christianity and Pagan Culture in the Later
Roman Empire* (Ithaca 1951) 28. The prejudice was hardly unilateral:
Canons 2, 3, and 56 of the Council of Iliberris in Spain (early fourth century)
forbade Christians who became duovirs from entering the Church, and
did not permit them to hold the flaminate or celebrate public games. See
C.J. Hefele *History of the Christian Councils* I (Edinburgh 1894) 138–9,
161; D.J. Kyrtatas *The Social Structure of the Early Christian Communities*
(London and New York 1987) 101.

28 Th. Mommsen *Gesammelte Schriften* I (Berlin, Dublin and Zürich 1965)
316; A.N. Sherwin White *The Roman Citizenship* 2nd ed (Oxford 1973)
256; J.F. Rodríguez Neila in *Actas del I Congreso de Historia de Andalucía*
(Córdoba 1978) 203; T. Spitzl *Lex Municipii Malacitani* (München
1984) 33; González *JRS* 76 (1986) 212

29 On the limited number of *curiae*, see *Mal.* 52–5; *Irn.* L (limit of eleven). Cf
Hardy *Charters* 102 n 16; E.S. Staveley *Greek and Roman Voting and
Elections* (London 1972) 224; Rodríguez Neila *Actas del I Congreso* 170;
Spitzl *Lex Municipii* 36–49. The presiding magistrate could not declare
the election of any person who failed to meet the prerequisites, *Tab. Her.*
98–107; however, *Mal.* 51 suggests that candidates were screened before
being allowed to stand for election.

30 For securities, see *Lex Mun. Tarent.* 7–11, 14–20; *Mal.* 60, 64; *Dig.*
50.1.38.6 Papir. Iust. Cf P.D. Garnsey *ANRW* II/1 (Berlin and New York 1974)
234. On aediles and public funds, see Mommsen *Gesammelte Schriften* I
342–3; González *JRS* 76 (1986) 217.

31 Rodríguez Neila *Actas del I Congreso* 204

32 Abbott and Johnson *MARE* 55, 89; Langhammer *Magistratus* 45; Jones *Later
Roman Empire* 730; cf J.F. Drinkwater *Britannia* 10 (1979) 89 and n 1.

33 On the irregularity of the quaestorship, see *Dig.* 50.4.18.2 Arcadius Charisius; cf Galsterer *Untersuchungen* 56; Clavel and Lévêque *Villes et
structures* 179. Jacques *Liberté* 466 interprets *in aliqua civitate* to mean 'in
some cities' rather than 'in any city.' Cf Alföldy *Gerión* 2 (1984) 199.
On irregularities of order outside of Spain, see, e.g., *ILS* 6146, 6259, 6264,

6482, 6489, 6529, 6536, 6542, 6551, 6594, 6620–1, 6694, 6820, 6968; *AE* 1916, 32–6; *AE* 1951, 153; *AE* 1956, 126; *ILAfr.* 384; *ILTun.* 729.

34 Cf Hardy *Charters* 107 n 28; Abbott and Johnson *MARE* 64; Langhammer *Magistratus* 158; Galsterer *Untersuchungen* 56; Mackie *Administration* 60. Rodríguez Neila *Actas del I Congreso* 205 suggests a shortage of candidates for quaestorships.

35 Stevenson *Administration* 172

36 Mackie *Administration* 59; Alföldy *Gerión* 2 (1984) 215

37 On 'q.' usually for quaestor, see J.E. Sandys *Latin Epigraphy* (London 1927) 307. Cf *AE* 1916, 32–6 (Cuicul) which record an 'aed., q., IIvir q.q.' – where 'q.' can only be 'quaestor.' L. Villaronga in *Estudios de numismática romana* (Barcelona 1964) 93 perversely interpreted 'QVAIC' as 'quinquennalis,' but has since recanted, accepting even 'q.' as 'quaestor' (*Aes Coinage* 13). Grant *FITA* 156 implausibly took 'Q.V.' and 'A.I.' as the names of 'C[ensores].'

38 Juba: *CIL* II 3417 = *ILS* 840 = *ILER* 6040. Members of royal and imperial families are not included in my Catalogue of local magistrates.

39 F. Beltrán Lloris *Numisma* 28 (1978) 173, 179; cf Galsterer *Untersuchungen* 26

40 Grant *FITA* 24–5; M.H. Crawford *Coinage and Money under the Roman Republic* (Berkeley and Los Angeles 1985) 341

41 On priesthoods following the duovirate in Gallia Comata, see Drinkwater *Britannia* 19 (1979) 94–5; on the problem of aedile shortages, see Alföldy *Gerión* 2 (1984) 202–3.

42 **891–2** (both Tarraco). Parallels: *ILS* 6485, 6826; *AE* 1951, 153; etc. Cf *ILS* 6586 (quaestor, decemvir), 7040 (quaestor, vergobret). Langhammer *Magistratus* 157, while maintaining that the quaestorship was not a prerequisite for the aedileship, assumes that a candidate for the duovirate must have held both of these lower offices.

43 *Tab. Her.* 89–90; González *JRS* 76 (1986) 215–16

44 On the origin of the singulars *duovir/duumvir* see chap. 1, n 15. The commonest orthography in Spanish epigraphy (including the municipal laws) is 'IIvir.' A Flavian or post-Flavian magistrate from Complutum (**663**) is explicitly *duovir*, and *Salp.* 26 exhibits the plural *duovir[i]*. *Irn.* generally prefers *duumvir/duumviri*, but in chap. 24 uses both *du[u]mviratum* and *duoviratum*. Both terms thus seem to have been equally current and acceptable in Roman Spain. For consistency I use the technically more correct nominative form *duoviri*.

45 On the first hypothesis, see Arnold *Roman System*³ 242; Abbott and Johnson *MARE* 59; A. Degrassi *Scritti vari di antichità* I (Rome 1962) 168–71;

challenged already by Liebenam *Städteverwaltung* 255–6. On the second, see F. Sartori *Problemi di storia constituzionale italiota* (Rome 1953) 157. On the third, see L.R. Taylor *The Voting Districts of the Roman Republic* (Rome 1960) 82; E.T. Salmon *The Making of Roman Italy* (Ithaca 1982) 179–81. On the fourth, see H. Rudolph *Stadt und Staat im römischen Italien* (Leipzig 1935) 90–1; A. Torrent *La 'iurisdictio' de los magistrados municipales* (Salamanca 1970) 74.

46 Stevenson *Administration* 171; Salmon *Making of Roman Italy* 179–81

47 Rudolph *Stadt und Staat* 90–1; S. Frere *Britannia* 2nd ed (London and Boston 1978) 237. F. Millar *The Emperor in the Roman World* (London 1977) 405 is not convinced that Sabora necessarily became a *municipium* in AD 77. At all events it adopted the Flavian name and switched from duovirs to quattuorvirs in that year.

48 For towns in other provinces having both duovirs and quattuorvirs, see Arnold *Roman System*³ 242 n 2; J.J. Wilkes *Dalmatia* (London 1969) 223, 249. For Sabora, see CIL II 1423 = ILS 6092 = FIRA I² 74.

49 Livy 43.4; AE 1981, 517; Taylor *Voting Districts* 82; H.-G. Pflaum *L'Afrique romaine* (Paris 1978) 380; Knapp *Roman Experience* 119–20, 213; J. González ZPE 55 (1984) 55

50 Degrassi *Scritti vari* I 126; A. García y Bellido in *Legio VII Gemina* (León 1970) 318–19

51 The mention of promagistrates in *Urs.* 125 and 127 is presumably a reference to these prefects: cf Hardy *Charters* 52 n 131. On the institution of prefects, see Tanfani *Contributo* 21–2; Hardy *Laws* 144–5; Abbott and Johnson MARE 11; P.A. Brunt *Italian Manpower* (Oxford 1971) 528–35; W. Simshäuser *Iuridici und Munizipalgerichtsbarkeit in Italien* (München 1973); M.W. Frederiksen JRS 65 (1975) 191–2; R.C. Knapp *Athenaeum* 58 (1980) 14–38; Salmon *Making of Roman Italy* 135–7. For prefects being appointed in the Imperial period, see A. Mócsy *Pannonia and Upper Moesia* (London and Boston 1974) 134; Drinkwater *Britannia* 19 (1979) 93–4.

52 Hyginus *Constitutio limitum* in C. Thulin ed *Corpus agrimensorum Romanorum* (Leipzig 1913) 135–6. Cf T.R.S. Broughton *Cahiers d'histoire mondiale* 9 (1965) 135.

53 Knapp *Roman Experience* 102; *Urs.* 68, 93–6, 126, 128–31, 134; *Salp.* 25

54 Mackie *Administration* 61 and n 28

55 On the appointment of a prefect, see *Salp.* 24; Hardy *Charters* 87 n 114; Abbott and Johnson MARE 62–3. Dual honorary duovirates are recorded in VM 166:4 = Gil 1757 (Germanicus and Drusus at Acci) and VM 152:2 = Gil 1773 (Drusus and Nero Caesar at Caesaraugusta). For Juba and Ptolemy, see VM 130:15 = Gil 1629; VM 131:5–6 = Gil 1642–3; CIL II

$3417 = ILS\ 840 = ILER\ 6040$; Avienus *Ora marit.* 280–3. On a possible
commercial motive for these appointments see below, chap. 7.

56 E.g., *cura templi, cura ludorum, cura operum publicorum*. See Langhammer
Magistratus 178–87. See also W. Eck *Die staatliche Organisation Italiens in der hohen Kaiserzeit* (München 1979) 190–3; G.P. Burton *Chiron*
9 (1979) 466. Abbott and Johnson MARE 63 are surely wrong in seeing
the *curator r.p.* as a constitutional descendant of the *praefectus Caesaris*.

57 Jacques *Liberté* 182

58 W. Liebenam *Philologus* 56 (1897) 293–7; cf Eck *Staatliche Organisation
Italiens* 198–205

59 Burton *Chiron* 9 (1979) 465–6, 474 n 38, 480–1

60 Abbott and Johnson MARE 88. Stevenson *Administration* 159 opines that
cities were at liberty to retain the old titles for their magistrates. See also Mackie
Administration 23.

61 J.B. Reid *The Municipalities of the Roman Empire* (Cambridge 1913) 246

62 E.g., at Narbo Martius, founded in 118 BC. For Italian examples, see Brunt
Manpower 529–30, 534; Salmon *Making of Roman Italy* 207 n 539.

63 Cf the situation in Gaul, where praetors are merely the Latin translation of
vergobrets: Liebenam *Städteverwaltung* 253; C. Jullian *Histoire de la
Gaule* IV 3rd ed (Paris 1924) 337–8. On councils of native *principes* cf G.
Alföldy *Noricum* (London and Boston 1974) 69. (As a modern parallel,
I recently observed the signature 'Chief and Council' on a trespass notice
outside the Indian reserve at Garden River, Ontario.) As for the senate
at Contrebia, the local governing body in a *municipium* was properly the
ordo decurionum (see chap. 1). But Contrebia was not even a *municipium* and the loftier appellation *senatus* sounds presumptuous. Similarly,
iudices are a peculiarly Roman office; in the provinces we expect *praefecti
iure dicundo* or the like.

64 ILS 2681, 3298, 5595, 5665, 6183, 6187, 6451. On the other possible interpretation, see Grant *FITA* 211–12.

65 ILAlg. 1297, 1341; Wilkes *Dalmatia* 193; Mócsy *Pannonia and Upper
Moesia* 70

66 For censors in Bithynia, see Pliny *Ep.* book 10; cf Knapp *Roman Experience*
119; and for Italy, see J.F. Rodríguez Neila *Gerión* 4 (1986) 67–8.

67 On the adjective *maximus*, see W. Kunkel *An Introduction to Roman Legal
and Constitutional History* 2nd ed (Oxford 1973) 14–15. For *decemvir*
possibly referring to a Punic institution, Broughton *Cahiers d'histoire mondiale* 9 (1965) 130.

68 Mackie *Administration* 23, 34

69 E.g., CIL IX 4543, Nursia; IX 4896, Trebula Metuesca; XI 5006, Trebiae; XI
5621, Plestia. These Italian octovirates had developed into quattuorvir-

ates by the Early Empire: cf H. Rudolph *PW* s.v. 'Octoviri'; Taylor *Voting Districts* 82–3; Salmon *Making of Roman Italy* 137. But Norba and Emerita (to either of which the octovir may belong) have duovirs.

70 Galsterer *Untersuchungen* 24. Norba was founded ca 35 BC, Emerita in 25. Admittedly the difference in dates is not extreme.

71 Cf. G. Wesener *PW* s.v. 'Quinqueviri'; Liebenam *Städteverwaltung* 266 n 6 for possible Italian examples.

72 Cirta: *ILS* 6858–64; *ILAlg.* 675–8; Mactar: Gascou *Politique municipale* 150–1; *undecemprimi*: *CIL* VIII 7041, 12006–7, 12302, 12331, 14755, 14875, 25808; B.D. Shaw *Museum Africum* 2 (1973) 3–10; cf fifteen magistrates at Massalia (Strabo 4.1.5).

73 Liebenam *Städteverwaltung* 254; Hardy *Charters* 57 n 152, 88. Known *interreges* from Italy and Gaul are conveniently listed by J. González in *Actas del I Congreso andaluz de estudios clásicos* (Jaén 1982) 224; for discussion of Italian *interreges* cf P. Castrén *Ordo populusque Pompeianus* (Rome 1975) 270–2.

74 D. Ladage *Städtische Priester- und Kultämter im lateinischen Westen* (Köln 1971) 80

75 On *honor* for priesthoods, see *CIL* II 3712–13 = *ILER* 1385, 1775 = Veny *Corpus* 124, 126; cf J.-N. Bonneville *MCV* 18 (1982) 30–1.

76 Alföldy *Gerión* 2 (1984) 195–6 n 9

77 *Irn.* F; *Dig.* 50.7.5.5 Marcian

78 *Urs.* 92; *Irn.* G; *Dig.* 50.7.1 Ulp.; 50.7.5 pr., 1 Marcian

79 Mackie *Administration* 23

80 On *domi nobiles* see Cic. *Cluent.* 23; Sall. *Cat.* 17.4; on Antium, Cic. *Att.* 2.6.1; Cf R. Syme *Mus. Helv.* 34 (1977) 137; J.F. Drinkwater *Latomus* 37 (1978) 834; M.I. Finley *Ancient Sicily* 2nd ed (London 1979) 156; P.D.A. Garnsey *Imperialism in the Ancient World* (Cambridge 1978) 229; M.K. Hopkins *Past & Present* 32 (1965) 13.

81 Cic. *Balb.* 6, 43; *Fam.* 6.8.1, 6.18.1, 9.19.1; Tac. *Ann.* 12.60; Gell. NA 17.9.1

82 Sen. *Controv.* 2 pr. 3–4. Cf now Talbert *Senate of Imperial Rome* 76–80.

83 Alföldy *Gerión* 2 (1984) 197, 218

84 R. Duthoy *Epigraphica* 36 (1974) 134–54

85 Etienne *Culte*; Alföldy *Flamines*

86 For the prestige of the augurate, see *Urs.* 66–7. Cf Ladage (n 74 above) 53, 99; and 115–16 on the augurate and the priest of the Imperial Cult representing Rome.

87 Etienne *Culte* 231–4; Mackie *Administration* 63

88 For points raised about theory vs. practice for the relationship between magistracies and priesthoods, see Ladage (n 74 above) 87 and 93; Alföldy

Flamines 54; and J.F. Rodríguez Neila *Revista de Estudios de Vida Local* 209 (1981) 91–118.

89 For the restriction of the Salii to the patrician and aristocratic classes of Rome and Saguntum, see Syme *RP* 1329; and Alföldy *Gerión* 2 (1984) 225–6 and 216–17.

90 Alföldy *Flamines* chap. 3

91 In nearly all cases the *cursus* in the inscriptions is given in correct sequence, e.g., 'aed., IIvir, trib. mil.' Very rarely is it inverted (e.g., **416**, **881**) and in only one instance is it apparently broken (**780**, where the most important office is given first, followed by the others in the order held).

92 One equestrian officer who rose from the ranks appears at **911**, a centurion and prefect who became decurion at Tarraco.

93 E. Birley *Roman Britain and the Roman Army* (Kendal 1953) 139

94 Th. Mommsen *Römisches Staatsrecht* III (Leipzig 1887) 535–6

95 *Dig.* 50.1.23 pr. Hermogenianus

96 *Cod. Theod.* 12.1.18, cf 12.1.48, 58; *Nov.* 15

97 R. Syme *Tituli* 5 (1982) 518–19

98 Annaei: R. Syme *Colonial Elites* (London 1958) 14; Ulpii: [Aur. Vict.] *Epit. de Caes.* 13.1

4

Duties of Magistrates

Local magistrates exercised a wide range of duties which embraced almost every conceivable sphere of activity – judicial, religious, economic, social, cultural. Many of these duties are punctiliously spelled out in the charters of Urso, Salpensa and Malaca, which have been extensively mined by modern commentators and by the standard handbooks on provincial administration; it would be pointless to reiterate at length the details of these provisions, which are as familiar to the specialist as they are tedious to the uninitiated. Whereas one could easily become bogged down in the cumbrous particulars of the charter regulations, there is obvious merit in an overview, which might summarize the disparate evidence in palatable form and permit an understanding of the 'job specifications' for each of the magistracies. Such a survey is especially necessary in light of the recently published *Lex Irnitana* fragments, which provide important new information on the duties of aediles, quaestors, and legates, areas hitherto largely conjectural. This chapter, then, will summarize the duties of each office as attested in a variety of sources, with some discussion of particular problems.

Decurions

The two principal matters with which the town council was concerned were public works and municipal finance. The extant portions of urban charters detail some of the specific duties of decurions, although there were undoubtedly others. Conversely, not all of the attested functions were necessarily applicable in every town. In particular, there may have been distinctions between conditions in colonies (such as Urso) and *municipia*, or changes effected over the course of time. Nonetheless, a summary of known duties is useful in illuminating the range and nature of decurial responsibility.

With regard to public works, the decurions had to approve the demolition of buildings, and the construction and repair of any public work (a function paralleled among city councils today). Once approved by decree of the decurions, the project would be supervised by the aediles. The creation or alteration of roads and waterways, the right-of-way for aqueducts, and the use of waste water on private property also required the approval of the decurions.[1]

In the financial sphere, the decurions received accounts of public business and decided upon the expenditure, loan, and investigation of public funds. They could pass decrees on the sale of property under a *lex praediatoria* (law concerning auctions) and on the annual inspection of sources of revenue in the town's territory. More importantly (although not mentioned in the surviving charter fragments), the decurions were responsible for ensuring the collection of taxes, although (to prevent any conflict of interest) they could not act as tax-farmers themselves.[2]

The Spanish evidence points to a number of other functions of the decurions. In the religious sphere, they set dates for sacrifices and festivals, and decided on the appointment of *magistri fanorum* (temple officials) and *seviri Augustales* (officials of the Imperial Cult). In the diplomatic sphere, they consulted with the duovirs on the appointment of ambassadors, patrons, and guests (*hospites*). In the social sphere, they allotted reserved seats for the games and the theatre (to members of the élite, we may be sure). In the sphere of defence, they could call out armed men in an emergency. In the judicial sphere, they acted as an appeal court for persons fined by the magistrates and as an advisory body to the duovirs in such matters as the manumission of public slaves and manumission by minors; and in some circumstances they could appoint guardians.[3]

The decisions of the decurions were called *decreta*. Numerous inscriptions recording building activity, donations by the city and honorific decrees bear the tag 'd[ecreto] d[ecurionum].' However, it is clear from both the Urso and Flavian charters that decrees were normally issued in close consultation with the duovirs.

According to such jurists as Papinian, Paul, and Ulpian, a father (*paterfamilias*) was legally responsible for the performance of all duties of a son who became a decurion (though a son was not responsible for his father's). The paternal liability in such cases has been seen as evidence of 'compulsory' local service at the beginning of the third century. However, all three jurists specify that this provision applies when the father 'consents' or 'desires' that his son become a decurion. In other words, the decurionate was still both voluntary and desirable.[4]

Duovirs

The duovirs were not merely the chief local dignitaries, but fulfilled a variety of practical and necessary tasks. One major function of these officials was the administration of justice. For this reason they are often called *duoviri i[ure] d[icundo]* or *quattuorviri i. d.* In their absence, law was dispensed by a prefect (*praefectus i. d.*).[5] Since no legal training was required for such positions, these magistrates were really justices of the peace or *corregidores*, rather than judges in the modern sense; we learn from chapters 85–6 of the Flavian municipal law that they were guided by a book of edicts, formulas, and rules issued by the provincial governor, and that (like the praetors at Rome) they appointed *iudices* from among the decurions to hear actual cases. Trials presumably took place in the basilica, a porticoed structure usually located alongside the forum. Basilicas are attested by epigraphic or archaeological evidence in a number of towns, including Abdera, Baelo, and Iliberris in Baetica, and Clunia in Tarraconensis. At Conimbriga in Lusitania, the basilica was adjacent to the *curia*.[6]

The judicial magistrate could deal with local civil cases such as the manumission of slaves and the appointment of legal guardians, and could award fines. He had jurisdiction over both local citizens (whether resident or not) and resident aliens. However, if the amount of money involved in a civil suit exceeded a certain figure (one thousand sesterces in the Flavian charter), it would be necessary to refer the case to the provincial governor.[7] Possibly the duovirs also had jurisdiction in certain criminal cases; at any rate the language of the Urso charter, with mention of *quaestio, delatores, accusatores*, and *subscriptores*, is appropriate to criminal trials, although the types of crime envisaged by this regulation are not specified.[8] Certainly chapter 84 of the *Lex Irnitana* makes it clear that the *IIvir i.d.* in a Flavian municipality could *not* try what are sometimes called *actiones famosae*: namely, cases involving violence, liberty, partnership, trust, mandate, tutelage, fraud, theft, injury, or accusation of wrongful intent. It therefore appears that in most instances the conduct of criminal proceedings would have to await the periodic visits of the governor or *legatus iuridicus* to the *conventus* capitals. Some legal matters could, however, be settled by correspondence: a letter from the *iuridicus* of Tarraconensis to the duovirs of Pompaelo in AD 119 authorizes them to use the powers of their office against officials who evade their responsibilities (*CIL* II 2959 = *EJER* 13). Magistrates could inflict moderate punishments upon slaves, and possibly had criminal jurisdiction over them.[9]

As the chief magistrates, the duovirs convened and presided over the local *ordo*. They were obliged to consult with the decurions regarding a diversity of matters such as festivals and sacrifices, payment of contractors, raising of loans, dispatch of embassies, expenditures on games and banquets, employment of public slaves, investigation of public funds and property, inspection of territories (fines) and sources of revenue (vectigalia), acquisition of land for aqueducts, and the use of water overflowing from a reservoir by private persons.[10] The duovirs also supervised the elections of magistrates, pontiffs, and augurs; celebrated games and dramatic performances, largely at their own expense; armed and commanded the populace in time of war (a rare scenario in Imperial Spain); appointed temple officials in the manner prescribed by the decurions; leased out public taxes and revenues, and published the contracts; acted as commissioners of roads; sent recaptured fugitive slaves to the office of the provincial governor; witnessed wills and reimbursed non-heirs who conducted a funeral. A recently published inscription suggests that they were also concerned with legacies. The duovirate was clearly no sinecure.[11]

Every five years, the duovirs conducted the local census and revised the roll of the local senate; in this capacity they were known as *duoviri quinquennales*. The census involved not only the names and ages of all Roman citizens in the town, but also the extent of their property; this information was required for taxation purposes. *Quinquennales* are not mentioned in the Flavian municipal law, nor attested in any known *municipium*; in such towns we can only assume that the census was indeed taken by the duovirs, but that they lacked a special title.[12] At the Julian *municipium* of Osset, a duovir (232) without the title *quinquennalis* is said to have conducted the census.

One of the safeguards provided by the collegial system was that a magistrate's power was counterbalanced by the equal power (*par potestas*) of his colleague. In practical terms, this meant that a duovir could veto a decision by his fellow duovir. In addition, the duovirs, having greater *potestas* than the aediles or quaestors, could apply *intercessio* against the acts of those magistrates, provided this was done within three days of a complaint being received. The one act which could not be vetoed was, of course, the holding of the annual elections (*Salp.* 27; *Mal.* 58).

Aediles

The Roman jurist Papinian, quoted in the *Digest* (43.10), lists the duties of the *astynomoi* or *astynomikoi*. Mommsen assumed that these were *curatores urbium*, but they were more probably aediles.[13] There is no way to prove whether they were aediles at Rome or in the Empire generally; Mommsen's plural *urbium* is hardly justified by the phase *kata tēn polin*. If it is true that municipal aediles performed the same functions as those at Rome, the question is in any case moot. It is interesting to note that Papinian's regulations correspond only roughly to the list of responsibilities for aediles at Rome given in the *Tabula Heracleensis*,[14] though it must be remembered that these documents are separated in time by some two centuries. However, the jurisdiction of Papinian's officials, which is limited to fining persons who damage the streets, seems more applicable to the aediles at Rome than to municipal aediles, who (as we now know) had much more sweeping legal competence.[15] But there is no compelling reason why such functions as Papinian does list could not obtain both at Rome and in provincial cities.

The duties enumerated by Papinian deal almost exclusively with public works. They include ensuring that streets are kept in order, that the overflow of water does not damage houses, and that bridges are built wherever necessary; inspecting the condition of walls (especially those facing a street) and requiring the owners to repair or rebuild them if necessary; ensuring that no one damages, undermines or builds upon the street, that no quarrels take place in the streets, and that no refuse is thrown into them.

The charter of Urso provides three further functions of aediles. They must celebrate games or dramatic spectacles, largely at their own expense; they can exercise jurisdiction in minor cases; and they must supervise the construction of buildings and other public works. Aediles probably used slave labour to install the city's water supply, for a lead pipe from Caesaraugusta, bears the name of an aedile (**504**) together with that of a public slave of the colony. With regard to jurisdiction, the charter of Malaca informs us that aediles could impose fines, but must report them to the duovirs. A curious passage in the *Digest* adds that municipal aediles had the right and duty to flog pedlars, who were commonly regarded as disreputable persons.[16]

A far broader spectrum of duties is provided in the recently unearthed chapter 19 of the Flavian municipal law. According to this important document, the responsibilities of the aediles include managing the grain supply (*annona*), shrines and sacred places, the town, its streets, neighbourhoods (*vici*), sewers, baths, markets, weights and measures.[17] Aediles also look after the *vigiliae* (fire department) when appropriate, seize pledges up to ten thousand sesterces, and award fines up to five thousand sesterces. This juridical power suggests not only that the local aediles fulfilled duties similar to those of the aediles at Rome, but also that they and the *duoviri i.d.* shared the legal duties corresponding to those of the Roman praetors. The title *quattuorviri i.d.*, which has hitherto been taken to mean 'those of the quattuorvirs who have juridical power' (i.e., the duovirs alone), should therefore be reinterpreted as including the aediles as well. Thus, while it may be an anachronism to describe the local aedile as a 'deputy mayor,'[18] he was clearly a key player in municipal government.

It is possible, as previous scholars have suggested, that the aediles may also have exercised responsibility for local finance, in towns which had no quaestors.[19] While there is no explicit evidence for this practice in Spain, it is clear that the duovirs controlled to a large extent the municipal purse strings, even at the *municipium Irnitanum* which did have quaestors; and one might rather expect *a fortiori* that in towns with no quaestors, the duovirs would carry the entire financial portfolio.[20]

Quaestors

Hardly anything was known with certainty about the role of the local quaestor, until the publication of the new *Lex Irnitana*, incorporating chapter 20 of the Flavian municipal law. This chapter gives quaestors the right and power to 'collect, spend, safeguard, administer and look after' the community funds, at the discretion of the duovirs. Thus in Flavian *municipia*, and probably in all towns which had quaestors, the duovirs could entrust the bulk of financial matters to these officials, who were in effect the town treasurers. The mention of the duovirs' discretion (*arbitratu*) reflects the degree of autonomy allowed to *municipia* in managing their own affairs. If there were towns which did not have quaestors, then (as suggested above) the duovirs themselves probably controlled the local finances.

Unlike a duovir or aedile, a quaestor could not impose a fine; but this limitation reflects more the quaestor's lack of judicial power than any restriction of his financial competence (*Mal.* 66). We know that at Rome the quaestor's duties included the witnessing of contracts for road maintenance; possibly this duty applied in some provincial towns as well (*Tab. Her.* 37–41, 46–9).

Was the quaestor also in charge of coinage? This was assuredly the case in certain cities, most notably the Augustan *municipium* of Emporiae, whose 'q.' coins have already been discussed. Yet the coinage of other Spanish cities names aediles, quattuorvirs, and (most commonly) duovirs – some of them quinquennial.[21] Responsibility for coinage is not spelled out in local charters as we have them – Flavian cities were not issuing their own coins anyway – and the variety of offices named on the coins suggests that the delegation of such responsibility was a matter of local preference. The underlying authority for issue of coins resided in the local senate, and on some Spanish monetary issues we actually find the legend 'ex d[ecreto] d[ecurionum]' or 'ex s[enatus] c[onsultu],' recalling the familiar sc on coins of Rome. But on coins with both types of legend we sometimes also find the names of the magistrates who supervised the minting.[22]

Prefects

The duties of the *praefectus i.d.* were identical to those of the duovir whom he replaced. Consequently the charters state, 'Let the duovir or the prefect [do so-and-so],' for the prefect had equal power. The same duties also applied to the *praefectus Caesaris* who represented the duovir-emperor (*Salp.* 24).

Curators

It is remarkable that none of the surviving passages from Ulpian's book on the duties of the curator (*De officio curatoris rei publicae*) mentions the word 'curator.' Indeed, the sections on the lending of public funds at interest, on bequests of legacies for public works, and on boundaries between public and private lands, state categorically that it is the duty of the provincial governor (*praeses provinciae*) to ensure that these matters are properly administered. Two other passages, one on the liability of donors to honour their promises, the other on the liability of their grandchildren, are merely clarifications of legal points and do not concern duties of officials at all.[23] A more ambiguous case is *Dig.* 50.9.4, which states that decrees of the decurions can be vetoed if their motive is suspect, but does not specify who has the power to veto them. If the title of Ulpian's book is to have any relevance to its contents, one must, I think, assume that it is the *curator r.p.* who has the power to nullify these local enactments, to enforce the payment of promised donations, and to act in place of the provincial governor in rectifying local financial administration. Burton, who adduced epigraphic evidence from the Eastern provinces for the exercise of these functions by curators, sees the curator as a sort of surrogate provincial governor, insofar as control of local finances was concerned.[24] Unlike the powerful but overworked governor, the local curator had the time and resources to monitor, and where necessary, intervene in civic financial management.

Two other passages, both from Papirius Iustus, elucidate the duties of the curator in the late second century. The first states that it is the duty of the curator to recover lands belonging to the city, even where someone had purchased them in good faith; the other says that, when property has been sold, the curator has a duty to collect money for the provision of grain (*annona*). These two provisions, and especially the former, serve to amplify Ulpian's ruling on the separation of private and public lands; they also show that it was the curator, as chosen representative of the governor, rather than the governor himself, who enforced the law.[25]

Burton and Jacques have both exposed the tendency of earlier scholars to over-emphasize the role of the curator as a constraining force on the auton-omy of the city. It should be stressed that the curator was the watchdog rather than the master of the city's finances, a definition borne out by the jurists: the passages from Ulpian suggest that the curator (or governor where there was no curator) stepped in only when the normal administrative apparatus was malfunctioning, while those from Papirius Iustus actually hold the curator liable for any abuse of his authority. The role of the *curator rei publicae* was in fact analogous to that of the *curator* or *tutor* who looked after the interests of minors and women. His mandate was not to supplant local government, but to ensure that it operated smoothly.[26]

Legates

The duties of an ambassador would of course depend upon the particular mission on which he was dispatched. A frequent function of *legati*, which is attested several times in Spain, was the arrangement of a guest-friendship (*hospitium*) with another town or of patronage (*patronatus*) with an individ-ual benefactor.[27] On another occasion (**724**), local *legati* act as representa-tives in a lawsuit.

In certain circumstances, legates were required to travel to Rome to pick up copies of decrees for their towns. Thus the *senatus consultum* of AD 19, honouring the deceased Germanicus, stipulates that the consuls 'will order the magistrates and legates of *municipia* and colonies to send a transcript [of the decree] to [their] *municipia* and colonies in Italy and to those colonies which are in the provinces.' Taken literally, this stipulation seems to imply that both *municipia* and *coloniae* in Italy, but only *coloniae* in the provinces, were required to provide envoys to make copies and send them home; but the fact that the extant copy was found in the vicinity of Siarum, a known *municipium* in Baetica (though of uncertain date), leaves open the question whether, as González supposes, Siarum was a colony at the time of this decree,[28] or whether, as I believe, the drafters of the decree intended *muni-cipia* as well as *coloniae* to be understood in the last clause. One might argue that *municipia* were inherently more autonomous than colonies; however, if Italian *municipia* were obliged to post the decree, there is no clear reason why others would be exempt. Moreover, since *municipia* were privileged indigenous foundations, it is hardly likely that a *colonia*, a non-indigenous foundation, could or would later become a *municipium*. That provincial *municipia* did send embassies to pick up decrees in the first century AD is shown by the *Lex Irnitana* of 91, where it appears that a legate (and possibly one of the duovirs as well) had to go to Rome to fetch the town charter. It is also likely that the bronze copy, found near Italica, of the *senatus consultum* which limited expenditures on gladiatorial shows (ca 177), was requested and brought back by an embassy.[29]

Embassies to the emperor were particularly prestigious, and required men who were ardent, courageous, and quick-witted (Plut. *Mor.* 805 A). On the other hand, they were also regarded as something of a burden, and much of *Dig.* 50.7 deals with liabilities for, and exemptions from, such service. According to the *Lex Irnitana*, exemption from embassies was granted only on account of age (over sixty) or illness, though a substitute could be provided with the permission of the *ordo*. Failure to undertake an embassy or provide a replacement brought a twenty thousand sesterce fine (*Irn.* G). Unless the envoy volunteered to undertake the embassy at his own cost, he was entitled to payment of his travel expenses (*viaticum* or *legativum*) at a daily rate determined by the decurions, to whom he had to submit his accounts upon returning.[30]

Accountability of Magistrates

'Our ancestors ... established the Senate as the guardian, protector, and champion of the state,' remarks Cicero. 'They wanted the magistrates to heed the advice of this order and to be, in a sense, the ministers of this veritable council' (Cic. *Sest.* 137). This concept of the relationship between senate and magistrates was enshrined not only in the minds of Romans but in the Spanish charters. The magistrates of Urso, for instance, were enjoined to obey the decrees of the decurions and to carry out their decisions (*Urs.* 129). They were also required to consult with the *ordo* on a wide variety of matters, some of them quite banal. Although performing their duties on an individual basis, magistrates were collectively accountable for their actions.[31]

Local magistrates were accountable in three areas of responsibility. Accounts of all public funds handled by the magistrates had to be rendered to the *ordo*. Also, magistrates were accountable for the performance of their duty. A candidate for office had to swear that he would perform his duty before he could be declared elected, and any magistrate who refused to execute that duty could be forced to do so by the provincial governor. Finally, any magistrate who promised to construct a public work, or to donate money towards one, or to pay an *honorarium* for his office, and who had accordingly begun to build or to make payment, was required to fulfil his promise.[32]

In order that he might be held accountable for these matters, a magistrate (or indeed any public official) was not permitted to change his domicile until his term of office was completed and all accounts rendered (*Dig.* 50.1.34 Modest.). Indeed, the charter of Tarentum in Italy did not permit duovirs and aediles to move from the town for six years after their tenure (*Lex Mun. Tarent.* 43–4). The Flavian municipal law more efficiently demands that accounts be rendered no later than thirty days after completing one's term, and prescribes the procedure for a trial in the event that accounts are not submitted or public monies not returned (*Mal./Irn.* 67–9).

The duties of local magistrates were thus not merely a moral obligation, still less a noble ideal, but a formal responsibility for which officials could be held legally accountable. Despite the corruption which can invade any administrative hierarchy, the Roman system of local government sought to provide honest and effectual management of a city's affairs and care for the welfare of its people through the mechanism of annual popular elections, written terms of reference for magistrates and decurions, and the necessary procedures to enforce them. An internal system of checks and balances, including magisterial veto against colleagues and subordinates, the obligation of duovirs and decurions to consult on many matters, and the examination of magistrates' accounts by the *ordo*, ensured competent administration and viable local self-government. Where this system broke down, a *curator r.p.* or urban guardian was appointed to help the community restore its affairs to order.

Notes

1 *Urs.* 75, 98–100; *Mal.* 62; *Irn.* 79, 82–3. On demolition of buildings, see P. Garnsey in *Studies in Roman Property* ed M.I. Finley (Cambridge 1976) 133–6. On the range of powers of decurions, cf Abbott and Johnson MARE 67–8.

2 For the sale of property and revenue inspection, see *Urs.* 69, 80, 96; *Mal.* 64, 67–8; *Irn.* 76–80. On ensuring tax collection, see *Dig.* 50.1.17.7, 50.2.6.2 Pap.

3 On functions of decurions in other spheres, see, e.g., the following. Religious: *Urs.* 128 (*magistri fanorum*); CIL II 1944 = ILER 297 ('sevir Augustalis decreto decurionum'); diplomatic: *Urs.* 92, *Irn.* F-G (embassies); *Urs.* 97, 130–1, *Mal.* 61 (patrons); cf J. Nicols ANRW II/13 (Berlin 1980) 537, 556; social: *Urs.* 125–6, *Irn.* 81; defensive: *Urs.* 103; judicial: *Salp.* 28–9, *Mal.* 66, *Irn.* 69, 72

4 *Dig.* 50.1.2 Ulp.; 50.4.17.1 Hermog.; 50.1.17.2, 50.4.15, 50.8.5.2(3.3)
   Pap.; 50.1.21.2, 50.1.21.6, 50.4.16.2, 50.8.9(7) Paul; Jacques *Liberté*
   365, cf 609–11.
5 *Urs.* 94. The power of one magistrate could be delegated to a lesser, e.g.,
   'aedilis IIvirali potestate' (**72**); 'praefectus IIIIvirali potestate' (**177**); 'IIvir
   II, IIvirali potestate III' (**139**).
6 On Spanish basilicas, see R. Etienne *Quaderni* 10–12 (1987) 42–8 (with
   plans).
7 For the judicial magistrate's jurisdiction, see *Salp.* 28–9; *Dig.* 26.5.19 pr.,
   1 Paul; 50.1.29 Gaius; and on the monetary limit, see *Irn.* 84, cf *Mal.*
   69. Similarly in Cisalpine Gaul, cases involving more than fifteen thousand
   sesterces had to be referred to the praetor at Rome (*Lex Rubria* 21–2).
8 *Urs.* 96, 102. See A. Torrent *La 'iurisdictio' de los magistrados municipales*
   (Salamanca 1970) 185; Mackie *Administration* 105.
9 *Dig.* 2.1.12 Ulp.; Cic. *Clu.* 64.180–66.187; Arnold *Roman System*[3] 62; cf
   W.W. Buckland *The Roman Law of Slavery* (Cambridge 1908) 91–3 on
   criminal liability of slaves. *Irn.* 84 does not allow the *duovir i.d.* to hear a
   case of theft brought against a slave if it pertains to his master.
10 *Urs.* 64, 69, 92, 96, 99, 100; *Salp.* 28; *Irn.* 76–83
11 *Urs.* 68, 70–1, 103, 128; *Mal.* 52–7, 63; Paul *Sent.* 4.6.2; *Dig.* 11.4.4 Paul;
   11.7.12.6 Ulp. On roads, see *Lex Agraria* 28; *Tab. Her.* 50; *Irn.* 82; *CIL*
   II 2886 = *ILER* 1966; *HAEp.* 736. For the new inscription see *AE* 1984, 511.
12 The title *quinquennalis* is taken by Clavel and Lévêque (*Villes et structures*
   178) to mean 'every four years,' by inclusive reckoning. However, local
   quinquennales were modelled on the Roman censors, who originally held
   the census every four years (*quinto quoque anno*) but after 209 BC held
   it every five. On the municipal census, see Mackie *Administration* 153–4;
   J.F. Rodríguez Neila *Gerión* 4 (1986) 61–81; H. Galsterer *JRS* 78
   (1988) 81.
13 See Liebenam *Städteverwaltung* 362, 405 n 3; Langhammer *Magistratus*
   149, 152; H.J. Mason *Greek Terms for Roman Institutions* (Toronto
   1974) 27. Mommsen is presumably thinking of the situation in the Late
   Empire, when curators had usurped the powers of the aediles.
14 Abbott and Johnson *MARE* 63–4. Cf P.D.A. Garnsey *Social Status and Legal
   Privilege in the Roman Empire* (Oxford 1970) 253 on a similar confusion
   over the term 'aedile' in Paul's *Sententiae*. See *Tab. Her.* 20–36, 46–52, 69
   for the responsibilities of aediles at Rome.
15 *Irn.* 19, 84; cf J. González *JRS* 76 (1986) 201–2.
16 On the further functions of aediles, see *Urs.* 71, 94, 98; *Irn.* 83; *Mal.* 66;
   cf Hardy *Charters* 114 n 49; and *Dig.* 50.2.12 Call.
17 On *vici*, see L.A. Curchin *Rev. Et. Anc.* 87 (1985) 327–43. The role of aediles

in maintaining streets, public buildings, and the *annona* was already divined by Stevenson *Administration* 172.

18 *Vizebürgermeister* is the term used by G. Alföldy *Gerión* 2 (1984) 195.

19 Cic. *Att.* 15.15.1; *CIL* x 219 = *ILS* 5330; Liebenam *Städteverwaltung* 265–6; Hardy *Charters* 107 n 28; Stevenson *Administration* 172; Langhammer *Magistratus* 150–1

20 According to Langhammer *Magistratus* 158, towns originally had no quaestors; financial administration was handled by the duovirs. As some towns became larger and finances more complicated, quaestors were appointed as financial assistants to the duovirs. By specializing in this single sphere of responsibility, the quaestors soon came to control the local treasury.

21 F. Beltrán Lloris *Numisma* 28 (1978) 185–6 asserts that there were no duovirs on Republican coins (only duoviral prefects and *quinquennales*), whereas under Augustus and Tiberius there appear a large number of duovirs. However, it is by no means certain that 'pr. IIvir' denotes a prefect (see above, chap. 3 on praetors). Moreover, there are numerous Republican monetal magistrates in southern Spain whose titles are not recorded (e.g., **189–209, 583–98**).

22 E.g., VM 128–9 = Gil 1806–15, Carteia

23 For these surviving passages, see *Dig.* 22.1.33, 50.9.4, 50.10.5, 50.12.1, 50.12.15. On the duties of the provincial governor, see 22.1.33, 50.10.5 pr., 1; and on the legal points, 50.12.1, 15.

24 G.P. Burton *Chiron* 9 (1979) 476–7

25 See *Dig.* 50.8.11.2, 50.8.12.2. Oddly, Burton 475 nn 40, 42 ascribes both passages to Ulpian, although the *Digest* attributes them unequivocally to Papirius' *Constitutions*. Papirius cannot be quoting from Ulpian, who flourished several decades later. See also *Dig.* 50.8.12.4, 50.10.5.1.

26 Burton *Chiron* 9 (1979) 479–80; Jacques *Liberté* 267–82, esp. 282.

27 Cf Nicols *ANRW* II/13 (1980) 537, 545–7

28 On points raised about the *Tabula Siarensis*, see González *ZPE* 55 (1984) 76, 83–5.

29 For embassies, see *Irn.* colophon, interpreted by González *JRS* 76 (1986) 238; and also *CIL* II 6278 = *ILS* 5163 = *FIRA* I² 49; cf R.J.A. Talbert *The Senate of Imperial Rome* (Princeton 1984) 307.

30 *Urs.* 80; *Irn.* H; *Dig.* 50.4.18.12 Arcadius Charisius; 50.7.3 Africanus; 50.7.11 Paul; 50.7.17 Pomp.; cf Hardy *Charters* 35 n 57; F. Millar *The Emperor in the Roman World* (London 1977) 383–4.

31 On consulting with the *ordo*, cf Hardy *Charters* 15–16; Stevenson *Administration* 171; and see *Dig.* 50.1.11 pr. Pap. for collective accountability.

32 For the three areas of responsibility, see, first, *Lex Mun. Tarent.* 12–14,

20–5; *Urs.* 80; *Mal.* 60, 67; secondly, *Dig.* 50.4.9 Ulp.; *Mal.* 59; cf CIL
II 2959 on magistrates evading their responsibilities; and thirdly, *Dig.*
50.4.16.1 Paul.; 50.12.1 Ulp.

5

Social Status

As members of the local élite, magistrates were persons of elevated status within the community. In chapter 3 it was demonstrated that admission to magistracies and to the local senate was limited to persons meeting the requisite birth, property, and character qualifications. The present chapter explores in somewhat greater detail the problems of birth and citizenship, as well as some related social considerations.

Free-born versus Freed

Local magistracies were the preserve of the free-born élite. The sole exception to this rule occurred under Julius Caesar, who allowed freedmen to serve as magistrates in his new Spanish foundations, whose colonists consisted largely of members of the urban *plebs* of Rome. Although this provision is included in chapter 105 of the charter of Urso, and although epigraphical examples of freedmen-magistrates are found in Caesarian colonies in Africa, Italy, and Dalmatia, there is no decisive proof that freedmen actually held magistracies in any town of Spain, even Urso itself.[1] After Caesar, this short-lived concession disappeared, and was indeed outlawed by the *Lex Visellia* of AD 24. As if there remained any doubt to be dispelled, the Flavian municipal law specifically debarred freedmen from local office.[2] Thus freedmen, in Spain and elsewhere, could hardly aspire to higher office than the 'semi-magistracy' of the sevirate, though it remained possible to become an 'honorary' decurion and to obtain the *ornamenta decurionatus*.[3]

Sons of freedmen had the possibility of becoming magistrates, but only if they were born free. Fabre's study of the epigraphic evidence from Spain reveals that the majority of freedman 'unions' (whether legal marriage or quasi-marital relationships) involved two freed partners rather than one freed and one free-born, and that the majority of children produced in unions of two freed partners were themselves freedmen, born before their parents were manumitted.[4] Thus many freedmen's sons did not meet the free birth prerequisite for holding magistracies. Even for those who were free-born, there was always a certain social stigma attached to being of servile descent. Moreover, Mackie has recently suggested that admission of freedmen's sons to the *ordo* may have entailed a hefty financial outlay on their part, in exchange for such a privilege; and while evidence is lacking, the suggestion is not implausible. The example of [Iu]nius Cornelianus of Carissa (**39**, unfortunately a fragmentary inscription), a sevir who furnished door fixtures for [name of building lost], apparently in return for the honorary title of decurion (reading '[pro honore] decurionatus'), certainly seems to refer to a *quid pro quo* donation by a freedman. And it is well established that freedmen paid for the position of *sevir Augustalis*.[5] If ex-slaves could purchase religious offices and honorary decurionates, their sons should have been able to purchase magistracies.

Several examples of freedmen's sons in local politics are known from the Spanish provinces. Q. Caecilius Philistio, the freedman of Caecilia Q. f. Severa of Mago, had a son, [Q Caecilius] Labeo (**796**), who became aedile and duovir there.[6] At Barcino, the aedile C. Iulius C. f. Pal. Silvanus (**446**) was presumably the son of two freedpersons, an unknown C. Iulius and Aurelia Nigella. His 'father' (probably step-father) C. Publicius Melissus is also a freedman, because he has another son who is a *sevir Augustalis*. The tribe Palatina confirms the servile origin of this aedile.[7] At Dertosa, a freedman's son, while not actually a magistrate, was granted *aedilicii et duomvirales honores*. This man, M. Porcius Terentianus (**677**), was the son of M. Porcius Theopompus (**676**), a *sevir Augustalis* who had himself received *aedilicium ius*. The grant of *honores*, rather than an actual magistracy, may suggest that Terentianus was born a slave; or, as Mommsen proposed, that he died a minor. It is curious that another man from Dertosa receiving *aedilicii honores*, P. Valerius Dionysius (**678**), was a *sevir Augustalis* and hence almost certainly a freedman.[8] At Arva and Lucurgentum in Baetica we find two *seviri* (one specifically called *libertus* and one whose Greek *cognomen* suggests a servile origin) who received *ornamenta decurionatus* (**13**, **170**), while at Tarraco, one Aemilius Valerius Chorintus (= Corinthus), who received *aedilicii honores*, has a *cognomen* appropriate to a freedman (**919**). Two other magistrates were probably but not certainly sons of freedmen: ... P. f. Pyramus (another Greek *cognomen*) was duovir at Corduba and Obulco (**223**), while L. Iunius Barbarus of Ulisi (**281**) was possibly the son of a freedman from Singilia Barba. Three more men, C.

Marius Verus of Gerunda and the Numisius brothers from Tarraco (**738**, **907–8**), all of the second century AD) bear the tribe Palatina and are therefore probably descendants of freedmen, though not necessarily sons. All three became provincial *flamines*, and the Numisii were both equestrians; this would be a dramatic social leap for sons of ex-slaves.

There are two known sons of free-born fathers and freed mothers. L. Calpurnius L. f. Iuncus (**427**), aedile, duovir, and flamen of Barcino, was the son of another L. Calpurnius Iuncus (**426**), aedile and duovir, and of the freedwoman Valeria. A recipient of the *ornamenta decurionalia*, M. Acilius M'. f. Phlegon (**251**) was the son of the *praefectus fabrum* M'. Acilius Fronto and the freedwoman Acilia Plecusa. His Greek *cognomen* and failure to obtain a real magistracy suggest that he was born while his mother was still a slave.[9] There are quite a few other magistrates whose mothers have Greek names, but whose status as sons of ex-slaves cannot be proved. One likely candidate is the son of Iunia Eleuthera, whose *cognomen* means 'free' or 'freed' (**29**).

Acquisition of Roman Citizenship

To gain the coveted Roman citizenship was a tremendous incentive toward local office-holding in the Early Empire. With rare exceptions a provincial could only gain this citizenship by service, either in the army or as a local magistrate of a privileged town.[10] One of the exceptions was P. Cornelius Macer, a duovir of Ammaia (**311**), who obtained the citizenship by an individual grant (*viritim*) from the emperor Claudius prior to Ammaia's receipt of municipal status.

While the élite of Roman colonies would from the beginning have comprised Roman citizens, *municipia* were usually native settlements whose upper class gained Roman citizenship under the terms of the so-called Latin right (*ius Latii*). This privilege, which Vespasian allegedly granted to 'all' of Spain according to Pliny, allowed the magistrates of each year, upon completion of their year of office, to assume the Roman citizenship for themselves and their families (Pliny *NH* 3.30; *Salp.* 21; Gaius *Inst.* 1.96). Since numerous Spanish cities are known to have become *municipia* under the Flavians, it is often assumed that *ius Latii* and municipal status went hand in hand. However, not all Spanish towns became *municipia*. We are therefore left to infer one of three possibilities: either Pliny is exaggerating when he says 'universae Hispaniae,' or he means the privilege was granted in all three provinces but not to every town, or, *ius Latii* is different from though often concomitant with the conferral of municipal status. The last option was advocated by two scholars in independent articles coincidentally published the same year. They argued that *ius Latii* was a process distinct from municipalization and bestowed Latin (as distinct from Roman) citizenship on the provincials; hence Pliny's statement would mean that all free persons in the Spanish provinces became Latin citizens instead of peregrines. This theory, though much discussed, remains controversial.[11] It would seem to draw support from the Flavian municipal law, particularly the recently published *Irnitana* fragments, where the *municipes*, while not Roman citizens, enjoy virtually all the privileges of Roman citizens, apparently including the use of *tria nomina* and enrolment in a voting tribe (*Irn.* 86). Elsewhere in the law it is made clear that all *municipes*, including even the freedmen, are Latin citizens (except, of course, those who are Roman citizens) (*Salp.* 28; *Irn.* 72).

One piece of evidence which disturbs this theory is the repeated mention in the law of *incolae* (residents) who are distinct from the *municipes* and have fewer privileges.[12] The Malaca copy of the municipal law, which has long been known and has provided evidence for proponents of the Latin citizenship theory, mentions assignment of *curiae* (voting bodies) in which '*incolae* who are Roman or Latin citizens may cast their ballot' (*Mal.* 53). *Incolae* assuredly has in these contexts the normal meaning of 'resident aliens,' persons who live in one town but are citizens of another. Hence they are not *municipes*; however, if they hold Roman or Latin citizenship from their home town they are allowed to vote in the *municipium*. By specifying '*incolae* who are Roman or Latin citizens,' the Malaca fragment seems to imply that there are some *incolae* who are not Roman or Latin citizens. But if, as has been claimed, 'there were no more peregrines in Spain, only Latin and Roman citizens,'[13] then the concept of non-citizen *incolae* makes little sense. The wording of the law clearly implies that only some of the *incolae* were Roman or Latin citizens, which in turn suggests that only certain towns received citizenship privileges. It therefore seems more plausible to associate *ius Latii* with municipal status, along the following lines. *Ius Latii* would be granted to towns when they became *municipia*; the *municipes* would all become Latin citizens and the magistrates would become Roman citizens. But inhabitants of towns without privileged status would remain peregrines, and if they took up residence at a *municipium* they would be *incolae* without Roman or Latin status. The debate will doubtless continue.

We know of several magistrates who explicitly state that they received Roman citizenship *per honorem* under the Flavians: three duovirs at Cisimbrium, an aedile at Igabrum, and two duovirs at Iluro (**73, 75–6, 111, 123–4**). The earliest of these, M. Aelius Niger (**111**), received his citizenship in AD

75, 'by the *beneficium* of the emperor Caesar Augustus Vespasianus.' If we accept the plausible thesis that Vespasian's grant of *ius Latii* occurred during his censorship in 73–4,[14] the new *municipia* will have held elections in 74 for the calendar year 75: this may make Aelius Niger one of the first two regular aediles of Igabrum, unless the grant was made early enough to allow elections in 73 for 74. Caecilius Optatus, duovir of the *municipium Irnitanum* in AD 91 and named in the town charter of that year (**134**) is surely another recipient of citizenship *per honorem*, as are most of the magistrates enrolled in the Flavian tribe Quirina (whose considerable number, as listed in Table 8, demonstrates the widespread effect of the Vespasianic grant).

Since so many towns in Spain were granted Latin rights by Vespasian, it is questionable whether Spain profited much from the introduction by Hadrian of the *ius Latii maius*, which gave citizenship to all decurions in towns acquiring this right (Gaius *Inst.* 1.96). We do know that at its own request, the *municipium* of Italica received from Hadrian a change of status to the theoretically inferior (i.e., less autonomous) grade of colony. Hadrian reportedly could not understand the logic of such a request, but the motive of the *Italicenses* may have been the hope of tax exemptions.[15]

By the infamous constitution of AD 212 the emperor Caracalla extended Roman citizenship to virtually all free inhabitants of the Empire. This act was perhaps inspired less by humanitarian motives than by financial, administrative, and political expedients: the increased revenue brought in from the 5 per cent inheritance tax applicable only to Roman citizens, standardization of personal status and legal rights, greater unity of the Empire, and the allegiance of all who benefited from the privilege of the new citizenship.[16] In fact the benefits were cheapened by this constitution, since widespread extension of the citizenship meant that being a Roman citizen was no longer an exclusive or prestigious privilege. What effect this constitution had upon the magistrates of Spain is difficult to gauge, since nearly all our recorded magistrates belong to the first and second centuries. The only third-century Aurelii (the *nomen* usually adopted by those owing their citizenship to Caracalla's constitution) are two *curatores r.p.* at Italica; since both of these are equestrian officials, and one of them a provincial governor, the origin of their *nomen* probably antedates the constitution. Certainly magistrates in the major towns, which had enjoyed privileged status since Flavian or earlier times, did not benefit from the Antonine Constitution; however, there may have been magistrates in hitherto unprivileged towns who did.

Families of Magistrates

One difference between local senates and the Senate at Rome was that membership in the latter was not hereditary. To enter the Roman Senate it was first necessary to be elected to a magistracy; being the son of a senator did not in itself confer admission. In local senates, where it was not necessary to hold a magistracy to belong to the *ordo*, sons of decurions attended as *praetextati* and were enrolled in the *album* – the only restriction being that they could not vote until they reached the requisite age of twenty-five.[17] Those who died before reaching this age were granted the decurial ornaments (e.g., **244**), and there is one example of a boy who died at age nineteen with the title *decurio* (**266**). Teenagers are sometimes attested with magistrates' honours, such as the *ornamenta duoviralia* held by C. Aemilius Faustinus of Urso (**294**). At Barcino we find not only a fourteen-year old with *aedilicii et duovirales honores* (**434**), but two teenagers actually called aediles (**442, 446**). While we can understand sons of decurions sitting in on senate meetings, there is no easy explanation for these teenage magistrates. Possibly their aedileships were honorary, or possibly a shortage of candidates necessitated a relaxation of the age limit.

Magistrates acquiring Roman citizenship *per honorem* automatically acquired it for their parents, wives, legitimate children, and grandchildren subject to the *patria potestas* (*Salp.* 21.2). Since these élite families made up the municipal aristocracy, it was from their ranks, i.e., the sons and grandsons of magistrates, that future magistrates were chosen. These magistracies therefore tended to become hereditary (as did priesthoods, which were also the preserve of the élite).[18] There are numerous examples in the Catalogue of sons of the élite who themselves became local magistrates in due course: undoubtedly this number would increase sharply if we had more complete local *fasti*.

Although the number of known magistrates and other members of the local aristocracy must represent but a small fraction of those who actually lived, it is still possible to detect in the *fasti* the prominence of certain élite families, such as the Baebii of Saguntum and the Pedanii of Barcino. For those not fortunate enough to be born into a powerful family, connections of influence or social mobility could be secured through marriage. The local magistrate L. Numisius Montanus of Tarraco (**907**), whose tribe Palatina suggests servile ancestry, married a provincial *flaminica* from the *gens Porcia* (whose roots in this province probably stretch back to the early second century BC); he was eventually made a knight by Hadrian. An even greater coup was scored by C. Varinius Fidus, magistrate at the undistinguished Baetican town of Segida (**247**): he managed to marry his daughter to a provincial governor. Not all marriages, however, were dynastic or diplomatic; there are examples of magistrates who married ex-slaves, either their own (**784**) or someone else's (**426**).

Despite the hereditary nature of local offices, and the understandable desire of local aristocracies to maintain a 'closed élite,' there is some reason to believe that persons who were not members of the 'family compact' might enter the ranks of the *ordo*. An obvious instance is provided by sons of freedmen, who (as discussed earlier in this chapter) sometimes aspired to magistracies or to equivalent honours. Moreover, we occasionally encounter explicit attestations of *novi homines* in local senates, such as the magistrate of Itucci (**154**) who boasts of being 'IIvir primus de familia'.

One possible reason for this upward mobility, not demonstrable for Roman Spain but well known to sociologists, is discontinuity in social stratification through a decline in 'élite fertility,' the ability of leading families to reproduce themselves. At Rome itself the most prominent senatorial families disappeared at a rate of 75 per cent per generation, and the syndrome is paralleled (though with less staggering statistics) among modern élites.[19] The causes of Roman élite infertility are inadequately understood and highly controversial. For instance, Hopkins posits a combination of sociological factors ('increased competition for status, individuation, secularisation, and the higher status of women'), while others adduce a range of medical problems ranging from lead poisoning to venereal disease.[20] The debate is further complicated by such equally controversial factors as the rate of infant mortality and the effectiveness of ancient birth control techniques. It is at least clear that if élite families were unable or unwilling to replenish their own numbers, opportunities would be created for upward mobility from the ranks of the community, probably with wealth as a major criterion for advancement. Evidence from elsewhere in the Roman world suggests that vacancies in local senates were regularly filled by wealthy *arrivistes*, who were often descendants of freedmen;[21] no doubt patronage, marital ties, and local economic requirements played as important a role as élite infertility in securing the advancement of these men.

A case-study of open and closed élites by Géza Alföldy has recently appeared, using the local magistrates and priests of Tarraco, Barcino, and Saguntum as examples.[22] Alföldy's findings are that Tarraco had three élite strata: the dominant, affluent families, whose members often 'skipped' the aedileship to become duovirs, and often ended up as equestrians; lesser locals, who had to follow the complete *cursus honorum* and only occasionally attained equestrian status or a provincial priesthood; and wealthy outsiders (mostly from other Spanish towns) who apparently purchased their magistracies. At Barcino, the local élite was smaller and less rich; hence there was even greater scope for rich foreigners to acquire local honours, and it was in fact this group which then advanced to higher offices. But at Saguntum, an old native town, unlike the two Roman colonies with their immigrants, the local aristocratic families operated a monopolistic, closed élite on a hereditary basis, with a standard, homogeneous *cursus*. Alföldy's study admirably illustrates the variety of 'family compacts' and differing degrees of social openness available in different towns. Of course, the three cities were chosen largely because of the comparatively large number of magistrates attested there. If we look at the magistrates of other important cities in Spain (e.g., Italica or Emerita Augusta), we simply do not have the same quantity of data on prominent families and on immigration to permit sweeping conclusions. Yet it is clear from the three towns sampled that there could be tremendous differences from one city to another, depending on local circumstances and the power of the ruling families.

Social mobility from one generation to the next can be seen not only in the case of ex-slaves whose sons become decurions, but in the advancement of decurions' sons into the equestrian and even senatorial orders. Several Roman senators and even consuls are thought to have been sons of local Spanish magistrates, though firm proof is lacking.[23] One of the most illustrious examples of a local magistrate's son is C. Licinius C. f. Gal. Marinus Voconius Romanus, the son of an *eques* (**862**) but adopted by a *clarior*, C. Licinius Marinus. A schoolmate of the younger Pliny, Voconius Romanus returned to Spain and became *flamen p.H.c.* in 96. Pliny recommended him to both Nerva and Trajan for adlection to the Senate, apparently without success, but did manage to obtain for him the *ius trium liberorum*, the privilege of a father of three children. Voconius, a man of letters and a lawyer by profession, retired to his native Saguntum, where he built a seaside villa. He owned a private fortune of four million sesterces inherited from his mother (well above the property qualification for admission to the Senate).[24]

Patronage

Personal patronage was an important social mechanism in the Late Republic and Early Empire. Although magistrates were elected to office, the provincial governor had considerable influence in ensuring an 'equitable' distribution of municipal honours;[25] and the patronage of the governor or of another senator was virtually *de rigueur* in aspiring to posts beyond the local level, or to other privileges such as citizenship, equestrian status, exemptions from duty, or the privilege of a father of three children. The letters of the younger

Pliny demonstrate his patronage as senator of the Spanish equestrian Voconius Romanus and of the Spanish poet Martial, as well as of various persons who came to Pliny's attention in the province of Bithynia. While Pliny's letters are probably typical of the sort of patronage exercised by Roman senators, they are atypical in that they survive. Lacking an Iberian equivalent of Pliny's letters to Trajan seeking favours for his friends, we can only assume that governors in Spain made similar requests for their provincial clients.

Our other source of information, epigraphy, is strangely tacit on this phenomenon. There are no commemorations of governors or other senators erected by grateful magistrates. If patronage flourished, it apparently did so under the table: magistrates seem reluctant to publicize the assistance of a patron. Yet it was perfectly acceptable to raise a memorial to the emperor (e.g., 8, 71, 123–4, 283) or to a member of the Imperial family (234, 355–6, 882). No motive for the commemoration is stated on these monuments. It is, however, remarkable that the monuments all date to the first century AD; thereafter, magistrates sometimes commemorate the emperor on behalf of their cities, but not on their own behalf. This shift may reflect a change in protocol, but it may equally indicate that first-century magistrates had a particular reason for wishing to thank the emperor. The extension of Roman citizenship to municipal magistrates under the Julio-Claudians and Flavians provides a likely motive for these memorials. As noted above, we know or suspect that several magistrates received the citizenship through holding local office, and three of these (8, 123–4) are among those commemorating an emperor. Other recorded favours, such as the *equus publicus*, or adlection to the five *decuriae iudicum*, clearly show beneficence by the emperor, almost certainly through an intermediary patron. Appointment to the provincial priesthood of the Imperial Cult also presumably required the emperor's approval. As noted in chapter 3, there are instances of decurions being adlected or excused by the emperor. One of the adlections (144) was apparently made by Trajan in his own home town of Italica. Special privileges by emperors to their fellow townsmen are hardly rare; Hadrian granted Italica the status of colony, while Septimius Severus promoted three procurators from his African birthplace, Lepcis.[26]

If magistrates were loath to acknowledge their debt to patrons, they were quite willing to be honoured as patrons themselves. Apart from epitaphs and honorific inscriptions erected by their *liberti* or *amici*, several magistrates are explicitly honoured as *patroni* by the *plebs*, the *municipes et incolae*, or the *provincia Hispania citerior* (6, 23, 130, 972). C. Laetilius Apalus (568) is honoured by the college of fishermen and sellers (perhaps of fish) at Carthago

Nova, and may be their patron. Many towns honour local magistrates for their munificence (cf chapter 7), though without designating them as patrons.

Status Symbols

While the holding of a magistracy or membership in the *ordo* was in itself a sign of elevated status in the community, there were also tangible indicators, in the form of special privileges, perquisites, and honours accruing to the local élite. Decurions had reserved seating at the games and in the theatre, wore distinctive dress, and enjoyed legal privileges such as exemption from certain penalties and the right of appeal to the emperor in certain cases. Magistrates, besides receiving the citizenship, wore the *toga praetexta*, were entitled to *fasces* and attendants (*apparitores*), and were exempt from liturgies during their tenure of magistracy.[27] The inscriptions from Spain record numerous examples of deceased decurions and magistrates being commemorated with statues, public funerals, eulogies, and other honours by the *ordo* – the cost of which was not uncommonly repaid by a flattered relative. Such privileges, no doubt restricted to distinguished individuals, found their prototype and inspiration at Rome, where they were likewise the gift of the Senate.[28]

Thanks to the Urso charter and the *Lex Irnitana* we have considerable information on magistrates' apparitors, or attendants. At Urso each duovir was entitled to two lictors, who were similar in title but not in number to the consuls' attendants at Rome,[29] two scribes, two messengers, an orderly, a copyist, a herald, a soothsayer, and a flutist, for a total of eleven apparitors. Each aedile had one scribe, one herald, one soothsayer, one flutist, and four public slaves. The apparitors (not counting the slaves) served for one year, were exempt from military service during that year, and received a stipend which varied in amount from position to position.[30]

The situation in the Flavian *municipia* was slightly different. Chapter 18 of the Flavian municipal law, listing the duovirs' attendants, is unfortunately lost, but we know from chapter 73 that the duovirs at least had scribes. Chapter 19 provides that the aediles are to have an unspecified number of public slaves, but there is no mention of scribes or other skilled trades. Furthermore, whereas the colonial charter fixes precise stipends for the servants, the municipal law allows the decurions to decide their wages. This difference reflects the greater independence of *municipia*, especially in financial affairs.

Some of these status symbols – except, perhaps, the attendants – could also be conferred upon deserving individuals who were ineligible for formal admission to the *ordo*, e.g., minors, freedmen, and deceased persons. Such individuals could be honoured with the *ornamenta* of a decurion, aedile, or duovir (but never quaestor), as several Spanish examples testify. Exactly what these *ornamenta* consisted of is not spelled out in the charters. However, we know that at Rome the magisterial *ornamenta* included use of the magistrate's title, the *toga praetexta*, reserved seats at public spectacles, and burial honours appropriate to the rank; and it is reasonable to suppose that *ornamenta duoviralia* and the like conferred similar privileges at the local level.[31] We do know, as mentioned earlier in this chapter, that sons of decurions who were minors could attend local senate meetings as non-voting observers, and this privilege was presumably another of the *ornamenta*.

Prestige

Although our sources do not explicitly discuss the prestige of magistracies, there can be little doubt that such offices attracted the status-conscious. The duovirate was sufficiently distinctive that it could be offered to the emperor or a member of the Imperial family as a compliment – and be accepted. Also, as Mackie has pointed out, the duovirate was the only magistracy worth holding more than once, as demonstrated by the pattern of *iteratio* in career inscriptions.[32] The aedileship, though clearly of lesser importance, was nevertheless an honour, and not devoid of prestige. We know, in fact, of one magistrate (**799**) who served three times as aedile; and another (**174**) may have served twice.

The local senate, too, enjoyed prestige through its political clout and social exclusivity. Its *dignitas* and sense of aristocracy are frequently emphasized in inscriptions by the superlative phrase *splendidissimus ordo*.[33] It should also be remembered that the privilege of entering the *ordo* or becoming a magistrate often involved a cash outlay, which implies that the honour these positions conferred must have made the expense worthwhile in the minds of those competing for them. Clearly, both the social prestige and tangible benefits of élite membership appealed to many men's *philotimia* (love of status), providing ample incentive for them to seek admission to the *ordo* and to run for local office.

Notes

1 *Urs.* 105; *CIL* III 1820 = *ILS* 7166; *CIL* VIII 977 = *ILS* 5320; *CIL* X 6104 = *ILS* 1945; cf Strabo 8.6.23; S.M. Treggiari *Roman Freedmen During the Late Republic* (Oxford 1969) 63–4. As Hardy *Charters* 49 n 116 rightly

observes, this unusual allowance was probably due to Caesar's inclusion of freedmen from Rome among the colonists. On the other hand, Carteia, as a *colonia libertinorum* (Livy 43.3.4) had presumably had freedmen magistrates since 171 BC.

2 *Mal.* 54; A.M. Duff *Freedmen in the Early Roman Empire* 2nd ed (Cambridge 1958) 66; A.N. Sherwin White *The Roman Citizenship* 2nd ed (Oxford 1973) 326–7

3 On the sevirate, see Etienne *Culte* 279–81. The *sevir Augustalis* of the Treveri (*civis Trever*) who held all magistracies among the Aedui (*CIL* XIII 2669 = *ILS* 7046) was a *libertus*, but such instances are exceptional. A *sevir Augustalis* might more easily advance if he were free-born, as approximately 15 per cent of them were, R. Duthoy *Epigraphica* 36 (1974) 140; and see J. D'Arms *Commerce and Social Standing in Ancient Rome* (Cambridge, Mass. 1981) 133 for becoming an 'honorary' decurion.

4 G. Fabre in *Actes du colloque 1973 sur l'esclavage* (Paris 1976) 425–6. On sons of freedmen holding local office, see M.L. Gordon *JRS* 21 (1931) 65–77 (dealing almost exclusively with Italy). *Irn.* 97 provides for sons of freedmen obtaining Roman citizenship *per honores* for themselves and their parents.

5 Cf Mackie *Administration* 56; and D. Ladage *Städtische Priester- und Kultämter im lateinischen Westen* (Köln 1971) 116.

6 Another magistrate named Caecilius (**403**) appears to be the son of a freedman, for his father has a Greek cognomen.

7 On this tribe cf P.D.A. Garnsey in *The Ancient Historian and His Materials* (Westmead 1975) 170–1.

8 More than 90 per cent of *Augustales* and *seviri Augustales* with a Greek cognomen are freedmen, as are about 80 per cent of those with a Latin one, Duthoy *Epigraphica* 36 (1974) 137–9.

9 J.F. Rodríguez Neila *Sociedad y administración local en la Bética romana* (Córdoba 1981) 42

10 For this reason, magistrates and veterans are sometimes difficult to distinguish, cf A. Mócsy *Pannonia and Upper Moesia* (London and Boston 1974) 137.

11 On the theory, see G. Alföldy *Latomus* 25 (1966) 37–57 and H. von Braunert in *Corolla memoriae Erich Swoboda dedicata* (Graz-Köln 1966) 68–83. For further discussion, see Galsterer *Untersuchungen* 37–50; Sherwin White *The Roman Citizenship*² 360–7; F.G.B. Millar *The Emperor in the Roman World* (London 1977) 401–6; Mackie *Administration* 201–14.

12 *Irn.* 94; J. González *JRS* 76 (1986) 237

13 On the possible meanings of *incolae*, see Mackie *Administration* 228–35; and for the claim, see Alföldy *Latomus* 25 (1966) 50.

14 R. Wiegels *Hermes* 106 (1978) 196–213

15 Gell. *NA* 16.13.4; E.T. Salmon *Roman Colonization under the Republic* (London 1969) 156

16 Dio Cass. 77.9 (overestimating the fiscal motive); *FIRA* I² 88. Cf W. Kunkel *An Introduction to Roman Legal and Constitutional History* 2nd ed (Oxford 1973) 62; Sherwin White *The Roman Citizenship*² 279–87, 380–94; Clavel and Lévêque *Villes et structures* 200–4; G.E.M. de Ste Croix *The Class Struggle in the Ancient Greek World* (London 1981) 461–2.

17 Cf T.P. Wiseman *New Men in the Roman Senate* (Oxford 1971) 95; and on *praetextati* in local senates, see *ILS* 6121–2; Arnold *Roman System*³ 257–8.

18 H. Castritius *Mitteilungen der Technische Universität Carolo-Wilhelmina zu Braunschweig* 8/3 (1973) 41; Garnsey *Ancient Historian and His Materials* 167; R. Syme *Mus. Helv.* 34 (1977) 138

19 P.D. Garnsey and R.P. Saller *The Roman Empire: Economy, Society and Culture* (Berkeley and Los Angeles 1987) 123, 144–5; cf L. Tepperman *Canadian Review of Sociology and Anthropology* 14 (1977) 285–93.

20 K. Hopkins *Death and Renewal* (Cambridge 1983) 78–107; L. and D. Needleman *Classical Views* 4 (1985) 63–94

21 Garnsey and Saller *The Roman Empire* (n 19 above) 125

22 G. Alföldy *Gerión* 2 (1984) 193–238

23 L. Antistius Rusticus (*cos. suff.* AD 90) is suspected to have been the son of the homonymous duovir of Corduba (**85**), W.M. Ramsay *JRS* 14 (1924) 179–81; R. Knapp *Roman Córdoba* (Berkeley 1982) 42–3. C. Calpurnius Flaccus cos. suff. AD 124 appears to be the son of C. Calpurnius Flaccus of Tarraco (**906**). T. Iunius Severus cos. suff. 154 could be the son of the homonymous magistrate and tribune of Dianium (**682**), Wiegels no. 283. L. Antonius Saturninus cos. suff. AD 83 is seen as the son of the homonymous duovir of Tarraco (**905**), R. Syme *Tacitus* (Oxford 1958) 596 and n 6. In addition, the proconsul L. Fabius Pollio (*PIR*² F 52) might be related to Fabius Pollio of Saepo (**243**).

24 Pliny *Ep.* 1.5, 2.13, 9.7, 9.28, 10.4; *CIL* II 3865a–66 = *ILER* 4382, 3959; *PW* 'Voconius (6)'; *PIR*² L 210; Wiegels no. 100

25 R.P. Saller *Personal Patronage under the Early Empire* (Cambridge 1982) 155–6

26 Saller *Personal Patronage* (n 25 above) 179

27 Regarding status symbols of decurions, see *Urs.* 66; 125; *Irn.* 81; *Dig.* 48.19.15; *PW* 'Decurio' cols. 2330–2; Abbott and Johnson *MARE* 66; P.D.A. Garnsey *Social Status and Legal Privilege in the Roman Empire* (Oxford 1970) 242, 244; and of magistrates, see *Urs.* 62, 81; Abbott and Johnson *MARE* 88. Togate statues, such as those at Segobriga, are believed to represent romanized local magistrates; M. Almagro *Segóbriga (ciudad celtibérica y romana)* (Madrid 1978) 64 and pls XXXV–VII.

28 R.J.A. Talbert *The Senate of Imperial Rome* (Princeton 1984) 364–71

29 On local lictors in Italy and Narbonensis see Liebenam *Städteverwaltung* 278 notes 1 and 5.

30 *Urs.* 62; discussion in L.A. Curchin *Gerión* 4 (1986) 185

31 For *ornamenta decurionatus*, see **13**, **108**, **244**, **251**; for *ornamenta aedilicia*: **900**; for *ornamenta duoviralia*: **294**; and cf Liebenam *Städteverwaltung* 236, 275; S. Borzsák PW XVIII, 1 (1939) 1110–22.

32 Mackie *Administration* 60–1

33 Rodríguez Neila *Sociedad y administración local* 37–9

6

Romanization

Romanization may be defined as the process of assimilation of Roman customs by non-Roman peoples. This was neither an instantaneous nor a simple process; some areas of the Empire, including parts of Spain, were never completely romanized. In each Roman province, however, the élite were among the first to be romanized, and indeed formed an essential nucleus for the romanization of the province as a whole. As Brunt has demonstrated, the romanization of local aristocracies was both a tenet of Roman policy and a cornerstone of Roman control.[1]

Romanization was effected through a variety of means: the influence of the Roman army, the presence of Italian merchants and colonists, the improvement of communications, the granting of Roman citizenship, and so on. But the crucial factor was the co-operation of the provincials themselves. This voluntary support was not always forthcoming and in many cases was achieved only after bitter fighting, the suppression or liquidation of recalcitrant elements of the population, and the resignation of the rest to Roman supremacy. Once it was clear that the Romans were permanently established in Spain, and that social advancement and advantage depended on co-operation with the new overlords, members of the local élite were induced to accept and indeed emulate Roman ways, so that, as Strabo remarks, they romanized themselves.[2]

It is difficult to measure the romanization of local magistrates. The fact that they adopted the system and titles of Roman magistracies is an important but rather elementary indication, which provides little insight into personal motivations or commitment to the Roman cause. The problem, of course, is that the ancient evidence – consisting almost entirely of inscriptions and coins – seldom tells us more about the magistrate than his name and appointment. Yet the name itself is a valuable clue to the progress of romanization. The willingness of the individual, even or perhaps especially in towns which had not yet received the Latin right, to adopt Roman nomenclature and to accept or affect citizenship is an indication of a commitment and indeed desire to become romanized and to 'blend in' with true Romans.

But the presence of 'true Romans' complicates the picture. If local magistrates in fact consisted largely of Roman immigrants, we can hardly think of them as becoming 'romanized,' although their presence may have contributed towards the romanization of the community as a whole. Similarly, immigrants from elsewhere in Italy, who by the first century BC were already largely romanized and in many cases practically Romans themselves, can hardly be said to have become 'romanized' in Spain.[3] Before attempting any detailed analysis of romanization, then, we must first consider whether the magistrates with whom we are dealing were really Spaniards, or immigrants from Roman Italy.

National Origin: Italian or Indigenous?

Prior to the introduction of the Roman magisterial system, towns or tribes were governed by local aristocratic families, acting either as autocrats (*reges, principes*) or as members of a local senate. The earliest magistrates attested on coins and inscriptions often bear non-Roman, indigenous names. However, the influx of Italians into the Peninsula – especially into Baetica, the east coast, and colonies such as Emerita and Caesaraugusta – resulted in at least a partial supplantation of the indigenous élite in some towns. In the beginning it is easy enough to identify a Roman or romanized Italian by his *duo* or *tria nomina*. However, once members of the old aristocracy begin to receive the Roman citizenship, or to affect it by the adoption of Roman nomenclature, it becomes increasingly difficult to distinguish indigenes from immigrants.

From the rapid romanization of Baetica and the east coast it is tempting to conclude that Italians had largely or entirely superseded the indigenous élite by the beginning of the Empire, if not earlier; hence, that most of the magistrates in these areas, and perhaps in other parts of Spain as well, were immigrants. This theory of supplantation was expounded by Rostovtzeff, and still finds many adherents. Undoubtedly, the magistrates of Roman colonies were mostly Italians; but colonies were in the minority. Moreover, since colonies were usually founded *ex nihilo*, there was no indigenous élite to be supplanted (though there is reason to believe that colonies sometimes did include select members from the native sector).[4] But the vast majority of incorporated towns were *municipia*, some of Julio-Claudian date but for the most part Flavian. These *municipia* were, by definition, originally pre-Roman towns which had subsequently been granted Roman, or more often, Latin rights. It is to these *municipia* that we must turn for evidence of any supplantation of the indigenous aristocracy by Italian settlers.

At once we encounter obstacles to Rostovtzeff's theory. An important result of Vespasian's grant of *ius Latii* to Spanish communities was that it enabled the local élite to acquire the Roman citizenship *per magistratum*. As already noted (in chapter 5), several Baetican magistrates inform us that they were enfranchised in this way, and the charter of Salpensa spells out the rules for obtaining the citizenship *per honorem*. If therefore we assume that local élites had long since been replaced by Italians, we must conclude that these Italians were not Roman citizens and therefore were in need of citizenship grants. Is this assumption probable?

By the *Lex Iulia* of 90 BC and the *Lex Plautia Papiria* of the following year, the Roman citizenship had been granted to all free men in Italian towns which had not revolted, and by 84 even the rebels had been enfranchised.[5] Therefore, any Italian immigrants to Spain after the Social War will already have been Roman citizens. Of those Italians who went to Spain prior to 90, the largest group will undoubtedly have been soldiers and veterans; but these too were Roman citizens. Another important group consisted of merchants and businessmen (*mercatores, negotiatores*), but these were largely Roman knights, as were the managers of the lucrative mines.[6] Those who were not knights were mostly the freedman-agents of noble houses; and they too were citizens. It is no coincidence that the *conventus civium Romanorum* in Spain consisted mostly of Italian businessmen. Which Italian immigrants were not citizens? Perhaps some itinerant potters, craftsmen and hawkers, some peasants, a few prospectors – hardly the ingredients of a new municipal aristocracy. In any event, as Brunt has effectively demonstrated, there were few Italian immigrants to Spain before the time of Caesar, and most of these were soldiers and organized businessmen; there was certainly no massive movement of peasants or self-enterprising individuals.[7]

By the time of the Flavian municipal grants there can have been few non-citizens of Italian stock, and such as did exist were probably of mixed blood. Livy attests the frequency of *hybridae* already in the 170s BC, when Carteia was founded as a 'freedman colony' for some four thousand mixed offspring of Italian soldiers and Spanish women (Liv. 43.3); Q. Varius Severus (tr. pl. 90 BC) was another such hybrid. By the mid-first century BC a large number of Italian soldiers could be counted as provincials by reason of their prolonged residence in Farther Spain (*B.Alex.* 53), which almost certainly included quasi-marital unions with local women. Both Julius and Augustus

Caesar settled fresh shipments of Italian veterans in Spanish colonies, but as Balsdon remarks, one wonders where they acquired their wives.[8] Even in the colonies, seaports, and *conventus*-capitals, where Italians are most likely to have abounded, ethnic purity cannot automatically be assumed. As for the remaining towns, mostly native settlements still unincorporated in Julio-Claudian times, I am inclined to see the municipal magistrates as consisting largely of romanized indigenes, who were subsequently rewarded by the Flavians with the gift of Roman citizenship *per honorem*.

Another obstacle to the supplantation theory is presented in the rescript of Vespasian to the Baetican *oppidum* of Sabora, granting it the title of a Flavian municipality and authorizing its move down into the plain (*CIL* II 1423 = *ILS* 6092 = *FIRA* I² 74). This letter illustrates an important point, namely that there were still tribes living in pre-Roman hill forts, even in Baetica, who were only now contemplating a descent into the open, and in the case of Sabora, this move was precipitated by economic hardships. It is scarcely credible that the newly enfranchised magistrates of such towns were really Italians who had been lurking there awaiting this opportunity since the second century BC. Surely they were romanized scions of the native aristocracy.

A further obstacle is presented by the onomastics of Spanish magistrates, particularly in Baetica and on the east coast. The *nomina* most frequently attested are those of Republican governors, yet there were no large-scale grants of citizenship in Spain before the time of Caesar. Knapp has taken great pains to prove, I think conclusively, that large numbers of Spaniards in the *clientela* of these governing families were assuming the *duo* or *tria nomina* even though they were not citizens.[9] These distinctive patrician *nomina*, such as Fabius and Cornelius, are readily identifiable, and would not normally have been borne by Italian soldiers, peasants, or knights. Their profuse presence among the local magistrates serves as a virtual guarantee that in these cases we are dealing with romanized natives rather than Italian immigrants.

While it is often difficult to distinguish Italian from indigene, a few immigrants can easily be identified as such. Several early magistrates (e.g., the coining officials of Carteia and Carthago Nova) bear *nomina* of Italian rather than Roman origin. L. Aemilius Rectus (**578**) was a native of Rome. A handful of immigrants have more exotic backgrounds: L. Caecilius Porcianus (**898**) and possibly L. Iunius Barbarus (**281**) were from Africa; C. Titius Similis (**349**) was born at Cologne; C. Domitius Maternus (**448**) apparently came from Aquincum in Pannonia. Mention has also been made (in chapter 5) of the Greek *cognomina* of a few magistrates, who may have been descendants of freedmen. Except for Italian colonists, however, there were probably few immigrant magistrates.

In conclusion, we must recognize that the magistrates of Roman Spain were not, by origin, a homogeneous lot. Some undoubtedly were Italians, though not as many as is sometimes assumed. A great many were of indigenous stock, while at least some would have been of mixed parentage.[10] Despite their varied backgrounds, however, these men were blended into a cohesive, and to all appearances harmonious, group in each community by the very process of romanization which had induced the establishment of magistracies in the first instance.

Nomenclature and Romanization

As even a casual glance through the Catalogue reveals, the local magistrates of Spain display a wide variety of nomenclature, from single names to *tria nomina*, from strikingly non-Latin names like Bodilcos and Iltirarker to fully romanized names which might equally have befitted a Roman senator. Various causes may be adduced to explain these discrepancies: the early dates of some examples, the predictably larger percentage of *tria nomina* in Roman colonies and *conventus*-capitals, the tendency for names on coins to be abbreviated for reasons of space. Even allowing all these factors, we may profit considerably from an overall analysis of the nomenclature, with particular reference to four characteristic features: various combinations of *praenomina*, *nomina*, and *cognomina*; the origin and significance of the *nomina* and *cognomina*; the manner of filiation; and the tribal designation.

While the assumption of *tria nomina* is no guarantee of Roman citizenship, it does intimate a desire on the part of the individual to have a Roman-sounding name. The development of this trend was gradual. The earliest magistrates, and those in remote areas, sometimes bear totally non-Latin names. The Spanish coin magistrates of the Late Republic generally sport the *duo nomina* (*praenomen* and *nomen*), as was common practice at the time. *Tria nomina* become the norm under Augustus and remain in vogue throughout the Early Empire. This relatively early adoption of the *tria nomina* in Spain is significant because, up until the Flavian period, *duo nomina* were still common among ordinary Romans, whereas the *tria nomina* were borne chiefly by the nobility.[11] Thus, in their zeal to become romanized, Spanish magistrates were actually exceeding their station by adopting such names. This trend to three names would have been understandable if local aristocrats were simply tacking the *duo nomina* in front of their old, non-Latin names, like C. Iulius Vercondaridubnus in Augustan

Gaul (Liv. *Per.* 139). But the *cognomina* adopted by the Spanish magistrates are usually respectable Latin names; moreover, even in the Late Republic, when *duo nomina* were first being adopted, it was very rare for the Spanish *cognomen* to be retained at the end. It appears, then, that the Spanish magistrates of the Julio-Claudian period were imitating the latest nomenclature fashions of the Roman nobility, as their ancestors had done with the *duo nomina* of the Republican nobility. In so doing they displayed a combination of snobbery and audacity which is typical of provincial aristocracies, and which perhaps attains its ludicrous extreme in the case of the African couple who proudly name their son Julius Cicero (*CIL* VIII 9114).

The preference for single, dual, or triple names is most readily determined by a count of the actual numbers of such names among the Spanish magistrates. The quantities of these various combinations of names for each province are indicated on a graph (Figure 1). Naturally Tarraconensis, which has the greatest number of attested magistrates, exceeds the other provinces in every category where the composition of the name can be determined, while Lusitania barely makes a showing at all. If however we represent each combination as a percentage of the total number of magistrates' names in the province, the results become more meaningful. Between 53 per cent and 62 percent of the magistrates in each province bear the *tria nomina* (Figure 2). The standard *duo nomina* (*praenomen* and *nomen*) represent about 14–20 percent of the magistrates in Baetica and Tarraconensis, although the figure is considerably lower for Lusitania, which was settled much later and has fewer attested magistrates of the Republican period. The dropping of the *praenomen*, leaving only *nomen* and *cognomen* (a practice common in the late second and third centuries AD) represents 2–6 per cent of examples from each province. The use of the *cognomen* alone accounts for no more than 11 per cent of all names; the use of the *nomen* alone scores no more than 5 per cent. The overwhelming preference for the *tria nomina* is unmistakable.

A wide range of *nomina* is exhibited by the magistrates, and even if we exclude those *gentes* with fewer than four representatives we are still left with some forty *nomina* (Table 2). In terms of frequency, pride of place must go to Cornelius, with forty-six attested examples; but most *nomina* have fewer than twenty. The predominant *nomina* among magistrates are for the most part the predominant *nomina* in Spain as a whole; indeed, a comparison of the 'top ten' *nomina* in each case shows remarkable consonance (Table 3), the five leaders being the same *nomina* (if not in the same order) in both lists. The origins of these *nomina* have relevance not only to the magistrates but to romanized Spanish society as a whole.

What is immediately striking about the vast majority of *nomina* in Table

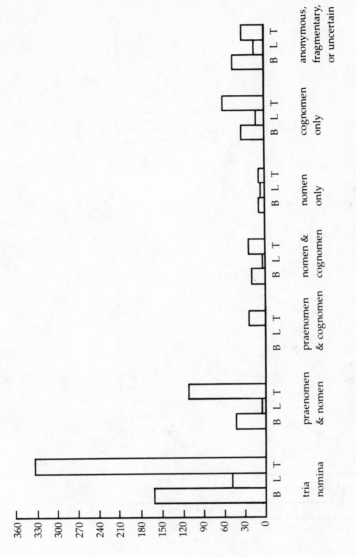

FIGURE 1 Nomenclature of Spanish magistrates – actual numbers.
B=Baetica, L=Lusitania, T=Tarraconensis

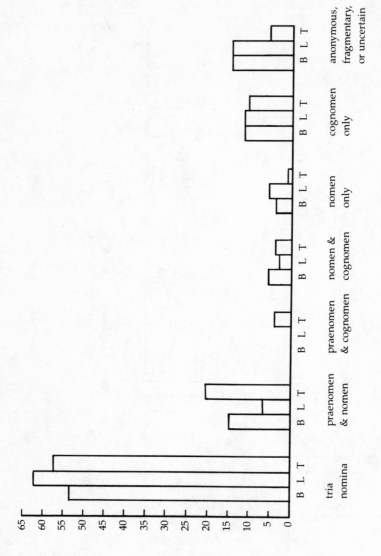

FIGURE 2 Nomenclature of Spanish magistrates – comparative percentages.
B = Baetica, L = Lusitania, T = Tarraconensis

TABLE 2

Frequency Table of Commonest *Nomina* among Spanish Magistrates

Rank	Nomen	B	L	T	Total	Rank	Nomen	B	L	T	Total
1	Cornelius	17	4	25	46	16	Fulvius	0	0	8	8
2	Valerius	10	0	31	41		Marcius	3	2	3	8
3	Iulius	9	9	14	32		Aufidius	3	1	3	7
4	Aemilius	9	1	20	30	17	Clodius	0	1	6	7
5	Fabius	16	0	12	28		Granius	1	0	6	7
6	Caecilius	2	2	21	25		Numisius	2	0	5	7
7	Iunius	10	1	8	19		Coelius	1	1	4	6
8	Antonius	4	1	12	17	18	Domitius	0	0	6	6
9	Licinius	4	1	11	16		Flavius	1	0	5	6
	Calpurnius	4	0	11	15		Postumius	0	0	6	6
10	Pompeius	2	2	11	15	19	Annius	3	1	1	5
	Porcius	4	1	10	15		Aurelius	2	2	0	4
11	Sempronius	3	0	11	14		Fabricius	0	1	3	4
12	Manlius	4	2	6	12		Helvius	1	0	3	4
	Aelius	6	0	5	11		Herennius	2	0	2	4
13	Baebius	0	0	11	11		Lucius	2	0	2	4
	Marius	2	0	9	11	20	Minicius	0	0	4	4
14	Terentius	4	0	6	10		Mummius	3	1	0	4
	Acilius	4	1	4	9		Pedanius	0	0	4	4
15	Lucretius	4	0	5	9		Pomponius	2	1	1	4
	Vibius	4	1	4	9		Quin[c]tius	3	0	1	4
							Sulpicius	0	1	3	4

B = Baetica   L = Lusitania   T = Tarraconensis

2 is that they are the gentilic names of prominent senatorial families of the Middle and Late Republic. 'Cornelius' recalls a host of governors, notably the famous Cornelii Scipiones. 'Valerius' invokes the memory of C. Valerius Flaccus, consul and proconsul in Hispania Citerior in the late 90s. Several governors bore each of the *nomina* Aemilius, Fabius, Caecilius, Iunius, Calpurnius, Manlius, Sempronius, and Marius. 'Antonius' perhaps refers to L. Antonius, proconsul in 40. 'Pompeius' is probably Cn. Pompeius Magnus (Pompey), proconsul in the 70s. 'Porcius' assuredly recalls the elder Cato who was consul in Hispania Citerior in 195. These illustrious *nomina* were not the sort one would expect to be borne by Italian soldiers or peasants, let alone by provincials.

How were these noble Republican *nomina* obtained by Spanish magis-

TABLE 3

Ten Most Frequent Nomina in All of Spain,
Compared with Their Frequency among Spanish Magistrates

Nomen	Rank in all of Spain*	Rank among magistrates**
Iulius	1	3
Valerius	2	2
Cornelius	3	1
Fabius	4	5
Aemilius	5	4
Licinius	6	9
Sempronius	7	11
Iunius	8	7
Caecilius	9	6
Pompeius	10	10

*Based on Knapp *Ancient Society* 9 (1978) 213
**Based on Table 2

trates? The assumption of the *duo* or *tria nomina* was supposedly the badge of Roman or Latin citizenship,[12] but there were few grants of citizenship in Spain before the time of Caesar. Knapp has conveniently assembled several examples of Republican Spaniards bearing Roman *nomina* yet who were not Roman citizens; perhaps most striking are the members of the *turma Salluitana*, a cavalry troop from the vicinity of the later Caesaraugusta, who bore Roman *nomina* prior to their enfranchisement in 89 BC. Knapp concludes that *nomina* were being 'usurped' by persons 'not legally entitled to use Roman names,' because they 'desired assimilation with *Romanitas*.'[13] However, the only evidence for such illegality is Suetonius's statement that the emperor Claudius 'forbade men of foreign status to use Roman names, especially the gentilic *nomen*' (Suet. *Claud.* 25.3). Quite apart from the negative criterion that this ban lacks any known precedent, Suetonius' inclusion of it in a chapter dealing with the emperor's innovative regulations suggests that the prohibition began with Claudius. If this is so, then the use of Roman names by peregrines must hitherto have been tolerated. If, then, the adoption of Roman *nomina* by non-citizens in the Republican period was not only practised (as Knapp has shown) but permitted (as Suetonius implies), it seems inappropriate to speak of usurpation and of illegal use of names, though it may be true that provincials desired a closer affinity with the Romans. It is indeed possible that the provincial governor tried to ensure or reinforce the loyalty of local aristocrats in his *clientela* by granting them the use of his prestigious *nomen*, without giving them citizenship.[14] Thus, local magistrates may have acquired Roman aristocratic *nomina* quite legitimately.

Dyson has recently attempted to link the geographic distribution of *nomina* in Spain with the military activities of Republican governors.[15] His thesis is that the concentration of inscriptions reflects the presence of these governors on the frontiers and their attempts to win the loyalty of the natives through 'onomastic identity with the Roman ruling class.' Since the inscriptions attesting these *nomina* are often centuries later than the campaigns in question, and since all the *nomina* are widespread across the Peninsula, the validity of this approach is not beyond question. Some of the patterns (e.g., Porcii in southern Baetica, or Fabii at Saguntum) show senatorial *nomina* where no governor is attested, or conversely, a scarcity of *nomina* where governors were especially active (e.g., a scarcity of Pompeii in the Ebro valley). On the other hand, the strong showing of Caecilii in Mallorca (conquered by Q. Caecilius Metellus) or of Cornelii at Italica (founded by P. Cornelius Scipio) can hardly be accidental.[16] In short, the prominence of Republican senatorial *nomina* seems in some cases to be the result of gubernatorial action, but one should beware of pushing the relatively late epigraphic evidence too far.

Three Imperial *nomina* merit special comment. 'Iulius' is clearly a reference to Julius, or possibly Augustus, Caesar. The Gallic aristocracy were nearly all Iulii, as a result of the influence and patronage of Julius Caesar. Spanish aristocrats had been adopting other illustrious *nomina* long before Caesar arrived; nonetheless, Iulius is the commonest *nomen* in Spain and one of the top three among the magistrates. As Knapp has demonstrated, the Iulii occur mostly in towns of Julian (i.e., Caesarian or Augustan) foundation, and represent those indigenes who were incorporated into Julian communities and who had not previously adopted a *nomen*. In the case of the local élite, then, the Iulii seem to comprise those magistrates who had not been romanized previously. In Lusitania, where romanization did not really get underway before the time of Caesar, Iulius is by far the commonest *nomen* of magistrates.[17]

The first century AD has been shown to be a period of 'free choice' of *nomina* by new citizens.[18] Thus, although Vespasian granted widespread citizenship to the magistrates of Spanish *municipia*, his *nomen* Flavius finds only six adherents among the Spanish magistrates. By that time, obviously, most magistrates of even the more remote *oppida* had already adopted Roman names prior to enfranchisement. That being said, it may seem even more surprising to find 'Aelius' well attested,[19] for there were no Aelii among the Republican governors, and the *nomen* is that of the emperor

Hadrian and his successors. But there are no grounds for supposing that our Aelii received their citizenship from Hadrian; on the contrary, nine of the eleven magistrates named Aelius are pre-Hadrianic, and three of them are Republican. Rather, the Spanish Aelii appear to be descendants of Italian immigrants, among them the ancestors of Hadrian himself; his family allegedly came from Picenum and moved to Italica during the age of the Scipios.[20] Ironically, there are no Aelii attested among the magistrates of Italica, though an Aelianus (**150**) may be suggestive of a family tie.

Several *nomina* occur exclusively or almost exclusively in Tarraconensis. This is partly because Tarraconensis has more magistrates, but partly because of the influence of certain governors of that province (e.g., the Caecilii and the Fulvii). Some *nomina* seem to have a special attachment to a particular city. For instance, of eleven Baebii, all from Tarraconensis, more than half come from Saguntum: there is indeed reason to believe that the *gens* Baebia was already established there by the time of the Second Punic War. Another group, the Pedanii, all come from Barcino, where this *gens* is strongly attested not only by magistrates but by five Roman senators.[21]

Some of the earliest and least romanized magistrates use an indigenous gentilic, ending in the genitive plural *-um* or *-orum*. Examples of these gentilics may be seen among the magistrates of Contrebia and Palantia (**665–70, 819–20**).[22] What is surprising is not that some magistrates retain these pre-Roman gentilic designations, but that so many others use Roman gentilic *nomina*, especially in the pre-Flavian period when relatively few magistrates could have acquired Roman or (so far as we know) Latin citizenship. I have argued above that the use of Roman *nomina* by non-citizens was probably not illegal until the edict of Claudius, and some *nomina* seem clearly linked to gubernatorial patronage. Whether all *nomina* were acquired by patronage, or whether magistrates wanting to appear romanized would simply abandon their indigenous names and adopt Roman ones, is unclear. Even in the case of indigenous magistrates who obtained the Roman citizenship through office-holding, we have no information on how they were allotted to a *gens* or whether they already had a Roman *nomen* before receiving the citizenship. The process by which indigenous gentilics were exchanged for Roman ones remains imperfectly understood, but the practice is so widespread and begins at such an early date as to leave little doubt that magistrates made the transition of nomenclature willingly.

Cognomina also play a significant role in tracing the romanization of the local élite. Magistrates with Iberian or Celtiberian names such as Balcacaldur, Sacaliscer or Deivorix are obviously unromanized indigenes. Often these names appear on early coins, in native script rather than the Latin

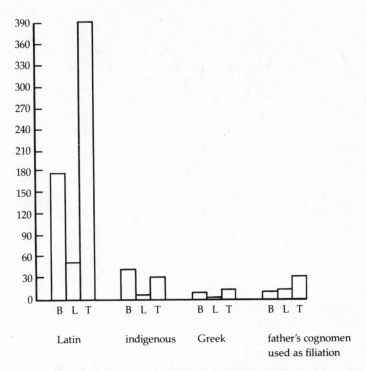

FIGURE 3 Cognomina of Spanish magistrates – actual numbers.
B = Baetica, L = Lusitania, T = Tarraconensis

alphabet. But for the most part, magistrates were willing to adopt Latin *cognomina* in much the same way as they had taken *nomina*. As shown in the graph (Figure 3), Tarraconensis, with the largest number of magistrates, is leading in Latin *cognomina*, while Baetica (with a large number of unromanized or semi-romanized Republican moneyers) leads in non-Latin *cognomina*.[23] The adjusted figures, however (Figure 4), show considerable consistency among all three provinces. Approximately 80–90 percent of the *cognomina* in each province are Latin; between 7 and 17 percent indigenous. Greek names are very few and probably indicate freedmen or their descendants (cf chapter 5).[24] This overwhelming preference for Latin *cognomina*, in spite of the fact (as witnessed by the *nomina*) that a great many of the magistrates were indigenes, is a tribute to the romanized tastes or ambitions of the aristocracy. The non-Latin names occur chiefly on early coins and on rare inscriptions from backwoods areas, most notably the *tabula Contrebiensis* of 87 BC (**665–70**).

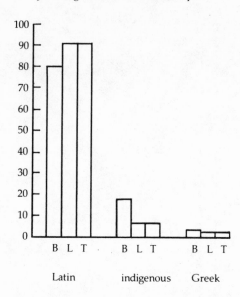

FIGURE 4 Cognomina of Spanish magistrates – comparative percentages.
B = Baetica, L = Lusitania, T = Tarraconensis

Filiation in a Roman name takes the form 'M[arci] f[ilius],' i.e., the father's *praenomen* forms the filiation. This manner of filiation was naturally adopted by the Spanish magistrates, and some include the *praenomina* of their grandfathers, great-grandfathers or even great-great-grandfathers to show how long the family had been romanized. If the father lacked a *praenomen*, the filiation was taken from his *cognomen*, e.g., 'Rustici f.' The fact that the son has a *praenomen* and *nomen* and the father does not is an indication of romanization on the part of the son, for if the father lacked a *praenomen* he probably lacked a *nomen* as well. Nonetheless, no small number of fathers have a Latin, rather than Spanish, *cognomen*. This 'indigenous filiation' is found chiefly in the early period; it is borne, for instance, by all six magistrates of Contrebia (e.g., Lubbus Letondonis f.). It is interesting that all the *cognomina* at Contrebia (both fathers and sons) take the endings of second or third declension Latin names, yet not one of them is Latin. In one case (**323**) the son apparently forms his *nomen* (Fidius) from the father's *cognomen* (Fidus); but this practice is more common in Gaul than in Spain.

Tribal enrolment is indicated by the insertion of the tribal abbreviation, e.g., 'Gal[eria]' or 'Quir[ina],' before the *cognomen*. Whereas *nomina*

TABLE 4
Magistrates' Tribes

Name of Tribe	Baetica	Lusitania	Tarraconensis	Total
Galeria	46	11	98	155
Quirina	30	5	31	66
Sergia	16	3	8	27
Papiria	4	1	4	9
Palatina	0	0	7	7
Velina	0	0	7	7
Aniensis	0	0	5	5
Claudia	0	1	0	1
Collina	0	0	1	1
Fabia	0	0	1	1
Teretina	0	0	1	1
Total number of magistrates with tribe mentioned				280

might be an affectation, tribal designation suggests that the magistrate was a legally enrolled Roman citizen. The two commonest tribes are Galeria, which indicates citizenship grants under Caesar or Augustus, and Quirina, which indicates citizenship under the Flavian grants of *ius Latii*.[25] The frequency with which these two tribes are found demonstrates that magistrates were not Italian immigrants but indigenes who were not receiving the citizenship until the Principate. 280 magistrates, or some 28 per cent, indicate their tribe (Table 4). Whether they do so merely by convention, or for ostentation, or as deliberate proof of citizenship, is a moot point. But none of these explanations accounts for those magistrates in cities where Roman citizenship was automatic for magistrates, yet who do not list their tribe. Obviously they had one; their silence suggests that it was not considered necessary to state it.

Occasionally we find an urban tribe, such as Palatina (seven occurrences) or Collina (**582**). These probably denote families of freedmen, perhaps of freedmen who had immigrated to Spain from Rome. There were also a few towns which had been assigned unusual tribes, such as the tribes Papiria (at Astigi), Aniensis (at Caesaraugusta) and Velina (at Palma and Pollentia). The presence of magistrates of these tribes in other cities is usually an indication of movement from one town to another.

Geographic Mobility

Pre-Roman society had been closely associated with and centred on the community. Towns were usually isolated entities established on fortified hilltops for protection. Romanization began in earnest when the inhabitants of these hill forts were coaxed down into the plain. As interurban commerce developed under the aegis of the *pax Romana*, there was a greater willingness to move from the home town in pursuit of one's career. The *flamines p.H.c.* who came to Tarraco from nearly every town in the province are an obvious example, but hardly a unique one. Within Spain there was a considerable degree of movement by local magistrates. This was only part of a much broader pattern of intra-peninsular relocation by large numbers of Spaniards.[26] This mobility of magistrates between towns is yet another indication of romanization.

Those magistrates who pursued careers in the army, civil service, and provincial priesthoods have already been considered (in chapter 3), but there was apparently much lateral movement as well. The movements of these 'mobile' magistrates may be traced in any of three ways. The first of these could be termed dual magistracy. At least seven magistrates held office in more than one town; usually they began as magistrates in their home town, then moved to a larger city and achieved municipal office there (**223, 444, 671, 739, 740, 762, 818**, possibly **928**). Another group of a dozen men held magistracies in a different town from that in which they were born. Again, this usually involved movement from a small town to a larger urban centre (**24, 92, 159, 274, 285, 347, 378, 419, 436, 891, 899, 917**, possibly **886**). The third category, dual loyalty, involves fourteen magistrates who appear to have some close connection with a town other than that in which they hold office, although the exact nature of this connection is unknown (**22, 132, 146, 160, 177, 331, 428, 437, 438, 480, 656, 800, 883, 899**). A recent study plausibly suggests that the relatively high number of 'outsiders' among the magistrates of Barcino shows that the local senate was selling these prestigious offices to rich parvenus from other towns for a substantial *summa honoraria*.[27]

The reasons for such geographic mobility are not easily traced. In some cases, movement may be due purely to the desire to pursue a political career in a more important centre. In other cases the association of a magistrate with more than one town may be due to commercial interests, multiple landowning, or family ties (e.g., a magistrate may have had parents from different towns, or a wife from another town). What is apparent and significant is the fluid atmosphere which supported the movement of magistrates from one romanized town to the next. This interchange and integration of élites is symptomatic of the breakdown of local isolationism and the increased unity of Spain under Roman rule.

Notes

1 P.A. Brunt in *Assimilation et résistance à la culture gréco-romaine dans le monde ancien* (Bucharest and Paris 1976) 161–73
2 Strabo 3.2.15 (for Baetica), 3.4.20 (for Celtiberia and Ebro valley)
3 This is not to deny that there is a distinction between romanization and Italianization, as can be seen, for instance, in the Italian flavour of Spanish Latin (cf Knapp *Roman Experience* 147). But the distinction is a relatively subtle one, and it would be pedantic to enforce it here.
4 On the supposed supplantation of local élites, see M.I. Rostovtzeff *Social and Economic History of the Roman Empire* 2nd ed (Oxford 1957) 211; on 'mixed' colonies of Romans and indigenes, see Strabo 3.2.1 (on Corduba) and R. Syme *Colonial Elites* (London 1958) 11.
5 A.N. Sherwin White *The Roman Citizenship* 2nd ed (Oxford 1973) 151–5
6 C.E. Goodfellow *Roman Citizenship* (Bryn Mawr 1935) 55
7 P.A. Brunt *Italian Manpower 225 BC–AD 14* (Oxford 1971) 233, 160–5; Knapp *Roman Experience* 151
8 J.P.V.D. Balsdon *Life and Leisure in Ancient Rome* (London 1969) 191
9 R.C. Knapp *Ancient Society* 9 (1978) 187–222; cf Knapp *Roman Experience* 162–3.
10 On the large proportion of natives in the municipal élites of other provinces, cf G. Alföldy *Noricum* (London and Boston 1974) 86–7; R.F. Hoddinott *Bulgaria in Antiquity* (New York 1975) 154; J.E. Ifie *Museum Africum* 5 (1976) 36–9; J.F. Drinkwater *Latomus* 37 (1978) 817–20; Drinkwater *Britannia* 10 (1979) 92–6.
11 J. Morris *Listy Filologické* 86 (1963) 36
12 On Latin citizens bearing *tria nomina*, see Knapp *Ancient Society* 9 (1978) 193 and the new fragment *Irn.* 86.
13 Knapp *Ancient Society* 9 (1978) 189–92; ILS 8888. Cf G. Alföldy *Latomus* 25 (1966) 38 on 'usurpation' of *tria nomina* by non-citizens under the Empire.
14 It is, of course, possible that some Spaniards may have been 'granted' citizenship by the governor – a procedure which was technically illegal unless ratified by the Roman Senate – and therefore thought they really were citizens, as did certain Alpine tribes under Claudius (CIL v 5050 = ILS 206). In such cases we would be dealing not with usurpation but with a legal problem, on which cf Sherwin White *The Roman Citizenship*[2] 294–5.

The most famous example is that of L. Cornelius Balbus Maior (uncle of 96), cos. suff. 40 BC and a native of Gades who was granted citizenship by Pompey during the Sertorian War. In 56 BC Balbus was put on trial at Rome for impersonating a citizen, but was successfully defended by Cicero (*Pro Balbo*). In this instance the governor's grant had been ratified by the *Lex Gellia Cornelia* of 72.

15 S.L. Dyson *Ancient Society* 11–12 (1980–1) 257–99

16 Knapp *Ancient Society* 9 (1978) 198–9. Knapp claims that Cato is responsible for the high percentage of Porcii at Tarraco, though one may question whether 1.74 is a high percentage. Dyson *Ancient Society* 11–12 (1980–1) 262 explains the large proportion of Porcii in Baetica (where no known Porcius was governor) by proposing a 'drift of Porcii' from Tarraconensis, but this suggestion seems to twist the evidence to fit the theory.

17 On the Iulii and the Gallic aristocracy, see Drinkwater *Latomus* 37 (1978) 818–19, 827–8; cf Knapp *Ancient Society* 9 (1978) 199–203. Further, J.F. Rodríguez Neila *Sociedad y administración local en la Bética romana* (Córdoba 1981) 50–1 associates the Lusitanian Iulii with presumed citizenship grants to the supporters of Caesar in the campaign of 61 BC. This theory is attractive but the evidence inconclusive.

18 Alföldy *Latomus* 25 (1966) 46–7

19 On Aelii in Spain cf J.M. Caamaño *Boletín del Seminario de Estudios de Arte y Arqueología* 38 (1972) 133–63.

20 Syme *RP* 620

21 For the Baebii see G. Alföldy *Los Baebii de Saguntum* (Valencia 1977) 25–6; Knapp *Ancient Society* 9 (1978) 201. For the Pedanii, see I. Rodá *Hisp. Ant.* 5 (1975) 223–68.

22 These indigenous gentilics are not counted as *nomina* in the tables.

23 I have counted as 'Latin' those *cognomina* recognized as such by I. Kajanto *The Latin Cognomina* (Helsinki 1965).

24 Comparative statistics from the Gallic, German, and Danubian provinces show that the proportion of magistrates and decurions with Greek *cognomina* ranges from zero per cent in Narbonensis to 6 per cent in Pannonia Superior, while Dacia, with 11.3 per cent, is exceptional, R. Duthoy *Epigraphica* 36 (1974) 137.

25 L.R. Taylor *The Voting Districts of the Roman Republic* (Rome 1960) 109 n 21. See now R. Wiegels *Die Tribusinschriften des römischen Hispanien* (Berlin 1985).

26 A. García y Bellido *Archivum* 12 (1963) 39–52; G. Fabre *Latomus* 29 (1970) 314–39

27 G. Alföldy *Gerión* 2 (1984) 210–12

7

Personal Wealth

The property qualification for admission to the *ordo* and the requirement for magistrates to provide games from their own pockets suggest that magistrates and decurions made up the financial as well as the political élite in their own communities.[1] Indeed, as we have seen, those without money and those engaged in lower-class jobs were specifically barred from office. That local magistracies were the preserve of the wealthy is therefore self-evident. The intention of the present chapter is to explore several more ambitious questions, namely, where did magistrates get their wealth, how much did they have, how and why did they spend it?

The connection between provincial élites and the means of production has long been recognized, but it is often difficult to identify which specific means of production was the chief source of magistrates' wealth. Some scholars have pointed to shopkeeping, others to landowning.[2] Commerce was frowned upon, at least in theory (Cic. *Off.* 1.150–1; *Dig.* 50.2.12 Call.), but even Roman senators engaged in it. No doubt both agriculture and trade, on a sufficiently large scale, were capable of providing a respectable income.[3] The question is, which of these professions did magistrates actually pursue; or rather, since wealth precedes office, from which walks of life were magistrates most often recruited?

The evidence from Spain could hardly be more frustrating in this regard. Outside of Italy, Spain was reputedly the richest province in the Empire (Pliny *NH* 37.203): her famed mineral resources, livestock, seafood, and crops are invariably praised by ancient authors and have been so exhaustively treated by modern scholars that to reiterate the long list of Spanish products here would be both onerous and redundant.[4] Against this vast literature, both antique and recent, on the flourishing Spanish economy must be set our almost total ignorance of where Spanish magistrates obtained their wealth, apart from the obvious and unhelpful assumption that it originated in one or more of the lucrative enterprises lauded by classical authors. Nonetheless, there do survive a few – too few – shreds of information which may provide some insight into the economic background of local magistrates.

Of the major Spanish industries (mining, commerce, farming) the first was controlled largely by the emperor or by equestrian companies. However, lead ingots from Carthago Nova on the east coast bear names similar to those of local magistrates (**551, 560, 568, 573**), and it may reasonably be inferred that local élite families were involved in the lead trade, which was a spin-off of the silver-mining operations in the Sierra Morena. The Aquinus family, which flourished at the end of the Republic or beginning of the Empire, is particularly well attested on these ingots, and the man 'C. Aquinus M. f.' whose name appears among those stamped in lead might just be the 'C. Aquinus Mela', quinquennial duovir around 30 BC (**551**). Future epigraphic finds may document the participation of other prominent lead-exporting families, such as the Planii, in local politics. An attractive suggestion has recently been made that the honorary duovirates granted to Juba II and Ptolemy of Mauretania were rewards from a local senate dominated by lead dealers to the dealers' African customers.[5]

Some magistrates may have made their money by merchandising, especially in harbour towns such as Emporiae and Gades. But at Emporiae, where commerce had been in Greek hands for centuries, there is only one magistrate with a Greek name (Nicomedes, **693**), whereas several early magistrates bear Iberian names. Did the Greek merchants decline to involve themselves in 'Roman' government? A magistrate from Carthago Nova (**568**), honoured by the 'fishermen and retailers' of the town was perhaps involved in the fish trade himself, and a magistrate of Mirobriga in Lusitania (**357**) was possibly a shipper. It is interesting to speculate that an African native who became a magistrate at Tarraco (**898**) may have been attracted to Spain through commercial interests, though this is conjectural and, even if true, may have been exceptional.[6] Painted names of olive oil shippers on Spanish amphorae may represent relatives of magistrates, if onomastic similarities are valid (**132, 274, 582**), and while there is no direct testimony that magistrates themselves were engaged in the oil exporting business, the concept should not surprise us.

While none of these possibilities can be, or need be, ruled out, all the positive evidence points to landowning. For one thing, landowning was the traditional source of wealth in Roman society. Agriculture was widely recognized as the safest and most honourable field for investment, and, as in pre-industrial societies generally, the socio-economic structure of the

Roman world depended on a landed aristocracy.[7] A few specific examples from Spain support this general assumption. C. Valerius Avitus (917), duovir at Tarraco, was owner of the 'Els Munts' villa, one of the most splendid on the east coast, while M. Cornelius Arrianus (745), duovir at Ilerda, apparently owned the large 'Els Viláns' villa near Aytona. The grandeur of these rural establishments is a patent index of the wealth derived from agriculture. Other magistrates (e.g., 362, 393) are attested on monuments located in the countryside far from any urban centre, and these were presumably landowners as well.

New evidence emerges in the recently published copy of the Flavian municipal law from Baetica, which contains a revealing provision whereby official business and court cases will be suspended for up to sixty days per year during harvest and vintage (Irn. κ): such prorogation strongly suggests that these agrarian activities called away so many decurions that senate meetings were impractical, and of course no justice could be dispensed if the appropriate magistrates were thus occupied. Nor does the provision in the Urso charter, requiring magistrates and decurions to live within a mile of town, preclude their owning rural estates as well as urban households (Urs. 91). The theory advanced by Sánchez León, of a conflict between urban and rural élites in the second century AD, loses much force if rural landowners were in fact members of the municipal élite.[8]

Thus, despite the lamentable paucity of hard evidence, we must conclude, both on general grounds and from specific instances, that agriculture was by far the likeliest source of wealth for the majority of local aristocrats. Production of the classic 'Mediterranean triad' – oil, wine, and grain – was probably largely in the hands of local magnates, though the possibility of alternate landowners (e.g., emperors acquiring provincial estates, or Italian senators investing in provincial land) cannot be discounted. No doubt some magistrates were involved in other pursuits – mining, fishing, manufacturing – but these magistrates, we suggest, were in the minority. The businesses in which they were engaged were determined by local resources or facilities, which might well have an impact on the economic structure of individual communities (e.g., port towns) without negating a predominantly agrarian model for Spain as a whole. Moreover, since land was the standard measure of wealth in antiquity, even those who made their fortune in commerce or other pursuits would probably have invested the profits in land, which in turn would yield further dividends. Thus, as one economic historian has justly noted, 'it was ... extremely rare in the Roman world for a man to be wealthy without being a landowner.'[9]

Given the power and prestige of local magistrates, one is entitled to wonder whether magistrates, yielding to temptation, might attempt to supplement their existing wealth by lining their own pockets while in office. Any student of Roman history will recall the seemingly inevitable extortion trial when a governor returned from his province, and the 'three fortunes' he supposedly needed to make in order to bribe voters and jurors and to ensure a comfortable retirement. No doubt some magistrates were less honest than others, but we have no explicit evidence of a local 'scam' in a Spanish city (though one magistrate, **96**, stole *provincial* funds). We do at least know that profits from office were officially discouraged. The charter of Urso provides that no person may be paid for holding office or performing his duty, nor may any magistrate accept a gift or reward in connection with a lease of public land (*Urs.* 93, 134). Moreover, the Flavian municipal law, in a clause reminiscent of modern governments' 'conflict of interest' guidelines, makes magistrates and their families ineligible to bid on contracts for taxes and public works (*Irn.* J).

But while magistrates and decurions could not legally profit from their office, they were entitled in certain cases to compensation for their out-of-pocket expenses. Reimbursement· could be made to municipal legates for their travel costs, provided the trip was authorized and they submitted receipts,[10] though some legates record that they undertook an embassy at their own expense. And at Urso, where the duovirs and aediles were obliged to spend a minimum of two thousand sesterces for games or theatrical performances, they were at least relieved of the necessity of paying the entire cost by means of subventions from the town treasury – two thousand sesterces per duovir, one thousand per aedile (*Urs.* 70–1).

If the origins of magistrates' affluence remain enigmatic, the extent of their personal wealth is somewhat easier to assess. Architectural evidence is only of limited assistance here. Villas are usually of anonymous ownership and do not necessarily belong to municipal magistrates. On the other hand, the splendid town houses (*domus*) excavated in various Spanish cities presumably belonged to members of the local élite. There is a common tendency in pre-industrial cities for the homes of the élite to be centrally located,[11] and although Spanish town houses (e.g., at Italica and Conimbriga) are often positioned closer to the circuit wall than to the forum, they do at least suggest that the aristocracy was inhabiting the urban environment rather than dwelling exclusively in the surrounding countryside.[12]

However, the majority of our information derives from inscriptions recording benefactions bestowed on towns by their magistrates. Some of these inscriptions state the exact price of the gift, thus furnishing us with some idea of the magistrate's personal affluence. Other benefactions, while not priced, are so large as to leave little doubt of the magistrate's wealth.[13]

The obligation of the magistrate to make such expenditures is well attested and indeed notorious, since in the Late Empire it led to disaffection among the magistrates themselves. The *Digest* defines a municipal magistracy as an administrative office which may or may not include a requirement for personal expense (*Dig.* 50.4.14 pr. Call.). In fact, there can have been few magistracies without such a requirement. The charter of the Caesarian colony of Urso, as we have mentioned, obliged the duovirs and aediles to contribute financially to the games. Moreover, for infraction of various regulations, a magistrate might be liable to a fine ranging from one thousand to one hundred thousand sesterces – no trivial amount. What applied under Caesar applied *a fortiori* under the Empire: a constitution of the emperor Trajan made all *ob honorem* promises of public works to a city legally binding, even upon the heir if the pledger died without completing the project (*Dig.* 50.12.14 Pomponius). Magistracies did not come cheaply.

In addition to the various *munera* which he was required to provide, an incoming magistrate might have to pay an admission fee (*honorarium* or *summa honoraria*), in effect purchasing his magistracy. For instance, as noted in chapter 6, the city of Barcino seems to have been in the habit of selling magistracies to outsiders. The technical difference between *munus* and *summa honoraria* seems to be that the latter usually comprised a fixed sum of cash, whereas a *munus* (which means 'duty' or 'gift') might include personal service, or the construction or repair of some public work. In fact the distinction is not always clear. For example, the requirement at Urso for magistrates to sponsor a gladiatorial or dramatic spectacle appears to be a *munus* or liturgy; but because the charter states that they must spend at least two thousand sesterces, Garnsey views this amount as a *summa honoraria*.[14] It should be noted, however, that this figure is a minimum, not a fixed price; nor is it a cash payment to the *ordo* as a *summa honoraria* would be, but an expenditure on goods and services. Clearly most *munera* (other than personal labour) cost money, whether the amount is stated or not; and spectacles are certainly to be reckoned in this category. Indeed, the word *munus* is itself often used as a synonym for 'gladiatorial show' or 'public building', which suggests that these were the usual benefactions.

There are a few epigraphic mentions of decurions (as opposed to magistrates) in Italian towns paying a *summa honoraria* or being exempted from it as early as the principate of Augustus. However, the practice seems not to have become widespread before the second century AD, and even then may not have been universal.[15] Occasionally the entry fee was waived: a decurion of Collippo (**328**) in the reign of Marcus Aurelius records that his *honorarium* and *munera* were remitted by the *ordo*. By the time of the Late Empire, when decurions were held liable for their towns' debts and expenses, elaborate legal regulations were established to limit the number of such exemptions (*Cod. Theod.* 12.1 *passim; Dig.* 50.5–6).

While compulsory *munera* and *honoraria* later became unpopular, local officials seem to have been willing enough to make benefactions in the Early Empire, whether these were required by law or not. Even obligatory payments worked to the advantage of the élite, by ensuring that magistracies were available only to the rich. The insistence on *summa honoraria* or other expenditure was a clear intimation that magistracies were sufficiently prestigious to be worth paying for. But magistrates often exceeded these requirements and made voluntary contributions of money, games, public works, or other benefits to the community. The rationale for such gifts has been discussed exhaustively by Paul Veyne.[16] They were motivated in part by ostentation, in part by civic pride. Munificence increased the donor's prestige and earned him the gratitude of the city by providing buildings or services which it could not otherwise have afforded. His status was enhanced in the public eye both by this immense display of wealth and by his assumption of the role of patron or benefactor (or, as Veyne expresses it, 'a Maecenas'). Can we doubt that this is the case when a duovir (**23**) is hailed as *munificentissimus* by the thankful citizenry, or when (as noted in chapter 5) magistrates are explicitly called *patronus* by their cities? Moreover, like modern politicians, a magistrate might hope to gain election or re-election by virtue of his generosity to the people. Of course, priests as well as magistrates made benefactions – usually of shrines, games (which were associated with cult festivals), and statues of the gods – but as noted earlier, magistrates and priests were often the same persons, or at least members of the same local élite. In short, benefactions were both a duty and a privilege, a sign of civic-mindedness but also of snobbery (or, in Veyne's own phrasing, 'narcissism').

Benefactions fall into four main categories: public works, spectacles, statues, and *sportulae*. Public works included temples, theatres, walls, baths, aqueducts, and the like; those donated by Spanish magistrates are listed in Table 5. The local charters gave magistrates permission to undertake construction or repair of public works, subject to the approval of the decurions.[17] In the case of city walls, which not all towns were allowed to have, the approval of the emperor or governor was necessary (*Dig.* 1.8.9 Ulp.). Two magistrates who construct a city gate at Ulia at their own expense during the Civil War (49 BC) mention in the dedication the provincial governor, Q. Cassius Longinus (**271–2**). Since governors are not named in any other building dedication by Spanish local officials, this exceptional mention may suggest official approval.

The value of benefactions may be approximated by reference to compara-

TABLE 5
Public Works Donated by Magistrates

Province	Town	Type of construction	Type of magistrate	Catalogue number
Baetica	Arva		honorary	
		marble benches and pilaster	decurion	13
	Astigi	ten furnished pools (lacus)	IIvir	19
	Aurgi	baths, aqueduct, woodland	IIvir	21
	Canania	marble colonnades	IIvir	38
	Ipolcobul-			
	cola	temple, forum	IIvir	127
	Italica	arches and colonnades	IIvir	139
		theatre (orchestra,		
		proscaenium, itinera, altars)	2 IIvirs	140–1
		possible temple	IIvir	975
	Lacippo	open-air crypt	vvir(?)	167
	Mellaria	aqueduct	IIvir	173
	Munigua	temple, forum, colonnades,		
		hall, record office	IIvir	179
	Obulco	shops	IIvir	218
	Ulia	gate	xvir and	
			aedile	271–2
	Villafranca	baths	2 IIvirs	298–9
Tarraconensis	Archena	aqueduct repairs	2 IIvirs	412–13
	Barcino	walls, towers, gates	IIvir	420
	Carthago			
	Nova	two walls	IIvir	552
		wall	aedile	553
	Emporiae	open area (campus)	IIvir	721
		shrine	IIvir	725
	Iacca	road repairs	IIvir	741
	Lucentum	tower(s)	prefect	789
	Numantia	road	IIvir	802
	Saguntum	wall and towers	2 IIvirs	851–2

ble donations elsewhere. In three cases, a duovir provides a temple or shrine, a structure which could cost, to judge by other Spanish examples, anywhere from six thousand to two hundred thousand sesterces, or even, to take an African example, as much as six hundred thousand sesterces.[18] Baths would probably cost between one hundred thousand and four hundred thousand sesterces, while the price of an aqueduct might reach two million. A city wall could cost several millions, and a road tens of millions of sesterces.[19] Two duovirs of Italica (**140–1**) who provided from their own pockets the *orchestra*, *proscaenium*, and *itinera* of that city's theatre probably incurred an expense of several hundred thousand sesterces.[20] Magistrates who could afford benefactions on this scale must easily have possessed the four hundred thousand sesterces necessary to meet the equestrian census; indeed, at Gades in the Augustan period, there were five hundred men (five times the supposedly 'standard'-sized municipal senate) in this category (Strabo 3.7.3).

The charter of Urso, it will be recalled, required each duovir and aedile to contribute at least two thousand sesterces to the games and shows. While this amount was small even for that early date, it was only a minimum. Candidates for magistracy would no doubt have promised much more than this meagre contribution in order to secure votes, and by the Antonine period expenditures on gladiatorial shows had gotten so far out of hand that they had to be reduced (ca 177). Parallel costs from Africa range from several hundred to fifty thousand sesterces per day.[21] In the fourth century, John Chrysostom complains that those who sponsor lavish shows and banquets receive effusive praise from the public but bankrupt themselves in the process (*De inani gloria* 4–11). 'Big spenders' apparently still existed in the Late Empire.

Baetican magistrates are attested as providing a variety of spectacles, including dramatic performances, gladiatorial combats, circuses (in one case for two days), or combinations thereof (Table 6). Tarraconensis provides only one example, which unlike the Baetican ones mentions the cost: one thousand sesterces per year for a boxing spectacle. This cost seems very modest for the Antonine age, yet in Africa in the same period a boxing match could cost less than one-quarter of this amount (though presumably it would have had fewer boxers).[22]

It was common practice in the Roman world for magistrates and other notables to erect statues, usually to a deity or emperor (himself sometimes a god). The erection of these statues was normally condoned by the city in view of their ornamental value, but the cost could not be reimbursed. Spanish statue costs range from one thousand to eight thousand sesterces;[23] however, no single statue dedicated by a magistrate bears a price tag. The only recorded cost is a stunning four hundred thousand sesterces for an unknown number of statues by a duovir of Corduba (Table 7); again, this amount was equivalent to the equestrian census. In five cases a weight of silver is attested, ranging from ten to two hundred fifty Roman pounds. It is difficult to calculate the equivalent value of these gifts in

TABLE 6
Spectacles Presented by Magistrates

Province	Town	Type of spectacle	Cost	Type of magistrate	Catalogue number
Baetica	Asido	XX paria gladiatorum	?	IIIIvir	15
	Canania	ludi scaenici	?	IIvir	38
	Corduba	munus gladiatorius et duae lusiones	?	IIvir	93
	Ilipula	circenses per biduum	?	decurion	114
	Isturgi	ludi scaenici	?	IIvir	136
	Lucurgen-tum	spectaculum per quadriduum ludorum scaenicorum	?	honorary decurion	170
	Tucci	ludi circenses et ludi scaenici	?	IIvir (at Aurgi)	22
Tarraconensis	Barcino	spectaculum pugilum	1000 HS annually	IIvir	445

sesterces; in Africa silver sold for about eight hundred sesterces a pound, but in Spain it was far more plentiful and undoubtedly less expensive.

Sportulae consisted of free handouts, to the general populace or to specific groups, of money, food or oil. For instance, a decurion of Axati (**24**) made testamentary *sportulae* to his fellow decurions, while a duovir of Barcino (**445**) arranged for eight hundred sesterces worth of oil to be distributed annually in the baths. Three other magistrates helped combat the high cost of food, either by financial relief to the *annona* or by free distribution of grain (**381, 402, 656**). An honorary decurion provided (perhaps by rental) a gymnasium for four days, as well as free admission for women to the baths (**170**). Many magistrates or their families sponsored a banquet (*epulum*) for the decurions or other groups on special occasions; however, the use of this device as an election ploy was outlawed.[24]

Finally, it is worth observing that the vast majority of benefactions come from Baetica and the east coast. The greater degree of munificence there helps confirm what we should in any event have expected, that the cities and magistrates of these two prosperous regions were considerably more affluent than those in the rest of the Peninsula. Unfortunately, however,

TABLE 7
Statues Dedicated by Magistrates

Province	Town	Weight/type of statue	Cost	Type of magistrate	Catalogue number
Baetica	Arva	?	?	hon. decurion	**13**
	Axati	?	?	decurion	**24**
	Corduba	?	400,000 HS	IIvir	**93**
	Ilurco	?	?	IIvir	**119**
	Ipolcobul-				
	cola	?	?	IIvir	**127**
	Italica	?	?	2 IIvirs	**140–1**
		100 pounds silver			
		(4 statues)	?	IIvir	**145**
		100 pounds silver	?	IIvir	**147**
	Lucurgen-				
	tum	?	?	hon. decurion	**170**
Lusitania	Norba	10 pounds silver	?	2 IIvirs	**364–5**
Tarraconensis	Carthago				
	Nova	250 pounds silver	?	aedile	**578**
	Emporiae	?	?	IIvir	**725**
	Tarraco	15 pounds silver	?	IIvir	**909**

since both regions owed their prosperity to a combination of agriculture and commerce, this localization brings us no nearer to defining the origin of their wealth. It may well be that the distinction is artificial, and that magistrates were often wealthy men from both agrarian and mercantile backgrounds; indeed, a given individual may have derived his income from a variety of sources. Undoubtedly, and especially in more remote regions, there were also poorer – or at any rate, less rich – magistrates, who barely met the property qualification for office, and who could scarcely afford benefactions. Whether magistrates were able to retain their affluence during the Late Empire, a time of financial crisis in the Roman world, will be considered in the following chapter.

Notes

1 Cf Stevenson *Administration* 172–3
2 Shopkeeping: P.D.A. Garnsey in M.I. Finley ed *Studies in Roman Property*

(Cambridge 1976) 130–1; G. Alföldy *Noricum* (London and Boston
1974) 121–2; landowning: M. Vigil *Historia de España Alfaguara* I (Madrid
1973) 379; A.H.M. Jones *The Roman Economy* (Oxford 1974) 40–2;
J.F. Drinkwater in A. King and M. Henig ed *The Roman West in the Third
Century* (Oxford 1981) 230–1

3 G.E.M. de Ste Croix *The Class Struggle in the Ancient Greek World* (London
1981) 467 suggests that landowning was the chief source of magistrates'
wealth in the large cities, whereas manufacture may have prevailed in smaller
towns. Trade was a less usual occupation (126–7).

4 Sources conveniently compiled and translated in C. Fernández-Chicarro
Laudes Hispaniae (Madrid 1948); and studied by J.J. van Nostrand in
Tenney Frank ed *Economic Survey of Ancient Rome* III (Baltimore 1937)
119–24; J.M. Blázquez *Economía de la Hispania romana* (Bilbao 1978)
and *Historia económica de la Hispania romana* (Madrid 1978)

5 A. Beltrán *Caesaraugusta* 51–2 (1980) 122–41; E. González Cravioto *Anales
de la Universidad de Murcia* 40/3–4 (1981–2) 25. On the ingots from
Carthago Nova see C. Domergue *MCV* 1 (1965) 9–25 and *AEA* 39 (1966)
41–72.

6 G. Alföldy *Gerión* 2 (1984) 205

7 P.D. Garnsey and R.P. Saller *The Roman Empire: Economy, Society and
Culture* (Berkeley and Los Angeles 1987) 45

8 M.L. Sánchez León *Economía de la Hispania meridional durante la dinastia
de los Antoninos* (Salamanca 1978) 213

9 K. Hopkins in P. Abrams and E.A. Wrigley ed *Towns in Societies* (Cambridge
1978) 74

10 *Irn.* H; *Dig.* 4.6.8 Paul; 50.4.18.12 Arcadius Charisius

11 B. Trigger *Time and Traditions* (Edinburgh 1978) 181

12 A. García y Bellido *Colonia Aelia Augusta Italica* (Madrid 1960) 81–102;
J.M. Bairrão Oleiro et al. *Conimbriga: Guide to the Museum and the
Ruins* 3rd ed (Coimbra 1975) 19–32

13 On Spanish personal wealth in general, see L.A. Curchin *Historia* 32 (1983)
227–44.

14 *Urs.* 70; P.D.A. Garnsey *Historia* 20 (1971) 313; for a *summa honoraria*
of four thousand to eight thousand sesterces in some eastern cities, cf
Pliny *Ep.* 10.112.

15 Garnsey *Historia* 20 (1971) 309–12

16 For the advantage of obligatory payments, see P. Veyne *Le pain et le cirque*
(Paris 1976) 162; Garnsey and Saller *The Roman Empire* 33; and on the
rationale of gift-giving, see Veyne *Le pain* 15–103. One dedicant (**145**)
explicitly records that his gift of statues is made *ob honorem duoviratus*.

17 *Urs.* 77 (= *Lex Mun. Tarent.* 39–42); on approval (*ex decreto decurionum*),

see *CIL* II 3541 = *ILER* 2043; *CIL* II 984 = *ILS* 5660 = *ILER* 2058. Cf in Italy
the formula *permittente ordine* (*ILS* 4381, Aequiculi).

18 *AE* 1974, 381; *CIL* II 964 = *ILS* 5402 = *ILER* 1760; *CIL* VIII 18226–7, Lambaesis

19 On baths, see R.P. Duncan-Jones *The Economy of the Roman Empire:
Quantitative Studies* 2nd ed (Cambridge 1982) 91; for an aqueduct, see
CIL XIII 596, Burdigala; on city walls and roads, see R.P. Duncan-Jones *JRS*
64 (1974) 80–2; on magistrates as millionaires, cf (for Africa) Apuleius
Apol. 23–4.

20 In Africa, the theatre in even a small town cost ca four hundred thousand
sesterces, while in a large city the *proscaenium* and *scaena* alone cost
five hundred thousand sesterces (Duncan-Jones *Economy*² 91–2, nos. 27–8,
63); but these examples date to the latter half of the second century AD,
whereas the theatre at Italica is Augustan.

21 On the *senatus consultum de sumptibus ludorum gladiatorum minuendis*,
see *CIL* II 6278 = *ILS* 5163 = *FIRA* I² 49, Italica; and cf Duncan-Jones *Economy*²
104–5 on the example from Africa.

22 *ILS* 5071, Gor (= Duncan-Jones *Economy*² 105, no. 288)

23 On statues, see Pliny *NH* 34.17; *Dig.* 43.9.2 Paul; *Urs.* 134; and cf Curchin
Historia 32 (1983) 243.

24 *Urs.* 132; Mackie *Administration* 121–2

8

Magistrates in the Late Empire

One of the primary symptoms of the 'decline' of the Roman Empire was the financial and moral collapse of its cities during the Late Empire. The theory, well rehearsed, can be found in any manual of Roman history. Hereditary membership in the decurionate became obligatory, a development now considered to have been virtually inevitable. Scholars differ in dating this process to the second, third or fourth century;[1] the earliest preserved edict on the subject is dated to 320 (*Cod. Theod.* 12.1.17). Magistracies were no longer an honour (*honor*) but a compulsory burden (*munus*); municipal offices had become (in Arnold's phrase) instruments of oppression.[2] To escape the crushing, obligatory expenses of local office, the élite abandoned the cities and fled in droves to the countryside with their wealth (which, somewhat paradoxically, the theory assumes they still possessed), thereby impoverishing the cities and precipitating their downfall. This migration, the theory concludes, resulted in the collapse of urbanism and contributed to the advent of the Dark Ages; cities would not recover until the rise of the bourgeoisie in the twelfth and thirteenth centuries.

That there were serious urban problems – especially, it seems, in the eastern half of the Mediterranean – no one can doubt. But the common assumption that the problems were identical throughout the Empire, or that there was a steady decline from the second century to the fifth, defies historical logic. Conditions are not the same everywhere, nor are trends constant; the fact that we do not have as much evidence for this period as we would like, hardly justifies painting every province and every century of the Late Empire with the same brush. Regional specialists must re-examine the extent to which these developments were occurring in different parts of the Empire, and in what period. The evidence, limited in quantity, will leave some questions unanswered, but it will also highlight differences.

The second century AD was a period of prosperity for Spain and her cities. Under what are often referred to as the five good emperors (Nerva, Trajan, Hadrian, Antoninus Pius, and Marcus Aurelius) the Empire prospered. In Spain the bulk of our epigraphic evidence for magistrates dates to this period. After about 180 the number of career inscriptions trails off: we have few from the early third century and almost none thereafter, and the last ones are mostly curators, the supposed destroyers of municipal independence. This sudden decline in the inscriptional evidence, accompanied by modern claims that there was a 'crisis' in Spain in the Antonine and Severan periods[3] and a presumed general decline in the entire Roman world, would seem to mark the late second and early third centuries as the beginning of the end.

This picture can no longer be supported. The diminishing number of attestations of magistrates is concomitant with a drop in the number of inscriptions generally, both in Spain and elsewhere. It is symptomatic, not of the decline of urban government, but of a discontinuation (for reasons still unclear) of the 'epigraphic habit.'[4] There is no evidence that honours were no longer avidly sought. Indeed, a recent, lengthy study has demonstrated that the decurionate and magistracies remained an aristocratic privilege throughout the Antonine and Severan periods, rather than a compulsory and hereditary burden.[5]

Frequent mentions of *munera* by third-century jurists do not imply the deterioration of *honores*, for the jurists were concerned with the legal responsibilities of office rather than their social or psychological advantages, and thus would be more likely to refer to the offices as *munera* than *honores*. *Honor* and *munus*, privilege and duty, had both been inherent in magistracies from the beginning. Honours had always entailed obligations. Cicero refers to the *munus* of the consulate (Cic. *Pis.* 23). A Spanish *sevir* in the reign of Marcus Aurelius mentions in the same breath the *honor* and *munera* of his office (*CIL* II 4514 = *ILER* 5838 = *IRB* 35). There was no implicit opposition in the terms, no question of *honores* 'becoming' *munera*.[6]

As for the 'crisis' of the Antonine and Severan periods, it is true that there were military disturbances (including raids on Baetica by the Moors), property confiscations by Septimius Severus, and rampant inflation. But there is no reason to suppose that any of these factors fomented a decline of cities. Galloping inflation in modern countries like Brazil and Israel has not made urban institutions obsolete. A very few cities in Lusitania and Baetica required curators to rectify their troubled finances (none is recorded in Tarraconensis in this period); as discussed in chapter 4, the role of the curator was to protect the city's interests, not to supplant them. So far as cities and magistrates are concerned, there is no justification for positing a 'decline' in the early third century.

An even greater 'crisis' is thought to have occurred during the military anarchy between the collapse of the Severan house in 235 and the accession of Diocletian in 284. For the central government at Rome the chaos was real enough; so was the continuing rampant inflation.[7] In Spain the immediate problem was the penetration of Germanic invaders around 260. If we believe the claims of some modern historians, the Franks destroyed every city in their path; the east coast of Spain was 'devastated'; Baetica was 'economically razed'; there was 'decadence of the city, ... downfall of ... industry and commerce, and loss of importance of the *municipium*.'[8] Fortunately, a more balanced assessment has now emerged.[9] From literary evidence we know only that Tarraco was 'sacked and almost destroyed' by the Franks (Aur. Vict. 33). Evidence for 'destruction' elsewhere is solely archaeological, but the cause of the damage is unknown, the dating evidence insecure. The effects of the Frankish invasion appear to have been exaggerated. There is no clear proof of destruction of cities or of the decline of municipal government. And the 'crisis' was in any event ephemeral.

One apparent after-effect of the Frankish invasion was the construction of defensive walls around several cities of northern Spain (Barcino, Ilerda, Lucus Augusti, Legio VII Gemina, Caesaraugusta, Asturica Augusta) as well as cities in many parts of Gaul. These architectural constructions may be indices of defensive need rather than prosperity. Nonetheless it has been suggested that the Late Roman town walls of Gaul, which are considerably smaller in circumference than those of Britain, may reflect a shortage of local magnates to pay for them.[10] By this reasoning the Late Roman circuit walls in Spain, which – unlike most of their Gallic counterparts – show no reduction in the size of the enclosed area, might point to a continuing supply of affluent local officials. However, another and perhaps more plausible explanation for the reduced size of the Gallic fortifications is that they were built in haste: the cities of Gaul, being much closer to Germany, lived in dread of a second Frankish invasion, whereas the Spanish towns, further removed from imminent danger, could take more time and care in constructing their defences.[11] But this explanation still presupposes that they had the resources to do so.

The early fourth century is often heralded as a 'renaissance' or 'golden age' of the Roman Empire, a final glimmer of glory between the third-century troubles and the 'fall' of the Western Empire. In Spain this period is marked by a flourishing of cities which had supposedly suffered destruction or financial collapse in the preceding period. Literary sources record that cities like Barcino and Bracara were booming in the fourth century. Tarraco, which is called a 'strong fortress' and was the seat of government of the diocese of Tarraconensis, had clearly not suffered permanent damage from the Frankish incursions.[12] However, the high cost of repairs and the expense (presumably borne by the decurions) of supporting the governor and his staff may account for the appearance of a curator in the fourth century. Archaeological evidence confirms the picture of urban prosperity, with attestation of building activity at several sites, most notably the Constantinian circus at Emerita. Dozens of milestones attest to the construction and repair of roads linking the cities of Spain in the late third and early fourth centuries.[13] The fourth century in Spain has rightly been praised as a period of prosperity and tranquility.[14]

Much of our knowledge of municipal upheaval in the Late Empire derives from the first 'title' (chapter) of book 12 of the Theodosian Code, which deals with decurions. Most of the problems described there refer to Italy, Africa, and the East; Gaul is mentioned once, Britain not at all, and Spain appears in only two passages, to be discussed below. Therefore the problems outlined in book 12, while applicable to much of the Empire, were apparently less serious in the westernmost provinces such as Spain, whose magistrates were not so oppressed financially as in the oriental provinces, and whose cities managed to survive repeated economic difficulties (as witness, for example, the paucity of Spanish *curatores r.p.*). Even in the East, it is doubtful whether the financial burden was as heavy as decurions complained that it was.[15]

Depletion of the *ordo* is the principal problem reflected in book 12. The unpopularity of the decurionate was due in large measure to the decurions being held responsible for collection of all taxes in the town's *territorium*; if their fellow citizens could not pay the tribute, the decurions were obliged to meet the deficiency from their own pockets. Many decurions tried to escape their responsibilities by moving to another town or to the countryside, or by joining the army, the civil service, or even the Roman Senate. These decurions, when apprehended, were returned to their towns to undertake compulsory decurial service, and were sometimes assessed an additional (e.g., monetary) penalty. Yet the need for repetition, under successive emperors, of decrees ordering the return of escaped decurions to their *patriae* suggests that the situation remained out of control.[16]

To maintain the size of the *ordo*, sons of decurions were enrolled against their will and the minimum age was reduced to eighteen. Furthermore, new decurions were drafted from among ex-counts and ex-governors, Imperial procurators, sons of veterans, and those members of the lower order (plebeians) who had both the merit and property necessary to discharge the task.[17] The admission of this last group destroyed the *discrimina ordinum dignitatumque* which had made the decurial order an exclusive, privileged aristocracy (Pliny *Ep.* 9.5), as well as undermining the solidarity and homogeneity of the *ordo*.

The *ordo* was now splintered into cliques based on social and financial status. Chief among these were the *principales*, a privileged group of powerful men who became a virtual oligarchy among the decurions. These *principales curiae* (known in some cities as *optimi, primi, primores, primates, primarii,* or *principes*) are particularly well attested in the abundant epigraphy of Roman Africa, but also appear in other western provinces.[18] In Spain they are represented three times, all in the fourth century. Mention of them first appears in a Constantinian constitution of 19 January 317, addressed to Rufinus Octavianus, count of Spain, requiring that candidates for the governorship (*praesidatus*, normally an equestrian post in this period) must have held all offices in turn in their own municipalities (*Cod. Theod.* 12.1.4). This measure was clearly aimed at preventing the *primates* from escaping compulsory office-holding through upward mobility, a well-known device for social advancement and preservation of wealth.[19] The second attestation appears on a bronze weight (*modius*) of ca 370 from northwestern Spain, with an inscription stating that the weight conforms to Imperial regulations. The inscription ends with the phrase, 'cur[antibus] Potamio et Quentiano principalibus,' signifying that the two named *principales* are in charge of administering the weights and measures law in their community.[20] Finally, an Imperial constitution of 7 May 396, addressed to the Spanish governor Petronius, provides that municipal enactments (*gesta*) require the presence of three *curiales* and a magistrate. The term *curiales* here presumably means *principales* rather than decurions in general, both because of the smallness of the number – the Urso charter had required a minimum of twenty decurions – and because a number of similar constitutions specify that documents must be witnessed by *primi curiae* or *primates*.[21]

Two facts are thus clear from the Theodosian Code: that decurions in many cities of the Empire were evading their responsibilities and that local *ordines* were often controlled by an oligarchic clique. It is remarkable that while the latter feature is attested several times in Spain, there is no evidence whatever for decurions and magistrates fleeing to the countryside. The fourth century sees a flourishing of grand villas in rural Spain;[22] yet this development is surely a reflection of the overall material prosperity of Spain during this period, a prosperity felt in town and country alike. There is no proof that these villas belonged to runaway magistrates. Indeed, the stringent provisions in the Theodosian Code for returning escaped magistrates to their towns by force should have made it dangerous for such a fugitive to construct a magnificent villa, thereby advertising his whereabouts and exposing himself to possible capture. Even if he evaded this fate, his open display of wealth would render him liable to decurial service in the town to whose territory he had fled.[23] The flaunting of affluence in these villas should rather suggest that their owners were members of the élite (municipal or senatorial) in good standing or of the Imperial bureaucracy. Since magistrates' wealth had always depended chiefly upon landowning, there is nothing suspicious about magistrates owning villas *per se*. Moreover, the villas of the Late Empire, while more luxurious on the whole than those of the Early Empire, are far less numerous. If only the archaeological and not the legal evidence had survived, we might conclude that most of the rural élite had migrated to the cities, rather than the urban élite to the country. In fact, urban and rural élites in the Roman world were rarely mutually exclusive groups. Recent research in Late Roman Britain and Gaul suggests not only that the native élite continued to exercise an important role in urban government, but also that villa owners were not in permanent residence on their lands.[24] In other words, the landowning élite may still have participated in the political, social, and cultural life of the towns.

A new picture of Late Roman Spain is thus emerging. While cities in the Eastern Empire were in a financial crisis which had to be remedied from the pockets of local officials, Spain enjoyed a healthier economic climate. Town and country were flourishing. There were few serious financial problems; few cities needed to be bailed out by the appointment of curators or by fleecing the local aristocracy.[25] Cities like Emerita, Toletum, and Barcino continued to prosper well beyond the Roman period. There is no trace in the Theodosian Code of a mass exodus of Spanish decurions; the single mention of candidates for provincial governorships trying to skip intermediate offices is hardly evidence of urban collapse. *Principales* assumed much of the responsibility of local government; these rich and powerful citizens may themselves be the owners of some of the sumptuous villas discovered outside the cities. There was also renewed social mobility for the Iberian élite. If the late second and third centuries were the grand era of admission of eastern provincials into the Roman Senate, the fourth century sees a resurgence of Spanish promotees, including Count Theodosius and his son, the emperor Theodosius I, to say nothing of other Spanish notables such as Pope Damasius and the poet-bishop Prudentius.[26] Against this background of material prosperity there was little reason for magistrates to flee their towns. But the decline of the 'epigraphic habit' leaves us without career inscriptions, making the Late Empire an age almost without history so far as municipal affairs are concerned.

Notes

1 On the virtual inevitability, cf M.G. Jarrett *AJPhil* 92 (1971) 532; A.H.M. Jones *The Later Roman Empire* (Oxford 1964) 741; and on dating, cf Arnold *Roman System*³ 262; P.D. Garnsey *ANRW* II/1 (Berlin and New York 1974) 242, 249–50; R. Ganghoffer *L'évolution des institutions municipales en Occident et en Orient* (Paris 1963) 28; Clavel and Lévêque *Villes et structures* 71.

2 Arnold *Roman System*³ 4

3 J.M. Blázquez *ANRW* II/3 (Berlin and New York 1975) 508–12

4 R. MacMullen *AJPhil* 103 (1982) 233–46

5 Jacques *Liberté* 603, 660

6 See Jacques *Liberté* 354–5.

7 K. Greene *The Archaeology of the Roman Economy* (London 1986) 59–61

8 J.M. Blázquez *La romanización* II (Madrid 1975) 253–5, reflecting the views of A. Balil, B. Taracena, and others

9 J. Arce *Hisp. Ant.* 8 (1978) 257–69

10 P. Salway in K.O. Morgan ed *The Oxford Illustrated History of Britain* (Oxford and New York 1984) 33. At Bordeaux, for instance, the Late Roman wall excludes not only the amphitheatre but even the forum.

11 I. Richmond *JRS* 21 (1931) 99

12 See (for Barcino and Bracara) Avienus *Ora mar.* 520; Auson. *Urb.* 13; and (for Tarraco) Auson. *Par.* 15.26.11–12.

13 See A. Chastagnol *Mélanges d'arch.* 88 (1976) 259–76; J. Arce *El último siglo de la España romana* (Madrid 1982) 94–99; and, for the roads, *ILER* 1788–2038 *passim*.

14 R. Collins *Early Medieval Spain* (London 1983) 4

15 Jones *Later Roman Empire* 756

16 On the penalties, see *Dig.* 50.5.1–2 Ulp.; *Cod. Theod.* 12.1 *passim*, 12.18.1–2; and cf Garnsey *ANRW* II/1 (1974) 229–30. We do know of one fourth-century Spaniard, Valerius Fortunatus of Emerita, who entered the Roman Senate to avoid being made a decurion in his home town (Symmachus *Orat.* 8); but he was already of senatorial family, not a devious upstart.

17 See *Cod. Theod.* 12.1.17, 19; and cf *Dig.* 50.2.6.4 on the *ordo* being made hereditary. For drafting into the *ordo*, see *Cod. Theod.* 7.22, 12.1.15, 32, 35 (veterans' sons); 12.1.26, 36, 42 pr., 44 (ex-governors etc.); 6.22.1 (procurators); 12.1.96, 133, 140, 148 (plebeians). On all of these, see Langhammer *Magistratus* 277–8.

18 See T. Kotula *Les principales d'Afrique* (Breslau 1982), especially chapter 1 and Appendix II.

19 R.M. Haywood *The Myth of Rome's Fall* (New York 1958) 111
20 Catalogue **973-4** with bibliography
21 *Cod. Theod.* 12.1.151; Kotula *Principales d'Afrique* 31 n 57 with complete references
22 Gorges *Villas* 48–56
23 On the liability of propertied newcomers to become decurions in the nearest city, see A. Chastagnol *L'évolution politique, sociale et économique du monde romain de Dioclétien à Julien* (Paris 1982) 283–5.
24 Salway in *Oxford Illustrated History* 37; A. Tranoy in J. Carpentier and F. Lebrun ed *Histoire de France* (Paris 1987) 80
25 Admittedly the decline in the 'epigraphic habit' accounts in part for the small number of attested curators. Undoubtedly there were more cities with curators than the inscriptional record indicates. Nonetheless, Spain seems to have had very few curators compared with some other provinces, even though the decline in the 'habit' was Empire-wide.
26 K.F. Stroheker *MM* 4 (1963) 107–32; A. Chastagnol *EREsp.* 269–92; M.T.W. Arnheim *The Senatorial Aristocracy in the Late Roman Empire* (Oxford 1972) 101

9

General Conclusions

This book has dealt with four main themes: the adoption of Roman institutions, the identity and nature of the municipal élite, the social dynamics of local government, and relation of wealth to power (or, in the Late Empire, to obligation). These do not correspond to the titles of the individual chapters, but rather overlap them, and indeed each other. Our final task must be to draw together the discrete inferences emerging from discussion of individual points and to sketch a composite scenario of the functioning of the local magisterial system as it relates to these central themes.

The creation of a romanized provincial élite was a crucial element in the acculturation of Spain and indeed of the entire Empire. The role of this élite in fostering romanization is usually illustrated by reference to provincial senators and knights, who left Spain and made their mark in Roman society (and eventually, in modern prosopography) by pursuing careers as Imperial officials and dignitaries. But one must challenge this view, for it is very questionable whether these *émigré* Spaniards really had much romanizing effect upon their stay-at-home compatriots. I think we must rather regard these senators and knights as the beneficiaries, not the agents, of provincial romanization. It was the local élite – the town magistrates – who exerted a continuing influence on their communities. The magistrates were the leaders and models of the romanizing process at the local level, which was after all the critical level. The governor in the provincial capital could desire and promote assimilation but he could not effect it. Roman garrisons and Roman law could be imposed, by force if necessary, but cultural affinity could not. Romanization was sanctioned by Roman policy but it was achieved by local co-operation and, more precisely, by the willingness of individuals to become romanized.

We can only speculate as to their motives for adopting Roman ways. For those wishing to leave the community and make a name for themselves in the world at large, personal ambition was the obvious incentive to assimilation. For those content with local honours, or with none, the motivation is less apparent. We are not aware of any regulation restricting office to those who were romanized. The explanation may rather be a psychological one. Informed native leaders eventually came to realize that revolts were futile, that the Romans were 'here to stay,' and that Roman civilization was both impressive and successful. It was prudent to accept the Roman presence, and tempting to imitate Roman manners. Roman citizenship, the badge of urbanity and privileged status, was dangled before their eyes and in due course made widely accessible through Vespasian's grant of *ius Latii*.

The Italian magisterial system was instituted in the colonies and soon emulated elsewhere. The smooth and almost imperceptible transition to this system on the southern and eastern coasts of Spain is attributable to the existence of organized cities in these regions before the Roman eagle arrived on their doorstep; the pre-Roman magisterial system in those cities was probably quite compatible with the Roman one. In the interior, the chiefs and nobles of tribes which had ceased their habitual migratory patterns, probably under Roman constraint, settled down and formed the nucleus of a proto-urban aristocracy, as the important *tessera* from Contrebia admirably illustrates. Local magistrates adopted not only this magisterial system but also Roman personal nomenclature even before citizenship was available; hence the widespread borrowing of the *nomina* of Republican governors, and the high incidence – nearly 60 percent – of *tria nomina*.

The identity of these magistrates can be ascertained by probes from diverse angles. The prosopographical method attempted in the Catalogue affords a sample or cross-section of known magistrates from various towns. The historical arguments presented in chapter 6 make it clear that, with the probable exception of the Roman colonies, the magistrates were mostly indigenes, not immigrants from Italy. Similarities in nomenclature and explicit mentions of family relations in the inscriptions suggest that the local élite was largely perpetuated along hereditary lines, despite the purchasing of offices in some towns and the hypothetical problem of infertility. We cannot be certain that the élite families of the pre-Roman period were still in charge. But the facts that the élite was largely indigenous, that sons of magistrates were often magistrates themselves, that there are at least a few recorded cases of the pre-Roman élite continuing (e.g., the Contrebian officials and the Balbus family), and that the liquidation of local élites was considered an unusual and extreme punishment worthy of historical notice, combine to suggest that the old aristocracy could and did continue to dominate local politics. Roman interference in local government seems to have been minimal; this 'hands-off' policy not only enabled old families to continue, but also allowed a certain degree of local variety in municipal institutions. To be sure, some cities seem to have retained a relatively 'closed' élite, while the more cosmopolitan centres were more amenable to the promotion of (preferably wealthy) parvenus. But local government remained the preserve of the local aristocracy.

The social mechanisms of the magisterial system were varied and complex. Advancement up the political ladder undoubtedly led to increased power and status in the community. However, we must differentiate between normal career progression and true social mobility, the latter involving an actual change of class. The entrenched view, furthermore, of a 'standard' *cursus honorum* is no longer tenable. The attested patterns of local office-holding display both variety and flexibility. The supposed first rung on the ladder, the quaestorship, was virtually an optional office, which could be held before, after, or instead of the aedileship, or omitted entirely; and many communities seem not to have had quaestors at all. The office of quattuorvir appears in some towns but not others, and appears to have been an alternate designation of the chief magistrates. An assortment of priesthoods was available but these were only an optional office in the *cursus*. Some communities maintained triumvirs, quinquevirs and other anomalous magistracies, probably remnants of pre-Roman government.

Relations between élites of different cities were apparently fluid, to judge from the large number of magistrates who held office in multiple towns or in a town other than their birthplace; this geographic mobility has implications not only for demography but for the romanization of Spain, as suggested in chapter 6. But real social mobility was far rarer. Magistrates could hold a range of local offices, and many of them must have met the equestrian census, but admission to the higher equestrian posts and to the Roman Senate was apparently closed to them. Local patronage could promote a man's career within the community, but advancement into the larger world required political pull which few could claim. The preserved career profiles reveal that a comparatively small number of magistrates achieved the military prefecture and tribunate (which in two-thirds of the cases were held after the local magistracy) while a smaller number sat on jury panels at Rome. The provincial priesthood of Tarraconensis (Hispania Citerior), originally the preserve of equestrian officers, was gradually made accessible to (apparently) non-equestrian magistrates, but the honour was undoubtedly cheapened in the process. The 'new men' from Spain who reached the top of the ladder – of whom L. Cornelius Balbus Maior and L. Annaeus Seneca are the most familiar examples – did so not by local office-holding but by serving outside of Spain. Such men took up a career pattern which differed radically from that followed by their fellow provincials content with local honours.

That local magistrates were often wealthy, particularly those in the larger cities, cannot be doubted. Parallel evidence suggests the likelihood of a property qualification for admission to the local senate; as Ovid appropriately remarked, 'curia pauperibus clausa est, dat census honores' (Am. 3.8.55; Fasti 1.217). Under the Early Empire rich benefactions are recorded, especially by magistrates on the prosperous eastern and southern littorals; whether these gifts were due to obligation, election promises, civic pride, or mere ostentation, is perhaps less important than the fact that local magistrates possessed the affluence necessary to bestow them. But if wealth was a necessary criterion for office, its sources are more difficult to verify. Landholding is the traditional explanation, which is now borne out by archaeological and epigraphic evidence from villas; moreover, the Theodosian Code insists that decurions possess twenty-five *iugera* of land. But the prevalence of landed wealth does not preclude the possibility of local aristocrats engaging initially in commerce or manufacture and then using their earnings to purchase land, which in turn would have produced revenue. Personal wealth from a multiplicity of sources may have been a far more common phenomenon than our surviving evidence indicates.

The role of local magistrates in provincial romanization has been long and undeservedly neglected. Spain provides the logical starting-point for a reassessment of the importance of local élites throughout the Empire. Because of its long history as a Roman provincial zone and of its precious series of colonial and municipal laws and records of personal careers, the Iberian Peninsula allows us to retrace both the development of local government and the social history of the urban aristocracy from the Hannibalic War to the fall of the Empire. Though less glamorous than the prosopographers' idols, the senators and *equites*, local magistrates had a crucial role to play in provincial society, and one which must now be recognized. By their personal and visible example – the adoption of Roman names and Roman titles, the implementation of Roman law, the construction of Roman buildings, the flaunting of Roman citizenship – they showed their compatriots that assimilation with the Romans was not only possible but beneficial. It was these local magnates who reorganized their civic institutions on Roman lines and led their townsmen along the road to *Romanitas*. In retrospect, they emerge as the initiators, models, exponents, and prime movers of romanization in every community.

SELECT BIBLIOGRAPHY

General

Abbott, F.F. and A.C. Johnson *Municipal Administration in the Roman Empire* Princeton 1926

Arnold, W.T. *The Roman System of Provincial Administration* 3rd ed Oxford 1914 (repr Freeport 1971)

Brunt, P.A. 'The Romanization of the Local Ruling Classes in the Roman Empire' in *Assimilation et résistance à la culture gréco-romaine dans le monde antique* 161–173 Bucharest and Paris 1976

Burton, G.P. 'The Curator Rei Publicae: Towards a Reappraisal' *Chiron* 9 (1979) 465–87

Callender, M.H. *Roman Amphorae* London 1965

Clavel, M. and P. Lévêque *Villes et structures urbaines dans l'Occident romain* Paris 1971

Devijver, H. *Prosopographia militiarum equestrium quae fuerunt ab Augusto ad Gallienum* Louvain 1976–80

Duncan-Jones, R.P. *The Economy of the Roman Empire: Quantitative Studies* 2nd ed Cambridge 1982

Duthoy, R. 'Curatores rei publicae en Occident durant le Principat: Recherches préliminaires sur l'apport des sources épigraphiques' *Ancient Society* 10 (1979) 171–238

Ganghoffer, R. *L'évolution des institutions municipales en Occident et en Orient au Bas-Empire* Paris 1963

Garnsey, P.D. *Social Status and Legal Privilege in the Roman Empire* Oxford 1970

– 'Honorarium decurionatus' *Historia* 20 (1971) 309–25

- 'Aspects of the Decline of the Urban Aristocracy in the Empire' *ANRW* II/1 (Berlin and New York 1974) 229–52
- 'Descendants of Freedmen in Local Politics: Some Criteria' in *The Ancient Historian and His Materials* ed B. Levick 167–80 Westmead 1975

Goodfellow, C.E. *Roman Citizenship: A Study of Its Territorial and Numerical Expansion from the Earliest Times to the Death of Augustus* diss, Bryn Mawr 1935

Grant, M. *From Imperium to Auctoritas: A Historical Study of Aes Coinage in the Roman Empire 49 BC–AD 14* Cambridge 1946

Hardy, E.G. *Six Roman Laws* Oxford 1911

Jacques, F. *Le privilège de liberté: Politique impériale et autonomie municipale dans les cités de l'Occident* Paris 1984

Jarrett, M.G. 'Decurions and Priests' *AJPhil* 92 (1971) 513–38

Kajanto, I. *The Latin Cognomina* Helsinki 1965

Langhammer, W. *Die rechtliche und soziale Stellung der magistratus municipales und der decuriones in der Übergangsphase der Städte* Wiesbaden 1973

Liebenam, W. *Städteverwaltung im römischen Kaiserreiche* Leipzig 1900 (repr Amsterdam 1967)

Pflaum, H.-G. *Les carrières procuratoriennes équestres sous le Haut-Empire romain* Paris 1960–1

Reid, J.B. *The Municipalities of the Roman Empire* Cambridge 1913

Schonbauer, E. *Municipia und coloniae in der Prinzipatzeit* Wien 1954

Schulze, W. *Zur Geschichte lateinischer Eigennamen* Berlin 1904 (repr Berlin 1966)

Sherwin White, A.N. *The Roman Citizenship* 2nd ed Oxford 1973

Stevenson, G.H. *Roman Provincial Administration till the Age of the Antonines* New York 1939

Syme, R. *Roman Papers* ed E. Badian and A.R. Birley, 5 vols Oxford 1979–87

Tanfani, L. *Contributo alla storia del municipio romano* Taranto 1906

Torrent, A. *La 'iurisdictio' de los magistrados municipales* Salamanca 1970

Toutain, J. 'Etudes sur l'organisation municipale du Haut-Empire' *Mélanges d'arch.* 16 (1896) 315–29 and 18 (1898) 141–63

Visscher, F. de 'L'expansion de la cité romaine et la diffusion du droit romain' *Mus. Helv.* 14 (1957) 164–74

Vittinghoff, F. *Römische Kolonisation und Bürgerrechtspolitik unter Caesar und Augustus* Mainz 1952

Wiseman, T.P. *New Men in the Roman Senate 139 BC–14 AD* Oxford 1971

Spain

Alarcão, J. and R. Etienne *Fouilles de Conimbriga* 7 vols Paris 1974–9

Albertos Firmat, M.L. *La onomástica personal primitiva de Hispania Tarraconensis y Bética* Salamanca 1966

Alföldy, G. *Fasti Hispanienses* Wiesbaden 1969

– *Flamines provinciae Hispaniae Citerioris* Madrid 1973

– *Die römischen Inschriften von Tarraco* Berlin 1975

– 'Drei städtische Eliten im römischen Hispanien' *Gerión* 2 (1984) 193–238

Alves Dias, M.M. 'M. Fabius Paulinus and L. Numisius Montanus: A Contribution to the Knowledge of the Hispanic Municipal Elites under Hadrian' *MM* 19 (1978) 263–71

Beltrán Lloris, F. 'Los magistrados monetales en Hispania' *Numisma* 28 (1978) 169–211

– *Epigrafía latina de Saguntum y su territorium* Valencia 1980

Broughton, T.R.S. 'Municipal Institutions in Roman Spain' *Cahiers d'histoire mondiale* 9 (1965) 126–42

Castillo García, C. *Prosopographia Baetica* Pamplona 1965

– 'Städte und Personen der Baetica' *ANRW* II/3 (Berlin and New York 1975) 601–54

Curchin, L.A. 'Personal Wealth in Roman Spain' *Historia* 32 (1983) 227–44

Dyson, S.L. 'The Distribution of Roman Republican Family Names in the Iberian Peninsula' *Ancient Society* 11–12 (1980–1) 257–99

d'Encarnação, J. *Inscrições romanas do conventus Pacensis* Coimbra 1984

Etienne, R. *Le culte impérial dans la Péninsule Ibérique* Paris 1958

Fabre, G. 'Le tissu urbain dans le nord-ouest de la Péninsule Ibérique' *Latomus* 29 (1970) 314–39

– et al. *Inscriptions romaines de Catalogne* 2 vols Paris 1984–5

Fatás, G. and M.A. Martín Bueno *Epigrafía romana de Zaragoza y su provincia* Zaragoza 1977

Francisco Martín, J. 'Los magistrados municipales en Lusitania durante el Alto Imperio' in *Estructuras sociales durante la Antigüedad* 227–45 Oviedo 1978

Galsterer, H. *Untersuchungen zum römischen Städtewesen auf der iberischen Halbinsel* Berlin 1971

García Iglesias, L. *Epigrafía romana de Augusta Emerita* diss, Madrid 1973

Gil Farrés, O. *La moneda hispánica en la edad antigua* Madrid 1966

Gómez-Pantoja, J. *El conventus iuridicus Caesaraugustanus: Personas y ciudades (a. 45–a.D. 192)* diss, Universidad de Navarra 1983

González, J. *Inscripciones romanas de la provincia de Cádiz* Cádiz 1982

– 'The Lex Irnitana: A New Copy of the Flavian Municipal Law' *JRS* 76 (1986) 147–243

Gorges, J.-G. *Les villas hispano-romaines* Paris 1979

Hardy, E.G. *Three Spanish Charters and Other Documents* Oxford 1912

Heiss, A. *Description générale des monnaies antiques d'Espagne* Paris 1870

Hübner, E. *Corpus inscriptionum Latinarum* II 2 vols Berlin 1869–92

Hurtado de San Antonio, R. *Corpus provincial de inscripciones latinas (Cáceres)* Cáceres 1977

Knapp, R.C. *Aspects of the Roman Experience in Iberia 206–100 BC* Vitoria and Valladolid 1977

– 'The Origins of Provincial Prosopography in the West' *Ancient Society* 9 (1978) 187–222

Lara Peinado, F. *Epigrafía romana de Lérida* Lérida 1973

McElderry, R.K. 'Vespasian's Reconstruction of Spain' *JRS* 8 (1918) 53–102 and 9 (1919) 86–94

Mackie, N. *Local Administration in Roman Spain AD 14–212* Oxford 1983

Mariner Bigorra, S. *Inscripciones romanas de Barcelona* Barcelona 1973

d'Ors, A. *Epigrafía jurídica de la España romana* Madrid 1953

Palomar Lapesa, M. *La onomástica personal pre-latina de la antigua Lusitania* Salamanca 1957

Pastor Muñoz, M. *Los Astures durante el imperio romano* Oviedo 1977

Pastor Muñoz and A. Mendoza Eguaras *Inscripciones latinas de la provincia de Granada* Granada 1987

Pflaum, H.-G. 'La part prise par les chevaliers romains originaires d'Espagne à l'administration impériale' in *Les empereurs romains d'Espagne* 87–121 Paris 1965

Richardson, J.S. 'The Tabula Contrebiensis: Roman Law in Spain in the Early First Century BC' *JRS* 73 (1983) 33–41

Rodríguez Neila, J.R. 'Las elecciones municipales en la Bética romana' and 'Observaciones en torno a las magistraturas municipales de la Bética romana' in *Actas del I Congreso de historia de Andalucía: Fuentes y metodología, Andalucía en la Antigüedad* 165–77, 203–10 Córdoba 1978

– 'Magistraturas municipales y funciones religiosas en la Hispania romana' *Revista de Estudios de Vida Local* 209 (1981) 91–118

– *Sociedad y administración local en la Bética romana* Córdoba 1981

Sagredo San Eustaquio, L. and S. Crespo Ortiz de Zárate *Epigrafía romana de la provincia de Palencia* Palencia 1978

Spitzl, T. *Lex municipii Malacitani* München 1984

Syme, R. 'La richesse des aristocraties de Bétique et de Narbonnaise' *Ktema* 2 (1977) 373–80

Thouvenot, R. *Essai sur la province romaine de Bétique* 2nd ed Paris 1973

Veny, C. *Corpus de las inscripciones baleáricas hasta la dominación árabe* Madrid 1965

Villaronga Garriga, L. 'Los magistrados en las amonedaciones latinas de Emporiae' in *Estudios de numismática romana* ed E. Ripoll Perelló 81–96 Barcelona 1964

– *The Aes Coinage of Emporion* Oxford 1977

Vives, A. *La moneda hispánica* 4 vols Madrid 1926–8

Vives, J. *Inscripciones latinas de la España romana* 2 vols Barcelona 1970–1

Wiegels, R. *Die römischen Senatoren und Ritter aus den hispanischen Provinzen* diss, Freiburg 1971

– *Die Tribusinschriften des römischen Hispanien: Ein Katalog* Berlin 1985

Parallels

Alföldy, G. *Noricum* London and Boston 1974

Cébeillac-Gervasoni, M. et al. *Les 'bourgeoisies' municipales italiennes aux IIe et I^e siècles av. J.-C.* Paris and Naples 1983

Debbasch, Y. 'Colonia Iulia Karthago: La vie et les institutions municipales de la Carthage romaine' *Rev. Hist. Dr. Fr.* 31 (1953) 30–53, 335–77

Drinkwater, J.F. 'The Rise of the Gallic Julii' *Latomus* 37 (1978) 817–50

– 'A Note on Local Careers in the Three Gauls under the Early Empire' *Britannia* 10 (1979) 89–100

Eck, W. *Die staatliche Organisation Italiens in der hohen Kaiserzeit* München 1979

Gascou, J. *La politique municipale de l'Empire romain en Afrique Proconsulaire de Trajan à Septime-Sévère* Rome 1972

Ifie, J.E. 'The Romano-African Municipal Aristocracy and the Imperial Government under the Principate' *Museum Africum* 5 (1976) 36–58

Kotula, T. *Les principales d'Afrique: Etude sur l'élite municipale nord-africaine au Bas-Empire romain* Breslau 1982

Mócsy, A. *Pannonia and Upper Moesia: A History of the Middle Danube Provinces of the Roman Empire* London and Boston 1974

Rudolph, H. *Stadt und Staat in römischen Italien* Leipzig 1935

Rupprecht, G. *Untersuchungen zum Dekurionstand in den nordwestlichen Provinzen des römischen Reiches* Kallmünz 1975

Salmon, E.T. *The Making of Roman Italy* Ithaca 1982

Simshäuser, W. *Iuridici und Munizipalgerichtsbarkeit in Italien* München 1973

Wightman, E.M. *Gallia Belgica* London and Berkeley 1985

Wilkes, J.J. *Dalmatia* London 1969

Catalogue of Magistrates

INTRODUCTION

This catalogue consists of five parts. Parts 1 through 3 list all known local magistrates from the Spanish provinces of Baetica, Lusitania, and Tarraconensis (Hispania Citerior), respectively. Part 4 contains addenda to the catalogue of historical magistrates. Part 5 lists supposed magistrates who appear to be spurious (e.g., attested in a fake inscription or adduced from a misreading of a coin) or dubious.

Each province has been subdivided into towns with known magistrates. These towns are listed alphabetically by their Roman names; if the ancient name is unknown, the modern toponym is substituted. When a magistrate is known to have held office at two towns, the primary entry will be found under the town of his first attested magistracy, and a cross-reference under the other town. Every effort has been made to assign magistrates to their recorded or probable towns, but certainty is not always possible, particularly if the provenance of an inscription is disputed or lies between two ancient towns. In a few cases where no probable town could be postulated, magistrates have been placed in a section of 'Uncertain Towns' at the end of the listings for their province. The location in the catalogue of any magistrate can quickly be determined by consulting the Index of Names.

Under each town, magistrates belonging to the same period (Republic, Early Empire, Late Empire) are grouped together. However, since many coins and inscriptions cannot be closely dated, and in some cases the date originally assigned to a document is later modified, a precise chronological sequence has not been attempted. In some cases (e.g., when an inscription is no longer extant or has been published without any discussion of date) no chronology is available at all.

Since this catalogue is essentially a synthesis of previously published data (despite occasional epigraphic comments on my part), it has seemed neither necessary nor practical to duplicate the variety of brackets, dotted letters and other critical signs employed in the *editio princeps* of an inscription. Square brackets have been used to indicate both expansion of abbreviations and restoration of missing letters, and an ellipsis (...) to indicate lost text. When an ellipsis occurs in place of a *praenomen* or filiation (e.g., ... Caelius ... f.), it indicates that these parts of the name were certainly or very probably mentioned in the inscription but are now lost or illegible.

1

Baetica

Abdera municipium (conv. Gaditanus)

1 Anonymus – flamen divi Augusti, praefectus cohortis ..., praefectus fabrum, iivir; son of ...lla, a local sacerdos
CIL ii 1979 = R. Lázaro Pérez *Inscripciones romanas de Almería* (Almería 1980) no. 2; *PB* Ignoti 13; Wiegels no. 362; *PME* Incerti 4

2 Anonymus – flamen divorum [Augustorum], praefectus ...; possibly a praefectus i.d; relative ...lia L. f. Anu[llina]
Lázaro Pérez *Inscripciones romanas de Almería* no. 25

Abra (conv. incertus)

3 Ueboeki – magistrate; second half of 2nd century BC
VM 98:1, 3–4 = Gil 372–3, 400
4 Takisnis – colleague of **3**
See **3**.

Acinipo (conv. Hispalensis)

5 L. Folce[nius?] – aedilis; ca 47–44 BC
The *nomen* Folcenius is Etruscan. Less plausibly, Castillo takes Folce as the ablative of an otherwise unattested *cognomen* Folcis.
VM 105:1 = Gil 1153; Schulze *Eigennamen* 169; *PB* xix; A. Balil *Hispania* 25 (1965) 362
6 M. Marius M. f. M. n. Quir. Fronto – pontificalis, iivir, patronus; late 1st or 2nd century
CIL ii 1348 = *ILER* 1509; *PB* 238

7 Anonymus – IIvir?
   CIL II 1351

Anticaria municipium (conv. Astigitanus)

8 L. Porcius Sabellus – IIvir; AD 76–77
   Since this inscription is dated shortly after Vespasian's censorship (73),
   Hübner thinks it may commemorate a grant of *ius Latii*. The inscription
   is dedicated to the emperor.
   CIL II 2041 = *ILER* 1083; *PB* 278

Arcilacis (conv. Gaditanus)

9 C. Avielius C. f. Pap. Paelignus – praefectus iure dicundo; 1st century AD
   Eph. Epigr. VIII 94 = *IRPC* 513

Arsa municipium Iulium V... (conv. Cordubensis)

10 K. Ae[lius] L. f. – magistrate; ca 47–44 BC
    VM 92:1 = Gil 1164; *PB* xxvii
11 M. Herennius M. f. Gal. Laetinus – aedilis, IIvir ter, pontifex, aug[ur] (or
    pontifex Augusti)
    CIL II 5547 = *ILER* 1537; *PB* 174

Arunda (conv. Hispalensis)

12 L. Iunius L. f. Quir. Iunianus – IIvir bis; son Iunius Gallus
    The tribe Quirina suggests a Flavian or later date (see chapter 6).
    CIL II 1359 = *ILS* 5498 = *ILER* 1745; *PB* 196

Arva municipium Flavium (conv. Hispalensis)

13 M. Egnatius Sciti lib. Venustus – sevir
    He received *ornamenta decurionatus* and a statue from the *ordo*. In
    return he paid for a statue, marble benches, and a pilaster. Cf another
    sevir so honoured at Lucurgentum (**170**) and three aedilic honours given
    at Dertosa (**676–8**).
    CIL II 1066 = *ILS* 5487 = *ILER* 1734; J.F. Rodríguez Neila *Sociedad y*
    administración local en la Bética romana (Córdoba 1981) 43

Asido municipium Caesarina (conv. Gaditanus)

14 Q. Fabius Cn. f. Gal. Senica – IIIIvir; Augustan
    CIL II 1315 = *ILER* 1498 = *IRPC* 4; *PB* 161

15 L. Fabius L. f. Gal. Cordus – iiiivir; provided twenty pairs of gladiators for local games
CIL II 1305 = ILER 1681 = IRPC 103; PB 148

16 M. Acilius M'. f. Gal. Silo – iivir, praefectus cohortis; probably Augustan
CIL II 1314 = ILER 5602 = IRPC 3; PB 9; Wiegels no. 204; PME A 11

Astigi colonia Augusta Firma (conv. Astigitanus)

17 Cn. Manlius Cn. f. Pap. – praefectus iure dicundo, iivir, praefectus cohortium, tribunus cohortis praetoriae; Augustan
CIL II 1477 = ILER 6390; PB 226; Wiegels no. 295; PME M 20

18 C. Cosconius L. f. Pap. Taurus – iivir
CIL II 1476 = ILER 3566; PB 129

19 ...ius M. f. Pap. Longinus – iivir bis, praefectus ter; donated ten fully equipped *lacus* to the public baths
CIL II 1478 = ILER 2052; PB Ignoti 5

20 L. Bercius Aper – iivir; wife perhaps named Aurelia
CIL II 1489 = M. Varela y Escobar *Bosquero histórico de la muy noble y muy real Ciudad de Ecija* (Ecija 1892) 29; PB 72

Aurgi municipium Flavium (conv. Astigitanus)

21 M. Sempronius C. f. Gal. Sempronianus – iivir bis, pontifex perpetuus; Trajanic; daughter Sempronia Fusca Vibia Anicilla; donated baths, an aqueduct and thirty-seven hectares of woodland
CIL II 3361 = ILER 2040; PB 289a; R.P. Duncan-Jones JRS 64 (1974) 85 n 53

22 M. Valerius M. f. Quir. Marcellus – aedilis, iivir; Trajanic; donated a clock, games and circuses to Tucci
The inscription was discovered at the site of Tucci.
CIL II 1685 = ILS 5623 = ILER 6079; PB 316

Axati municipium Flavium (conv. Hispalensis)

23 C. Iuventius C. f. Quir. Albinus – aedilis, iivir munificentissimus, patronus patriae; Flavian or later
CIL II 1054 = ILER 1457; PB 207

24 L. Lucretius Severus – decurio; a native of Corduba and resident alien at Axati; provided in his will for a statue, and for sportulae to the decurions
CIL II 1055 = ILS 6916 = ILER 1730

Baelo municipium Claudium (conv. Gaditanus)

25 Q. Manlius – magistrate [aedilis?]; ca 47–44 BC
VM 91:1 = Gil 1362; PB xxxiii

26 P. Cornelius – colleague of **25**
   PB xiii; and see **25**.

27 Falt[o?] – aedilis; ca 47–44 BC
   The name was formerly read 'Fat,' but Villaronga's photograph clearly
   shows an 'AL' ligature. Falto is a known variant of the Latin *cognomen*
   Falco.
   VM 91:3 = Gil 1363; Grant *FITA* 24; L. Villaronga *Numismática antigua
   de Hispania* (Barcelona 1979) 165

28 L. Apo[nius] – colleague of **27**
   Grant's reading 'L. Ap. Q.' is erroneous.
   PB v; and see **27**.

29 Q. Pupius Q. f. Gal. Urbicus – iivir; first half of 2nd century AD; parents
   Q. Pupius Geneti[v]us and Iunia Eleuthera
   J.C.M. Richard et al., *MCV* 8 (1972) 577 = *AE* 1971, 172 = *AE* 1975,
   495 = *IRPC* 68

Barbesula municipium (conv. Gaditanus)

30 L. Fabius Gal. Caesianus – iivir, flamen perpetuus; Trajanic; heirs Fabia C.
   f. Fabiana and Fulvia Sex. f. Honorata
   The former is presumably a sister or niece, the latter may be the
   daughter of the local *flamen* Sex. Fulvius Lepidus mentioned in *CIL* II
   1939 = *ILER* 1000.
   CIL II 1941 = *ILER* 1556 = *IRPC* 77; Etienne *Culte* 203; *PB* 46

31 C. Cervius Quir. Quintianus – iivir; reign of Trajan; father Cervius
   Honoratus Ostorianus Rufus (cf Honorata under **30**)
   CIL II 1940 = *ILER* 1739 = *IRPC* 76; *PB* 93

Batora (conv. Astigitanus)

32 P. Fabius P. f. Gal. Iulianus – iivir bis, pontifex; mother Iunia M. f. Severa
   CIL II 1677 = *ILER* 1425; *PB* 151

Baxo (conv. Cordubensis)

33 M. Fabius Q. f. Rufus – legatus; AD 34; arranged *hospitium* between the
   senate and people of Baxo and the Colonia Claritas Iulia (Ucubi)
   J.F. Rodríguez Neila and J.M. Santero Santurino *Habis* 13 (1982) = *AE*
   1983, 530 = *AE* 1985, 564; C. Puerta and A. Stylow *Gerión* 3 (1985) 328

34 C. Terentius P. f. Macer – colleague of **33**
   See **33**.

Bujalance (ancient name unknown; conv. Cordubensis)

35 C. Pomponius Quir. Marullus – ɪɪvir; Flavian or later; uncle L. Aemilius
Avitus, and brother C. Pomponius Lupus
   CIL ɪɪ 2150 = *ILER* 1722; *PB* 271

Callenses Aeneanici (conv. Hispalensis)

36 ...ius Fabianus – ɪɪvir; perhaps a member of the *gens* Fabia
   Although the identity of the town is uncertain, the inscription naming
   this magistrate and his colleague was discovered only five km from
   another inscription (*CIL* ɪɪ 1372) which appears to mention the *res publica
   Callensis*.
   A.M. Canto *Habis* 9 (1978) 293 = *AE* 1979, 351
37 ...ius Senecio – colleague of 36
   See 36.

Canan[i]a municipium Flavium (conv. Hispalensis)

38 L. Attius Quir. Vetto – flamen, ɪɪvir; Flavian or later; constructed marble
   porticos and provided a dramatic spectacle and banquet at his own expense;
   son L. Attius Vindex, daughter Attia Autumnina, granddaughter Antonia
   Procula
   His *cognomen* is the name of a Lusitanian tribe (Vettones) and his family
   may have come from that region.
   CIL ɪɪ 1074 = *ILS* 5544 = *ILER* 6071; Etienne *Culte* 204; *PB* 64

Carissa Aurelia (conv. Gaditanus)

39 [Iu]nius Cornelianus – sevir cor[poratus?], [honor] decurionatus; dedicated
   wooden door jambs (*valvae*) in return for these honours
   As Duthoy has demonstrated, *sevir corporatus* is probably equivalent to
   sevir Augustalis
   IRPC 100; cf R. Duthoy *Epigraphische Studien* 11 (1976) 208

Carmo municipium (conv. Hispalensis)

40 L. Iunius L. f. M. n. L. pron. Gal. Rufus – ɪɪɪɪvir, pontifex, aug[ur] (or
   Augusti), quattuorvirali potestate
   He was honoured by the *equites Romani*, may therefore have been a
   knight himself, and probably was of Italian descent if his lengthy pedigree
   is authentic.
   CIL ɪɪ 1380 and p 701 = *ILS* 5080a = *ILER* 1481; *PB* 203
41 ... Fonteius C. f. Calp... – ɪɪɪɪvir
   CIL ɪɪ 1379 = *ILER* 1480

Carteia colonia Latina; later municipium (conv. Gaditanus)

42 Anonymi – legati Carteienses; 45 BC
   BHisp. 36

43 C. Curman... – magistrate; second half of 1st century BC
   VM 126:11–12 = Gil 1222–3; *PB* xvi

44 L. Marcius – magistrate; second half of 1st century BC
   VM 126:13–14 = Gil 1227–8; possibly also VM 129:9–10 = Gil 1225–6; *PB* xxxiv

45 M. Cur[ius] – magistrate; second half of 1st century BC; colleague of L.M.
   (perhaps 44) and perhaps a relative of 49
   VM 129:9–10 = Gil 1225–6; *PB* xvii

46 M. Sep[tumius] – magistrate; second half of 1st century BC
   VM 126:8 = Gil 1229; *PB* xlix

47 Num[isius?] – magistrate; second half of 1st century BC
   VM 127:10 = Gil 1230; *PB* xl

48 C. Ninius – q[uaestor?]; second half of 1st century BC
   VM 127:2 = Gil 1231; *PB* xxxix

49 Curius – q[uaestor? Quintus?]; second half of 1st century BC
   VM 126:7 = Gil 1232; *PB* xv

50 Opsil[ius?] – q[uaestor? Quintus?]; second half of 1st century BC
   VM 127:3–4 = Gil 1233–4; *PB* xlii

51 Pedecaius – q[uaestor? Quintus?]; second half of 1st century BC
   The *nomen* is rare.
   VM 127:7–8 = Gil 1235–6; *PB* xliv = xlv

52 C. Vibius – aedilis; second half of 1st century BC
   VM 127:9 = Gil 1237; *PB* lvi

53 Cn. Mai[us?] – aedilis; second half of 1st century BC
   Cf **60** for a possible relative.
   VM 127:5–6 = Gil 1238–9; *PB* xxxi

54 L. Arc[ius?] – aedilis; colleague of 53
   PB vii; and see **53**.

55 L. Raius – censor; second half of 1st century BC
   Censors often occur in Latin towns. A Raius Plebeiius (**142**) is attested at
   Italica.
   VM 127:1 = Gil 1240; *PB* xlviii; cf Knapp *Roman Experience* 119

56 L. Agrius – colleague of 55
   PB ii; and see **55**.

57 Anonymus – censor; second half of 1st century BC
   VM 126:4 = Gil 1241

58 P. Iulius – q[uaestor?]; second half of 1st century BC
   VM 126:9–10 = Gil 1242–3; *PB* xxv

59 Anonymi – IIIIviri; before 19 BC
VM 128:11, 12, 14, 129:5 = Gil 1805–7, 1809

60 C. Maius C. f. Pollio – IIIIvir; before 19 BC
Castillo infers two men from this coin legend, L. (*sic*) Maius C. f. and Pollio, but since all the other magistrates of this town appear to have *nomina*, the *cognomen* Pollio is less likely a separate name than a complement to Maius.
VM 128:2 = Gil 1810; *PB* xxxii, xlvi

61 Aufidius – IIIIvir; before 19 BC
VM 129:14 = Gil 1811; *PB* ix

62 Maecilius – IIIIvir; before 19 BC
VM 129:1 = Gil 1812; *PB* xxx

63 P. Mion... – IIIIvir; before 19 BC
The name is perhaps indigenous.
VM 129:7 = Gil 1813; *PB* xxxvi

64 M. Falcidius – IIIIvir; before 19 BC
With his uncommon *nomen*, he is perhaps related to C. Falcidius of Reate in Italy.
VM 128:1 = Gil 1814; *PB* xviii; Wiseman *New Men* no. 170

65 L. Atinius – IIIIvir; before 19 BC
VM 128:3–4 = Gil 1815–16; *PB* viii

66 C. Nucia – colleague of **65**
His rare *nomen*, not listed in Schulze *Eigennamen*, is considered indigenous by Albertos.
Albertos *OPP* 171; and see **65**.

67 C. Vibius – IIIIvir it[erum]; before 19 BC
VM 128:5–9 = Gil 1817–21; *PB* lviii

68 C. Minius Q. f. – IIIIvir it[erum]; colleague of **67**
VM 128:5–9 = Gil 1817–21; *PB* xxxv

69 C. Minius C. f. – IIIIvir it[erum]; before 19 BC; perhaps the son of **68**
VM 128:10 = Gil 1822

70 C. Curvius C. f. Ser. Rusticus – IIIIvir iterum; late 1st century BC or early 1st century AD
D.E. Woods in *V Symposium Internacional de Prehistoria Peninsular* (Barcelona 1969) 254 = C.F. Chicarro y de Dios *Rev. Bellas Artes* 1 (1970) 60 = *IRPC* 92

Cartima municipium civium Latinorum (conv. Gaditanus)

71 Vestinus Rustici f. – xvir; AD 53–4; son Rusticus
The inscription is dated by its dedication to Claudius. The office of

decemvir antedates the granting of *ius Latii,* as shown by the inscription. Note that Vestinus lacks both *praenomen* and *nomen.* The family tree can be reconstructed from CIL II 1952–3 and 1962:

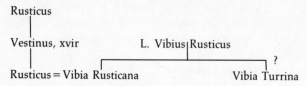

Rusticus

Vestinus, xvir   L. Vibius Rusticus

Rusticus = Vibia Rusticana   Vibia Turrina   ?

CIL II 1953 = ILS 5504 = ILER 1071; PB 332; J. Muñiz Coello *Hisp. Ant.* 6 (1976) 20–1

Ceret (conv. Gaditanus)

72 ... f. Serg. Vernus – aedilis IIvirali potestate; probably 1st century AD
   CIL II 1306 = ILER 1502 = IRPC 104

Cisimbrium municipium Flavium (conv. Astigitanus)

73 ... Valerius C. f. Quir. Rufus – IIvir; AD 77; citizenship granted per honorem
   CIL II 2096 = A.U. Stylow *Gerión* 4 (1986) 292–4; PB 320; Galsterer *Untersuchungen* 43 n 53

74 C. Valerius C. f. Gal. Valerianus – IIvir, pontifex perpetuus; granddaughter Flavia Valeriana
   CIL II 2098 = ILS 5356 = ILER 1443; PB 323; cf Alföldy *Fasti* 190

75 Q. Annius Quir. Niger – IIvir; AD 84; received the Roman citizenship per honorem; dedicated a statue to Venus Victrix
   J. González MCV 17 (1981) 39–41 = AE 1981, 496 = Stylow *Gerión* 4 (1986) 290–1

76 Anonymus – IIvir; perhaps Flavian; received Roman citizenship per honorem together with his son Annianus
   CIL II 1635; A.U. Stylow *Gerión* 4 (1986) 294–5

Corduba colonia Patricia (conv. Cordubensis)

77 Cn. Iulius L. f. – q[uaestor]; before 49 BC
   Grant and Castillo suggest that he was quaestor of the province rather than a local magistrate. He is not listed in Broughton MRR.
   VM 118:1–3 = Gil 1263–5; Grant FITA 4–7; PB xxiv; Galsterer *Untersuchungen* 57 n 66; C. Castillo *Hisp. Ant.* 4 (1974) 193

78 A. At[ilius] – possible magistrate, named on a leaden tessera
   CIL II 4963.9; cf R. Knapp *Roman Córdoba* (Berkeley 1982) 33

79 L. Ai(milius) – colleague of **78**
  See **78**.

80 T. Marius Mercello Persinus – aedilis, IIvir
  With the rare *cognomen* Mercello we may compare Mercelio (or
  Mergilio) of Italica in *B.Alex.* 52.3, 55.4
  CIL II 2226 = *ILER* 1454; *PB* 242

81 ...lius L. f. Cinna – praefectus, IIvir aedilicia potestate; possibly Augustan
  CIL II 5525 = *ILER* 1449; *PB* 109; Knapp *Roman Córdoba* 34

82 L. Fulcinius Pacatus – IIvir; daughter Fulcinia Prisca, flaminica
  A. García y Bellido *BRAH* 168 (1971) 184 = *AE* 1971, 185

83 L. Manlius A. f. A. n. Bocchus – tribunus militum legionis XV, IIvir,
  praefectus i.d.
  An early date is suggested by the absence of a *cognomen* for the legion.
  It is probably XV Apollinaris, created by Augustus; otherwise XV
  Primigenia, created by Gaius.
  CIL II 2225 = *ILER* 1692; *PW* 'Legio' cols 1747, 1756–8; *PB* 228; Wiegels no.
  296; *PME* M 21

84 L. Valerius Poenus – IIvir; possibly mid-1st century AD
  The *cognomen* suggests Punic origin.
  CIL II 2242 = *ILER* 3442; *PB* 317

85 L. Antistius Rusticus – colleague of **84**
  He is possibly related to the senator of the same name (cos. suff. AD 90)
  PB 52; and see **84**.

86 L. Iulius M. f. Q. n. Gal. Gallus Mummianus – tribunus militum cohortis
  maritimae, IIvir, flamen divorum Augustorum prov. Baeticae; early 2nd
  century; received an equestrian statue; wife Aelia Flaviana (perhaps the
  daughter of a Flavian freedman)
  CIL II 2224 = *ILS* 6905 = *ILER* 1718; Etienne *Culte* 129; *EREsp.* 93; *PB* 186;
  Wiegels no. 273; *PME* I 67

87 Iunius Bassus Milonianus – IIvir, praefectus fabrum; probably Trajanic
  CIL II 2222 = *ILER* 1691 = E. Serrano Ramos and R. Atencia Paez
  Inscripciones latinas del Museo de Málaga (Madrid 1981) no. 13; *PB* 194

88 L. Aelius L. f. Faustinus – IIvir; 2nd century; daughter Aelia Faustina
  CIL II 5524 = *ILER* 1448; *PB* 14

89 M. Iunius L. f. L. n. Gal. Terentianus Servilius Sabinus – IIvir, flamen,
  pontifex perpetuus, patronus
  CIL II 1347 and p 701 = *ILER* 1742; *PB* 205

90 M. Lucretius Marianus – IIvir; perhaps 3rd century
  CIL II 2216 = *ILER* 6049 = Serrano Ramos and Atencia Paez *Inscripciones
  latinas del Museo de Málaga* no. 12; *PB* 217

91 Q. Vibius Laetus – colleague of **90**; IIvir, perhaps curator; possibly 3rd century

    CIL II 2207; *PB* 334; R. Duthoy *Ancient Society* 10 (1979) 195; and see **90**.

92 M. Marcius Gal. Proculus – IIvir; native of Sucaelo; daughter Marcia Procula

    AE 1935, 6 = *ILER* 5505; *PB* 232

93 L. Iunius P. f. Serg. Paulinus – pontifex, flamen perpetuus, IIvir, flamen prov. Baeticae; late 2nd or early 3rd century; dedicated statues costing four hundred thousand HS; provided two plays and a gladiator show

    He is presumably a knight. Also, the tribe Sergia is distinctive, cf *AE* 1976, 285.

    CIL II 5523 = *ILS* 5079 = *ILER* 1720; Etienne *Culte* 130, 203; *PB* 2010

94 ... P. f. Pyramus – see **223**.

Epora municipium Foederatorum (conv. Cordubensis)

95 L. Modius Priscus – IIvir

    CIL II 2161 = *ILER* 1451; *PB* 247

Gades municipium Augustum (conv. Gaditanus)

96 L. Cornelius P. f. L. n. Balbus Minor – IIIIvir of Gades 44–43 BC, quaestor prov. Hispaniae ulterioris 44, proquaestor 43, propraetor ca 40–39, cos. suff. 32, procos. prov. Africae 21–20, pontifex, patron of Norba; born ca 74 and enfranchised as part of the family of his uncle, L. Cornelius Balbus Maior, in the 70s

    Balbus Minor served as an agent of Julius Caesar during the Civil War and was subsequently admitted to the Senate. His high-handed conduct as quaestor allegedly included robbing and torturing the provincials, throwing Roman citizens to the beasts in the amphitheatre, renewing his own quattuorvirate at Gades, and holding the elections for two years in two days. When the provincial governor declared himself inimical to Caesar, Balbus absconded with the provincial treasury. After a successful campaign against the Garamantes he was granted a triumph in 19 BC, and in 13 BC opened a theatre in Rome. He was also the author of a *fabula praetexta* and probably of the *Exegetica*. His daughter Cornelia married C. Norbanus Flaccus, cos. ord. 24 BC. Since Balbus was provincial quaestor at the time of his quattuorvirate, the latter was probably intended as an honorary appointment. Rodríguez Neila (1976) argues that Balbus was a IIIIvir quinquennalis.

    Cic. *Fam.* 10.31–2; Vell. Pat. 2.51.3; *ILER* 6053/6788 = *AE* 1962, 71; *PIR*² B 1331; Broughton *MRR* II 344; L. Rubio *AHAM* 2 (1950) 142–99; Wiegels

no. 56; J.F. Rodríguez Neila *Los Balbos de Cádiz* (Sevilla 1973);
Rodríguez Neila *Gerión* 4 (1986) 84–97

97 L. Fabius L. f. Gal. Rufinus – IIvir, praefectus iure dicundo ab decurionibus
creatus
CIL II 1731 = *ILS* 6908a = *IRPC* 127; *PB* 158; J.F. Rodríguez Neila *El
municipio romano de Gades* (Cádiz 1980) 74

98 L. Antonius Q. f. Gal. Antullus – IIIIvir aedilicia potestate
For a possible relative, cf L. Antonius C. f. Gal. Antullus sacerdos, in *CIL*
II 1728 = *ILS* 8131 = *ILER* 3783 = *IRPC* 124
CIL II 1727 = *IRPC* 123; *PB* 54; Rodríguez Neila (see 97) 71

99 Q. Antonius C. f. Gal. Rogatus – decurio
CIL II 1729 = *ILER* 3544 = *IRPC* 125; Rodríguez Neila (see 97) 51

100 ...s P. f. Gal. ...us – aedilis, possibly IIvir, sacerdos; 1st century AD
There is no justification for restoring the name P. Antonius P. f.
Antullus, as in *IRPC* and Rodríguez Neila.
Eph. Epigr. IX 236 = *IRPC* 346; *PB* 56 = Ignoti 2; Rodríguez Neila (see 97)
71; L.A. Curchin *ZPE* 47 (1982) 108

101 M. Antonius M. f. Syriacus – IIvir; 1st or 2nd century
Hübner thinks the letters in the inscription are Antonine, while García y
Bellido favours a Flavian date. Rodríguez Neila is surely wrong in
assuming that the mention in this inscription of the mun[icipium]
Aug[ustum] Gad[itanum] implies an Augustan date
CIL II 1313 = *ILER* 1486 = *IRPC* 2; A. García y Bellido *Esculturas romanas
de España y Portugal* (Madrid 1949) no. 299; *PB* 57; Rodríguez Neila (see
97) 51

102 L. Valerius Fecula – IIIIvir; 2nd century or later; died at age eighty
The *cognomen* is unique.
AE 1920, 79 = *IRPC* 361; Kajanto *Cognomina* 340; Rodríguez Neila (see 97)
71

103 C. Breccius Secundianus – aedilicia potestate; 2nd century or later
CIL II 1730 = *ILER* 3074 = *IRPC* 126; Rodríguez Neila (see 97) 71

104 Anonymus – IIIIvir
M.J. Jiménez Cisneros *Emerita* 30 (1962) 297 = *HAEp.* 1978 = *IRPC* 445;
PB 20

Hispalis colonia Iulia Romula (conv. Hispalensis)

105 L. Blatius L. f. Serg. Ventinus – tribunus militum legionis v, item tribunus
militum legionis x Gemellae, aedilis, IIvir; Augustan
If the order of offices given in the inscription is correct, Ventinus held

equestrian posts before assuming municipal appointments. He is perhaps related to L. Blattius Traianus (**140**).

CIL II 1176 = *ILER* 6039; *PB* 73; Wiegels no. 228; *PME* B 25

106 L. Horatius L. f. Gal. Victor – IIvir bis; honoured for his munificence to patria and populus

CIL II 1185 = *ILER* 1461–2; *PB* 177

107 Q. Pomponius Clemens Serg. Sabinianus – aedilis, IIvir, pontifex, aug[ur] (or Augusti); parents Q. Pomponius Clodianus and Sabina

CIL II 1188 = *ILER* 1464; *PB* 270

108 Q. Iunius Quir. Venustus – received posthumously the *decurionatus ornamenta* and a funeral oration; father Q. Iunius ..., who reimbursed the colony for the funeral expenses

CIL II 1186 = *ILER* 1463

109 L. Vibius L. f. Gal. Tuscus Aurelius Rufinus – praefectus cohortis I Ausetanorum, possibly aedilis; 2nd century or later.

The Ausetani were Latin citizens of Tarraconensis.

CIL II 1181 = *ILER* 6402; cf Pliny *NH* 3.23; Ptol. 2.4.70; *PB* 338; Wiegels no. 347; *PME* V 107

110 Iulius Ho... – egregius vir, curator; 3rd century

CIL II 6283; *PB* 187

Igabrum municipium Flavium (conv. Astigitanus)

111 M. Aelius M. f. Niger – aedilis; AD 75; granted Roman citizenship per honorem

CIL II 1610 = *ILS* 1981 = *ILER* 174 = A.U. Stylow *Gerión* 4 (1986) 296–8; *PB* 18

Iliberris municipium Florentinum (conv. Astigitanus)

112 L. Galerius L. f. Gal. Valerianus – IIvir, possibly pontifex perpetuus; late 1st or early 2nd century AD

Hübner suggests reading 'IIvir [po]nt.' for the improbable 'IIvi VI.' The *nomen* is rare in Spain, but compare the younger Seneca's uncle, C. Galerius (*PIR*² G 25).

CIL II 2081 = *ILER* 1434 = *ILGranada* 44; *PB* 170

Ilipa (conv. Hispalensis)

113 M. Calpurnius Lucius – decurio; early 3rd century

CIL II 1088 = *ILER* 5798; cf A.M. Canto *Habis* 8 (1977) 421

Ilipula (conv. Hispalensis)

114 M. Curiatius Quir. Longinus – decurio; Flavian or later; presented circuses lasting two days
  CIL II 954 = *ILER* 392
115 M. Cornelius – possibly IIvir; reign of Antoninus Pius
  CIL II 955

Ilipula Laus (conv. Astigitanus)

116 Valerius Ter[entianus?] – magistrate, ca 47–44 BC
  VM 1161 = Gil 1326; *PB* lv
117 L. Flavius L. f. Quir. Gallus – IIIIvir, IIvir bis
  CIL II 1470 and p 702 = *ILER* 1478

Iliturgicola (conv. Astigitanus)

118 L. Porcius L. f. Gal. Maternus – IIvir
  CIL II 1648 = *ILER* 6017; *PB* 276

Ilurco (conv. Astigitanus)

119 P. Cornelius P. f. Quir. Callicus – IIvir; late 2nd or early 3rd century; erected a statue of his mother complete with her ornamenta
  M. Sotomayor *NAH* 8–9 (1964–5) 354, *NAH* 10–12 (1966–8)
  275 = *ILGranada* 60; L.A. Curchin *Historia* 32 (1983) 231–2
120 C. Annius Seneca – IIvir; AD 165–6
  CIL II 5511 = *ILER* 1128 = *ILGranada* 106; *ILER* 1143 = *ILGranada* 96; *PB* 45
121 Q. Cornelius Macer – colleague of **120**
  For a possible relative, cf P. Cornelius Q. [f?] Macer (**311**).
  PB 113; and see **120**.
122 ... Cornelius Rus[ticus] – possibly [II]vir; mid-2nd century
  P. Rodríguez Oliva *Jábega* 25 (1979) 14–20 = *AE* 1981, 515 = *ILGranada* 114

Iluro municipium (conv. Gaditanus)

123 L. Munnius Quir. Novatus – IIvir; reign of Domitian; granted Roman citizenship per honorem
  CIL II 1945 and p 704 = *ILS* 1982 = *ILER* 1090; *PB* 255
124 L. Munnius Quir. Aurelianus – colleague and relative of **123** and enfranchised at the same time
  PB 254 and see **123**.
125 C. Fabius Vibianus – IIvir; mother Vibia Lucana; heir Fabia Firma
  CIL II 1947 = *ILER* 1768; *PB* 163

Ipolcobulcola (conv. Astigitanus)

126 P. Iunius Abitus – iivir
   CIL II 1646 = *ILER* 5338; *PB* 193
127 L. Porcius Quir. Quietus – iivir, pontifex; Flavian or later; built a temple, statue and forum on his own land at his own expense; son T. Porcius Quietus
   CIL II 1649 = *ILER* 2075; *PB* 277

Ipsca municipium Contributum (conv. Astigitanus)

128 Anonymus – iivir
   CIL II 1576
129 Anonymus – iivir
   CIL II 1577
130 C. Sempronius C. f. Quir. Lucretius Salvianus – iivir, patronus, praestantissimus civis; perhaps 2nd century
   CIL II 1597 = *ILER* 1712; *PB* 289

Iptuci (conv. Gaditanus)

131 C. Trebecius Lucanus – one of three men who enacted hospitium between Iptuci and Ucubi in AD 31
   The men were presumably *legati*.
   EJER no. 20 = *AE* 1955, 21 = *HAEp.* 547; *PB* 307
132 C. Attius Severus – colleague of **131**
   For a possible relative, cf. P. Attius Severus, attested in painted amphora inscriptions as an exporter of Spanish oil.
   EJER no. 20 = *AE* 1955, 21 = *HAEp.* 547; *PB* 63; M. Beltrán Lloris *Las ánforas romanas en España* (Zaragoza 1970) 225
133 L. Catinius Optatus -- colleague of **131**
   He is presumably related to Catinia L. f. Sila, also of Iptuci, mentioned in
   CIL II 5484 = *ILER* 1001
   EJER no. 20 = *AE* 1955, 21 = *HAEp.* 547; *PB* 92

Irni municipium Flavium (conv. Hispalensis)

134 ... Caecilius Optatus – iivir; AD 91
   Together with **135** he arranged for the inscribing of the Lex Irnitana and Domitian's letter on marriage. Another Caecilius Optatus, possibly related, appears at Barcino (**445**).
   Irn. colophon
135 Caecilius Montanus – legatus; AD 91; named in conjunction with **134**
   González suggests that he brought both the municipal law and the letter

back from Rome to be promulgated locally by Caecilius Optatus, for *Irn.* 95 stipulates that one of the IIvirs must see that the law is inscribed and publicly displayed.

Irn. colophon; J. González *JRS* 76 (1986) 238

Isturgi municipium Triumphale (conv. Cordubensis)

136 A. Terentius A. f. Gal. Rusticus – aedilis, IIvir, pontifex; Antonine; provided a dramatic spectacle at his own expense.

CIL II 2121 = *ILER* 6076; *PB* 301

137 Sempronius Fau[stus?] – legatus; arranged hospitium between Isturgi and Licinius Iulianus

The latter is doubtless a patron.

AE 1942, 23 = *AE* 1969–70, 746

138 Anonymus – colleague of **137**

See **137**.

Italica municipium, later colonia Ulpia or Aelia Augusta (conv. Hispalensis)

See also Addenda **975**.

139 L. Herius L. f. – IIvir iterum, IIvirali potestate ter, pontifex creatus Augusto primus; built arches and colonnades for the *municipium*

Since **140** and **141** were also *pontifices creati primi* there appear to have been at least three charter members in the local pontifical college (cf same situation at Urso, *Urs.* 67). The foundation of the *municipium* may be dated on numismatic evidence – coins with the image of Augustus and legend 'per[missu] Aug[usti]' – to ca 15 BC. The lack of a personal *cognomen* is also suggestive of an early date, as is the absence of 'divo' with 'Augusto.' The inscription was found in the theatre, which dates to the principate of Augustus. On other Herii at Italica, see *CIL* II 1150–1.

A. Blanco Freijeiro *BRAH* 180 (1983) 13–15 = *AE* 1983, 522

140 L. Blattius L. f. Traianus Pollio – IIvir designatus iterum, pontifex primus creatus

This man and his colleague (**141**) built at their own expense the orchestra, proscaenium, parodoi, altars, and statues in the Augustan theatre. This is the first appearance in history of a Traianus; Italica also later produced Trajan the emperor.

AE 1978, 402; A.M. Canto in *La religión romana en Hispania* (Madrid 1981) 143–5

141 C. Fabius C. f. Pollio – colleague of **140**

AE 1978, 402

142 L. Raius L. f. Serg. Plebeiius – iivir ter.
   CIL II 1129 = *ILER* 1677

143 Anonymus – curator; ca reign of Trajan
   CIL II 1122; *PB* Ignoti 12

144 ...Caecilianus – adlectus [a Tr]aian[o].
   He was presumably adlected to the local *ordo* by the emperor, if the
   restoration is correct.
   unpublished inscription from the theatre, now in the Italica Museum

145 M. Cassius Serg. Caecilianus – flamen perpetuus divi Traiani, flaminalis
   prov. Baeticae, iivir; 2nd century, possibly reign of Marcus Aurelius;
   erected four statues to the *genius* of the colony
   P. León Alonzo in *Italica (Santiponce Sevilla)* (Madrid 1982) 117 = *AE*
   1982, 520 = Blanco Freijeiro *BRAH* 180 (1983) 2–7

146 C. Agrius Rupus Silonis f. – adlected as a decurion of Italica.
   He was perhaps a native of Mirobriga in Lusitania, whence the inscription.
   AE 1964, 276 = *HAEp.* 2685; J. Gagé *Rev. Et. Anc.* 71 (1969) 75

147 M. Sentius M. f. Serg. Maurianus – aedilis, iivir, augur perpetuus; mid-2nd
   century; a native of Italica; made a dedication to Apollo, perhaps a statue
   Blanco Freijeiro *BRAH* 180 (1983) 7–8 = *AE* 1983, 520

148 ...cus – [aedilis?], iivir, possibly praefectus militum sagittariorum
   unpublished inscription from the theatre; now in the Italica Museum

149 Licinius Victor – iivir under Marcus Aurelius
   He is perhaps related to the Licinii Victores of Munigua (cf **180**). The
   inscription mentioning this magistrate and his colleague refers to enemy
   activity in Baetica – presumably the Moorish invasion of ca 172 (S.H.A.
   Marc. 21.1).
   CIL II 1120 = *ILS* 1354 = *ILER* 1470; A. d'Ors *Emerita* 18 (1950) 329; *PB*
   213

150 Fabius Aelianus – colleague of **149**
   PB 145 and see **149**.

151 M. Lucretius Q. f. Quir. Iulianus – equo publico [donatus], procurator
   Augustorum trium prov. Baeticae, item procurator kalendari Vegetiani, item
   procurator vigesimae hereditatium prov. Baeticae et Lusitaniae, curator rei
   publicae Italicensium; between 209 and 211
   A.M. Canto *Habis* 4 (1973) 311–18 = *AE* 1972, 250; R. Duthoy *Ancient
   Society* 10 (1979) 195

152 Aurelius Ursinus – vir egregius, curator rei publicae Italicensium; AD 276
   The title *vir egregius* suggests that Aurelius Ursinus had been a
   procurator.
   CIL II 1115 = *ILS* 593 = *ILER* 1199; *PB* 68a

153 Aurelius Iulius – vir perfectissimus, agens vices praesidis under Florianus
   (AD 276); curator rei publicae Italicensium under Probus, (276–82)

CIL II 1115 = ILS 593 = ILER 1199; CIL II 1116 = ILER 1200; PIR² A 1539;
Alföldy *Fasti* 174

Ituc[c]i colonia Virtus Iulia (conv. Astigitanus)

154 M. Pompeius Q. f. Gal. Icstnis – IIvir; Augustan
He is the first known duovir from the *familia* Pompeia and his *cognomen*
is obviously non-Roman.
CIL II 1585 = ILER 1675; PB 268; Albertos OPP 276; J.F. Rodríguez Neila in
Actas del I Congreso de Historia de Andalucía (Córdoba 1978) 206

155 Cn. Pompeius Cn. f. Afer – aedilis, IIvir; Augustan
He is possibly related to **154**; however, the *nomen* is very common.
CIL II 1596; PB 267

156 Q. Mummius L. f. Gal. Gallus – IIvir
CIL II 1584 = ILER 1674a; PB 248

157 Numisius Si... Stabilis – possibly praetor tutelarius; late 2nd or 3rd
century
The inscription is very fragmentary, and contains a later mention of
'annona plebi.'
CIL II 1599

Iulipa municipium (conv. Cordubensis)

158 M. Cornelius Proculus – aedilis
Eph. Epigr. IX 253 = A. García y Bellido and J. Menéndez Pidal *El distylo
sepulcral romano de Iulipa (Zalamea)* (Madrid 1963) no. 13 = ILER 5553;
PB 116

159 L. Attius L. f. Gal. Optatus – decurio; a native of Arsa
García y Bellido (see **158**) no. 26 = ILER 6845

160 ...lius ... – IIvir, decurio; possibly a native of Emerita
García y Bellido (see **158**) no. 25 = ILER 6846; PB 180

Lacilbula (conv. Gaditanus)

161 M. Fabius ... – possibly legatus; AD 5
He was one of four magistrates who enacted *hospitium* with Q. Marius
Balbus.
CIL II 1343 = ILS 6097 = ILER 5833; PB 143; Thouvenot *Essai*² 225

162 M. Manilius ... – colleague of **161**
PB 221 and see **161**.

163 P. Cornelius ... – colleague of **161**
PB 100 and see **161**.

164 C. Fabius ... – colleague of **161** and possibly his brother
PB 142 and see **161**.

Lacippo perhaps municipium (conv. Gaditanus)

165 Anonymus – ııvir
CIL ıı 1936 and p 875 = ILER 1547
166 Rusticus – colleague of **165**
See **165**.
167 Q. Fabius Q. f. Varus – pontifex, vvir; AD 14–37; dedicated an open-air
crypt to *divus Augustus* at his own expense.
This is the only quinquevir attested in Spain, but the reading of the stone
is unequivocal. Etienne prefers, however, to see it as a mason's error for
'ıvvir.'
R. Puertas Tricas and P. Rodríguez Oliva *Mainake* 1 (1979)
99–104 = same authors, *Estudios sobre la ciudad romana de Lacipo*
(Valladolid 1980) 23–7 = R. Etienne *ZPE* 43 (1981) 135–42 = AE 1981,
504 = E. Serrano Ramos and R. Atencia Paez *Inscripciones latinas del
Museo de Málaga* (Madrid 1981) no. 8

Lascuta (conv. Gaditanus)

168 A. Irthi – magistrate; ca 57 BCcmBeltrán Martínez suggests reading
'Hirthi[us].' Such a variant of Hirtius is certainly not implausible.
VM 92:9 = Gil 1414; A. Beltrán Martínez *Numismática antigua*
(Cartagena 1950) 448; PB xx
169 Scuic... – magistrate, ca 47–44 BC
The name appears to be indigenous.
VM 92:2 = Gil 1416

Lucurgentum (conv. Hispalensis)

170 M. Helvius Anthus – sevir Augustalis; provided games, theatre shows, and
a gymnasium for four days, as well as free admission for women to the
baths, and a statue
He was granted ornamenta decurionatus by the ordo (cf the sevir
similarly honoured at Arva, **13**.
HAEp. 166 = AE 1953, 21 = ILER 1732

Malaca municipium Flavium (conv. Gaditanus)

171 L. Octavius L. f. Rusticus – aedilis
CIL ıı 1967 = ILER 503; PB 260

172 L. Granius M. f. Balbus – aedilis, colleague of **171**
PB 171 and see **171**.

Mellaria municipium (conv. Cordubensis)

173 C. Annius C. f. Quir. Annianus – IIvir bis, pontifex perpetualis; Flavian or
later; provided a water supply (presumably an aqueduct) for the city
CIL II 2343 = ILER 2047; PB 36

Montemolín (ancient name unknown; conv. Hispalensis)

174 L. Norbanus ...f. Mensor – perhaps aedilis bis, IIvir; 1st century AD
CIL II 6337; PB 257

Munigua municipium Flavium (conv. Hispalensis)

175 L. Lucceius L. f. – magistrate under Augustus or Tiberius
Alföldy Fasti 182–3 = ILER 5831; PB 215
176 L. Octavius M. f. Silvanus – legatus; held office at the same time as **175**
PB 261 and see **175**.
177 L. Servilius L. f. Pollio – IIIIvir bis, praefectus C. Caesaris IIIIvirali potestate,
pontifex or flamen sacrorum publicorum municipalium under Tiberius,
pontifex divi Augusti.
A male relative, possibly his son, lent a large sum of money to the town,
the repayment of which was enforced by a rescript of Titus (AE 1962,
288). His wife Postumia Q. f. Prisca was perhaps related to Q. Postumius
Hyginus and Postumia Cypare of Carmo, where Servilius Pollio was
buried. She is not likely to have been their daughter, as Bonsor had
proposed: indeed, their inscription (CIL II 5422 = ILER 4660) appears to date
to the 2nd century. Thouvenot even considers them freedmen.
CIL II 5120 = ILER 5680; G. Bonsor *Archaeological Sketch-book of the
Roman Necropolis at Carmona* (New York 1931) 111–12; Etienne *Culte*
202; PB 295; Thouvenot *Essai²* 555; Galsterer *Untersuchungen* 5 n 34;
M. Bendala Galán *La necrópolis romana de Carmona* (Sevilla 1976) 83
178 Anonymi – IIIIviri, AD 79
AE 1962, 288 = Alföldy Fasti 159
179 Valerius Quir. Firmus – perhaps IIvir bis; Flavian; built a temple, forum,
etc. for the city
F. Collantes and C. Chicarro AEA 45–7 (1972–4) 366–8 = AE 1972, 268–9
180 C. Licinius Victor Annianus – probably a magistrate; wife Aelia L. f.
Procula
He was undoubtedly a relative of L. Licinius Annianus who made a
dedication to a Flavian emperor. A Licinius Victor also made a dedication
to Titus. The double *cognomen* suggests a possible lineage:

L. Licinius Annianus
|
...Licinius Victor
|
C. Licinius Victor Annianus

Collantes and Chicarro *AEA* 45–7 (1972–4) 364 = *AE* 1972, 264; cf *CIL* II 1050–1 = *ILER* 1248, 6051

181 L. Quintius L. f. Quir. Rufinus – IIvir bis; early 2nd century
Collantes and Chicarro *AEA* 45–7 (1972–4) 362–4

182 Anonymus – perhaps IIIIvir; early 2nd century
This inscription might, however, refer to a [II]IIIIvir.
Collantes and Chicarro *AEA* 45–7 (1972–4) 386

183 T. Aemilius T. f. Quir. Pudens – IIvir bis; mid–2nd century; wife Fulvia
Collantes and Chicarro *AEA* 45–7 (1972–4) 365–6, 368–9 = *AE* 1972, 265–6

184 L. Quintius L. f. L. n. Quir. Rufus – son of **181**; IIvir bis; late 2nd century
Collantes and Chicarro *AEA* 45–7 (1972–4) 345 = *AE* 1972, 252; Collantes and Chicarro *AEA* 45–7 (1972–4) 392–4

185 T. Aemilius T. f. T. n. Quir. Pudens – son of **183**; IIvir bis; late 2nd or early 3rd century
Collantes and Chicarro *AEA* 45–7 (1972–4) 391 = *AE* 1972, 267 = *CIL* II 1378 = *ILER* 1476; *PB* 27; L.A. Curchin *ZPE* 47 (1982) 108–9

Naeva municipium Flavium (conv. Hispalensis)

186 L. Aelius Quir. Aelianus – IIvir; Flavian or later; wife Egnatia M. f. Lupercilla
CIL II 1191 = *ILER* 1472; *HAEp.* 1027 = *AE* 1958, 39 = *ILER* 1735; *PB* 11, 303

Oba (conv. Gaditanum)

187 L. Cornelius Herennius Rusticus – IIvir; 2nd century AD; grandson of L. Herennius Herennianus, whom he buried on 9 March 151
CIL II 1330, 1332–3 = *ILER* 1501, 5845, 6536 = *IRPC* 523, 525–6; *PB* 112

188 M. Sentius Restitutus – colleague of **187**
CIL II 1330 = *ILER* 1501 = *IRPC* 523; *PB* 291

Obulco municipium Pontificiense (conv. Cordubensis)

189 Situbolai – magistrate; mid–2nd century BC
VM 94:7 = Gil 409, 413; A. Arévalo González *Revista de Arqueología* 74 (June 1987) 32

190 Urkail – colleague of **189**

'Urka-' is a common Iberian prefix.

Albertos *OPP* 256; and see **189**.

191 Iskeratin – magistrate; second half of 2nd century BC

The Iberian element 'Isker-' appears also at Emporiae (**686**).

VM 95:1, 3 = Gil 410–11, 416; Arévalo (see **189**) 33; Albertos *OPP* 125

192 Tuitubolai – colleague of **191**

See **191**.

193 Iltireur – magistrate; second half of 2nd century BC

VM 94:8–9, 95:2 = Gil 414–15; Arévalo (see **189**) 33

194 Ka...suritu – colleague of **193**

The undeciphered Iberian symbol between 'ka' and 's' is possibly to be read 'ku' or 'ba.'

See **193**.

195 Sikai – magistrate; second half of 2nd century BC

VM 96:3 = Gil 421–2; Arévalo (see **189**) 33

196 Otaiis – colleague of **195**

See **195**.

197 Urkailtu – magistrate; second half of 2nd century BC

The name appears to be a compound of Urkail (**190**).

VM 95:5–6 = Gil 417–19; Arévalo (see **189**) 33; Albertos *OPP* 256

198 Neseltuko – colleague of **197**

See **197**.

199 [E]koeki – magistrate; second half of 2nd century BC

The first letter of the magistrate's name is quite uncertain.

VM 95:7–10, 96:1, 4 = Gil 420, 423–5, 427–8; Arévalo (see **189**) 33

200 Botilkos – colleague of **199**

'Bot-' or 'Bod-' is a common Iberian prefix.

Albertos *OPP* 57; and see **199**.

201 Ilteratin – magistrate; 2nd century BC

Both elements of this Iberian name can be seen in others from Obulco, viz Iltereur (**193**) and Iskeratin (**191**).

VM 96:2 = Gil 426, 429; Arévalo (see **189**) 33; Albertos *OPP* 123

202 Kolon – colleague of **201**

See **201**.

203 Tuituiboren – magistrate; second half of 2nd century BC

For a similar name, cf Tuitubolai (**192**)

VM 95:4 = Gil 412; Arévalo (see **189**) 33

204 ...ntuakoi – colleague of **203**

The reading of the first syllable is disputed.

See **203**.

205 Ilno – magistrate; probably second half of 2nd century BC, as are **207–9**.

Gil dates the coin with this magistrate's name to ca 47–44 BC; Arévalo to
the mid–2nd century BC. The reason for the dating difficulty is that the
obverse and reverse designs are those of the 2nd century but the names
of the magistrates are in Latin, not Iberian, characters.

VM 94:3 = Gil 1471; Arévalo (see **189**) 32; *PB* xxi, xxxvii

206 Naal – colleague of **205**
VM 94:3 = Gil 1471; Arévalo (see **189**) 32

207 Bodilcos – magistrate; ca 120–90 BC
The spelling is clearly a Latinized version of the Iberian name Botilkos (cf
200), though it does not necessarily refer to the same individual.
VM 97:5 = Gil 435; *PB* xi; Albertos *OPP* 57

208 [Insani?] – magistrate; second half of 2nd century BC
The name is perhaps indigenous. Arévalo reads 'Mihsam,' but the
photograph is indecisive.
VM 97:6 = Gil 439; Arévalo (see **189**) 34; *PB* xxii. On the name, see F.
Beltrán Lloris *Numisma* 28 (1978) 185; but Schulze (*Eigennamen* 175–6)
records an Etruscan name *insni*, whence Latin 'Insianus' etc.

209 Sisiren – colleague of **208**
The name is Iberian.
VM 97:6 = Gil 439; Arévalo (see **189**) 34; *PB* li; J. Untermann *Elementos
de un atlas antroponímico de la Hispania antigua* (Madrid 1965) 162; Albertos *OPP* 210

210 Co[rnelius] Ni[ger?] – pr[aefectus?]; ca 120–90 BC
VM 94:2 = Gil 408; cf VM p 56; *PB* xiv

211 L. Aemilius – aedilis; ca 120–90 BC
VM 96:6 = Gil 430; Arévalo (see **189**) 34; *PB* iii

212 M. Iunius – colleague of **211**
PB xxvi; and see **211**.

213 Atiti[m?] – perhaps magistrate
The name appears to be non-Roman, with parallels in Upper Germany
('Atitio') and Spain ('Atitta'). However, Castillo proposes the reading 'A.
Titi[us],' perhaps rightly.
VM 97:10; *PB* liv; Albertos *OPP* 39; cf M. Beltrán Lloris *Las ánforas
romanas en España* (Zaragoza 1970) 121 no. 36

214 Nig[er?] – magistrate; ca 67 BC
For another Niger, cf **210**.
VM 97:12–14, 98:1, 173:4 = Gil 1461–4, 1467; Arévalo (see **189**) 35; *PB*
xxxviii

215 Cn. [Nic]om[edes] – magistrate; ca 67 BC
VM 98:3 = Gil 1468

216 Anonymus – possibly IIIIvir; ca 67 BC

The coin bears the legend 'IIII'; but a different interpretation is not excluded.

VM 98:6 = Gil 1470

217 C. Cornelius C. f. C. n. Gal. Caeso – aedilis, flamen, IIvir; Vespasianic. His homonymous son was a *sacerdos* and possibly *pontifex*.

CIL II 2126 = *ILS* 6911 = *ILER* 1777; Etienne *Culte* 202; *PB* 107

218 [Q?] Quintius Q. f. Q. n. Q. pron. Q. abn. Gal. Hispanus ...us – aedilis, flamen, IIvir, pontifex, [pro?]curator Baetis, praefectus cohortis primae ...rum equitatae, comes et adsessor legati ad census accipiendos, comes et adsessor proconsulis prov. Galliae Narbonensis; 2nd century AD.

He provided 'tabernas et posthorreum' at his own expense. No one has explained the otherwise unattested word *posthorreum*: I would instead propose reading 'tabernas et post horreum,' i.e., 'shops, even behind the granary' (where they perhaps were not very visible or were outside the existing commercial zone). The restoration '[pro]curator' is uncertain, although a 'procurator Augustorum ad ripam Baetis' is known (*CIL* II 1180 = *ILS* 1403).

CIL II 2129 = *ILS* 1404; Pflaum *Carrières* 61, 1049; *EREsp.* 108–12; *PB* 286; Wiegels no. 322; *PME* Q 2

219 Cornelius L. f. Gal. ... – aedilis; sister Cornelia L. f. Anus

CIL II 2130 = *ILS* 5497 = *ILER* 1713; *PB* 99

220 [L?] ...nicius L. f. L. n. L. pron. Gal. Mento Man... – aedilis, IIvir i.d., praefectus IIvirali potestate, praefectus fabrum, pontifex, aug[ur] (or pontifex Augusti)

CIL II 2149a and p 886 = *ILER* 1542; *PB* Ignoti 6

221 L. Porcius L. f. Gal. Stilo – aedilis, IIvir designatus; received an equestrian statue

CIL II 2131 = *ILER* 5375; *PB* 280

222 M. Valerius M. f. M. n. Q. pron. Pullinus – IIvir, legatus perpetuus municipii, praefectus fabrum, flamen, pontifex, aug[ur] (or pontifex Augusti)

CIL II 2132 = *ILS* 6908 = *ILER* 1415; *PB* 319

223 ... P. f. Pyramus – IIvir at Corduba and Obulco; probably 2nd century; buried at the latter town, aged seventy

Given the Greek *cognomen*, perhaps he was the son of a freedman.

CIL II 2133 = *ILER* 5396; *PB* Ignoti 8

Onuba (conv. Cordubensis)

224 C. Aelius – magistrate; ca 47–44 BC

VM 102:1–3 = Gil 1488–90; *PB* i

225 Q. Publilius – colleague of **224**
   PB xlvii; and see **224**.
226 P. Terentius – magistrate, ca 47–44 BC
   VM 102:4 = Gil 1487; *PB* lii
227 Colp. – colleague of **226**
   The name is indigenous, or an abbreviation for 'Co[rnelius] L ...
   pr[aefectus]' or the like.
   PB xii; and see **226**.

Osqua municipium (conv. Astigitanus)

228 C. Licinius C. f. Agrinus – 11vir bis
   His *cognomen* is otherwise unknown but presumably a variant of
   Agrianus. His father and son are both named C. Licinius Agrippinus.
   CIL II 2030 = *ILS* 5488 = *ILER* 1751; E. Serrano Ramos and R. Atencia Paez
   Inscripciones latinas del Museo de Málaga (Madrid 1981) no. 52 = *AE*
   1981, 506; *PB* 209
229 P. Coelius ... f. Rutilus – possibly 11vir
   The crucial line of the text may be read either '11v[ir]' or 'Ilu[ronensis].'
   CIL II 2032 = *ILER* 2551

Osset municipium Iulia Constantia (conv. Hispalensis)

230 L. Luc[ius?] – magistrate; late 1st century BC
   VM 111:2 = Gil 1506; *PB* xxix
231 P. Vet[tius?] – colleague of **230**
   PB lvii; and see **230**.
232 L. Caesius L. f. Pollio – aedilis, 11vir and census-taker ('censu et duomviratu
   bene acto'); 1st or early 2nd century AD
   CIL II 1256 = *ILS* 6918 = *ILER* 1469; *PB* 80
233 Q. Cornelius Q. f. Quir. Senex – 11vir quater; Antonine; daughter Cornelia
   Fabulla
   As Zevi and D'Arms point out, a fourth term of office as duovir is rare,
   at least in Italy, after the Augustan age.
   CIL II 1258 = *ILER* 1678 = A.M. Canto *MM* 20 (1979) 333; *PB* 123; cf F.
   Zevi *Mélanges d'arch.* 85 (1973) 555–78; J.H. D'Arms *Bulletin of the
   American Society of Papyrologists* 21 (1984) 49–54

Ostippo oppidum liberum (conv. Astigitanus)

234 Q. Larius L. f. Niger – xvir maximus; ca AD 15–20
   He dedicated an inscription to the younger Drusus. Cf note at **71** on the
   decemvirate.
   CIL II 5048 = *ILER* 1057; *PB* 208

Sabora municipium Flavium (conv. Astigitanus)

235 C. Cornelius Severus – iivir; AD 77
  CIL II 1423 = *ILS* 6092; *PB* 124; Galsterer *Untersuchungen* 41 n 34
236 M. Septimius Severus – colleague of **235**; perhaps father of Septimia M. f. Severa in *CIL* II 1432
  PB 292; and see **235**.

Sacili municipium Martialium (conv. Cordubensis)

237 Ola f. – magistrate; second half of 1st century BC
  The name is indigenous.
  VM 113:2 = Gil 1519; *PB* xliii; Albertos *OPP* 172
238 L... – magistrate; second half of 1st century BC
  VM 113:5 = Gil 1520
239 V. f. [P?] – magistrate; second half of 1st century BC
  Gil 1521
240 L. Acilius L. f. Gal. Barba – iivir; 2nd century AD; daughter, or perhaps sister, Acilia L. f. Lepidina
  CIL II 2188 = *ILER* 6361; *PB* 5
241 L. Acilius L. f. L. n. Gal. Terentianus – iivir, possibly flamen; son of **240** wife Cornelia Q. f. Lepidina
  PB 10; and see **240**.

Saepo municipium V[ictrix?] (conv. Gaditanus)

242 Fabius Senecio – iivir; late 2nd century AD
  CIL II 1340 = *ILER* 1131 = *IRPC* 540; *PB* 160a
243 Fabius Pollio – iivir, colleague of **242**.
  PB 155; and see **242**.

Salpensa municipium Flavium (conv. Hispalensis)

244 L. Marcius L. f. L. n. L. pron. C. abn. Quir. Saturninus – 2nd century AD
  He was awarded the *ornamenta decurionatus*, a funeral and an equestrian statue by the city upon his death at age eighteen. His father remitted the expense. The long pedigree suggests an important local family.
  CIL II 1286 = *ILER* 1741

Sanlúcar la Mayor (ancient name unknown; conv. Hispalensis)

245 Anonymus – iivir; apparently Neronian
  CIL II 1266

246 C. Lucius ... – perhaps iiiivir, but might be a [ii]iiiivir
    CIL II 1271 = *ILER* 1740

Segida Restituta Iulia (conv. Hispalensis)

247 C. Varinius Fidus – aedilis, iivir, flaminalis prov. Baeticae; end of 2nd or beginning of 3rd century; daughter Varinia Flaccina, who was wife of Licinius Serenianus, governor of Cappadocia under Maximinus
    CIL II 983 = *Eph. Epigr.* VIII 89 = *ILS* 6904; Etienne *Culte* 129–30; *PB* 329

Siarum municipium Fortunale (conv. Hispalensis)

248 Cn. Servilius Cn. f. Gal. Niger – iivir, interrex; late 1st century BC
    He is the only attested interrex in Spain, although *Urs.* 130 allows for such an appointment.
    J. González Fernández in *Actas del I Congreso andaluz de estudios clásicos* (Jaén 1982) 223 = *AE* 1982, 511 = González *ZPE* 55 (1984) 85

Singilia Barba municipium Flavium liberum (conv. Astigitanus)
See also Addenda **976**.

249 C. Fabius Rusticus – apparently a iivir; reign of Marcus Aurelius
    CIL II 2015 = *ILS* 1354a = *ILER* 1487; Pflaum *Carrières* 586; *PB* 160
250 L. Aemilius Pontianus – colleague of **249**
    CIL II 2015 = *ILS* 1354a = *ILER* 1487; *PB* 26
251 M. Acilius M'. f. Quir. Phlegon – son of the local *patronus* M'. Acilius Fronto and his wife/freedwoman Acilia Plecusa (*CIL* II 2016, 2019–20 = *ILER* 1488, 5454–5), sister Acilia Sept[umina]
    He received the *ornamenta decurionalia*. His Greek *cognomen* suggests that he might have been born before his mother's manumission.
    CIL II 2017–18 = *ILER* 1489–90; J.F. Rodríguez Neila *Sociedad y administración en la Bética romana* (Córdoba 1981) 42

Torre de Albolafia (ancient name unknown; conv. Cordubensis)

252 ... Crassus – iivir; AD 80–120; honoured after his death with a eulogy, statue, and funeral by the decurions
    C. Puerta and A.U. Stylow *Gerión* 3 (1985) 333–7 = *AE* 1985, 565

Tucci colonia Augusta Gemella (conv. Astigitanus)

253 Q. Iulius Q. f. T. n. Serg. Celsus – aedilis, IIvir bis; Augustan
    CIL II 1666, 1679 = *ILER* 1023, 6084; *PB* 183

254 L. Iulius L. f. Serg. Culleo – IIvir
  CIL II 1680 = *ILER* 6378; *PB* 185

255 C. Iulius C. f. Serg. Scaena – decurio equitum, centurio hastatus primus
  legionis IIII, IIvir; daughter Iulia Laeta, flaminica
  He probably served in *legio* IIII *Macedonica*, which was stationed in Spain
  until AD 43.
  CIL II 1681 = *ILER* 5672; E. Birley *Roman Britain and the Roman Army*
  (Kendal 1953) 117; *PB* 188

256 L. Mummius Serg. Rufus – IIvir, pontifex
  CIL II 1684 = *ILER* 1676; *PB* 252

257 L. Licinius ... – praefectus
  CIL II 1683

258 Anonymus – aedilis
  CIL II 1688

259 Q. Antonius ... – praefectus
  CIL II 1675

260 P. Cornelius Firmus – aedilis, IIvir; 2nd century or later
  CIL II 1676 = *ILER* 5554; *PB* 110

261 ... Cornelius L. f. Savo – aedilis, IIvir, pontifex
  HAEp. 2274 = *AE* 1965, 78 = *ILER* 1420

262 Iulius Claudius – curator [rei publicae?]; AD 280
  CIL II 1673 = *ILS* 596 = *ILER* 1203

Ucubi colonia Claritas Iulia (conv. Astigitanus)

263 T. Iulius T. f. ... – aedilis
  CIL II 2223 = *ILER* 1453; *PB* 181

264 Anonymus – possibly aedilis designatus
  CIL II 1560

265 Anonymus – IIvir, praefectus Imp. Caesaris
  CIL II 1558; *PB* Ignoti 17

266 C. Lucretius Fronto Fabianus – decurio; died at age nineteen
  unpublished inscription in the Córdoba Museum

267 Valerius [Chalcidicus?] – curator, procurator Augusti, curator rei publicae
  colonorum Claritatis Iuliae; AD 196
  S. de los Santos Gener *Memorias de los Museos Provinciales* 4 (1943) 83
  and pl XVIII, 1; *PB* 314a

Ugia municipium Martiense (conv. Cordubensis)

268 P. Mummius P. f. Gal. Ursus – legatus; AD 6; sent to Emerita to establish
  hospitium
  AE 1952, 49 = *EJER* no. 18 = *HAEp.* 546 = *ILER* 5830

269 M. Aemilius M. f. Gal. Fronto – colleague of **268**
See **268**.

Ugultuniacum municipium Contributa Iulia (conv. Hispalensis)

270 Q. Manlius Gal. Avitus – IIvir bis; possibly pre-Flavian; daughter Manlia Avita
    CIL II 1029 = *ILER* 5306; *PB* 227

Ulia municipium Fidentia (conv. Astigitanus)

271 Binsnes Vercellonis f. – xvir maximus; 49 BC
    He and M. Coranus (**272**) constructed a city gate (*porta*) at their own expense during the Civil War. The mention of the governor Q. Cassius Longinus indicates that Ulia was pro-Caesarian.
    C. Castillo *Stud. Doc. Hist. Iur.* 52 (1986) 377

272 M. Coranus Acrini f. Alpis – aedilis; 49 BC
    For his building activity, see **271**. His *nomen* is rare.
    See **271**.

273 L. Cornelius L. f. Gal. Niger – IIvir, pontifex sacrorum; beginning of 1st century AD
    A.M. Canto *Habis* 5 (1974) 222 = *AE* 1974, 373

274 P. Aelius P. f. Fabianus Pater – aedilis, IIvir, praefectus C. Caesaris, praefectus iterum, pontifex sacrorum, flamen divi Augusti under Tiberius; a native of Corduba
    C. Aelius Fabianus, attested in painted amphora inscriptions as an exporter of Spanish oil, is possibly a relative.
    CIL II 1534; Etienne *Culte* 202; *PB* 13; M. Beltrán Lloris *Las ánforas romanas en España* (Zaragoza 1970) 217–18

275 L. Aemilius M. f. M. n. Cato – aedilis, IIvir, praefectus
    CIL II 1535 = *ILER* 1673; *PB* 23

276 L. Calpurnius L. f. Gal. Pannonius – IIvir
    CIL II 1536 = *ILER* 1674; *PB* 83

277 L. Fabius L. f. Gal. Tuscus – IIvir
    CIL II 1537 = *ILER* 1450; *PB* 162

278 L. Calpurnius L. f. Gal. Danquinus – aedilis, IIvir, praefectus; 2nd century
    The *cognomen* appears to be a variant spelling of the common Lusitanian name Tancinus. He is perhaps a relative of **276**
    Canto *Habis* 5 (1974) 222 = *AE* 1974, 373

279 Q. Caesius M. f. P. n. P. pron. Hirrus Aelius Pairvinus Fabianus – aedilis, IIvir, flamen quinquennalis divorum Augustorum, pontifex sacrorum perpetuus

Cf Aelius Fabianus (274) for a possible relative.

HAEp. 1023 = *ILER* 1545; *PB* 79

280 M. Maenius Cornelianus – curator annonae; AD 212

It is unclear whether this official is an elected magistrate or a public servant.

CIL II 1532 = *ILER* 1701; *PB* 219

Ulisi (conv. Astigitanus)

281 L. Iunius Barbarus – native of Ulisi; municipal decurion at Ulisi or a neighbouring town; late 2nd century

Canto would make him the son of L. Iunius Maurus, *magister Larum Augustalium* at Singilia Barba (*CIL* II 2013 = *ILER* 230), on the assumption that their *cognomina* both reflect an African origin. By virtue of his title, Maurus is a *libertinus*, but sons of freedmen are sometimes decurions.

A.M. Canto *Habis* 8 (1977) 420–2 = l.M. González-Pardo AEA 50–1 (1977–8) 57–76 = AE 1977, 442 = *ILGranada* 137

282 C. T[erentius?] Fabianus – perhaps IIvir; late 2nd century

CIL II 5499 = *ILER* 5456 = *ILGranada* 92

Urgavo municipium Albense (conv. Astigitanus)

283 L. Aemilius L. f. Nigellus – aedilis, IIvir; dedicated an inscription to Augustus in AD 11–12

CIL II 2106 = *ILER* 1030; *PB* 25

284 A. Cantilius ... – IIvir bis

The *nomen* is unusual, presumably formed from Cantius; cf below 377.

CIL II 2113; *PB* 88

285 M. Horatius M. f. Gal. Bodon – IIvir; native of Iluro; wife Lucretia L. f. Sergeton

CIL II 2114 = *ILER* 1427; *PB* 176

286 L. Calpurnius L. f. Gal. Silvinus – IIvir bis, flamen sacrorum publicorum, pontifex domus Augustae

CIL II 2105 = *ILS* 6910 = *ILER* 210; Etienne *Culte* 203; *PB* 87

287 M. ...vius M. f. Gal. Novatus – IIvir, pontifex divi Augusti under Tiberius

Castillo restores the *nomen* 'Helvius' on the basis of *CIL* II 2116 = *ILER* 1560

CIL II 2115 = *ILER* 1444; Etienne *Culte* 202; *PB* 173

Urso colonia Genetiva Iulia Urbanorum (conv. Astigitanus)

288 L. Ap. Dec. – q[uaestor?]; 1st century BC

He is possibly a quaestor of Rome rather than a local magistrate, though the evidence for this hypothesis is now questionable (see discussion in chapter 4).

VM 112:3–8 = Gil 1570–2; Grant *FITA* 24; *PB* vi

289 Anonymi – legati; 45 BC; murdered by a Pompeian partisan
BHisp. 22

290 Anonymi – principes; 45 BC; presumably magistrates of some sort, who were treacherously murdered by adherents of the Pompeian faction
BHisp. 22

291 C. Vettius C. f. Serg. – centurio legionis xxx, IIvir iterum.
The Thirtieth Legion was created by Julius Caesar in 49 or 48 (*BAlex.* 53.5). Vettius will then have been one of the first duovirs of the colony at Urso.
CIL II 5438 = *ILS* 2233; *PB* 333

292 ...ius L. f. Gal. Gallus – [IIvir?], praefectus fabrum; 1st century AD
CIL II 5442 = *ILER* 6655; *PB* 284

293 M. Valerius M. f. Serg. Sabinus – IIvir, pontifex perpetuus
CIL II 5441 = *AE* 1952, 120 = *ILER* 1543; *PB* 321

294 C. Aemilius C. f. Serg. Faustinus – awarded the ornamenta IIviralia upon his death at age nineteen
J. González Fernández *Habis* 8 (1977) 437 = *AE* 1978, 416

295 Anonymus – curator under Commodus
Thouvenot, followed by Ganghoffer, erroneously attributes him to Astigi; in fact, the inscription comes from Urso and is dedicated by the *res publica Ursonensium*.
CIL II 1405 = *ILER* 1135; Thouvenot *Essai*² 221 n 2; R. Ganghoffer *L'évolution des institutions municipales en Occident et en Orient au Bas-Empire* (Paris 1963) 157 n 11

Vesci (conv. Gaditanus)

296 Sisdn – perhaps a magistrate; ca 48–47 BC
The name is presumably indigenous.
VM 91:3 = Gil 1579; *PB* 1

297 C. Livius – magistrate; ca 48–47 BC
VM 91:5 = Gil 1580; *PB* xxviii

Villafranca de los Barros (ancient name unknown; conv. Hispalensis)

298 C. Aufidius C. f. Gal. Vegetus – IIvir bis, curator; middle or late 2nd century AD; built a bath in honour of the Imperial cult
CIL II 5354 = *ILER* 2050; *PB* 66

299 C. Aufidius C. f. C. n. Gal. Avitus – IIvir designatus; son of **298**
PB 65; and see **298**.

Uncertain Towns

300 Kankinai – magistrate; second half of 2nd century BC
VM 99:1–2 = Gil 402–3

301 [Tokikakalbos?] – colleague of **300**
See **300**.

302 P. Terent[ius] Bodo. – magistrate; ca 47–44 BC
His city, once thought to be Lascuta, is uncertain. His *cognomen* should
perhaps be restored as Bodon, like **285**; or Bodo. might be the name of
his town, though no such toponym is otherwise attested.
VM 92:1 = Gil 1367; PB liii

303 L. Numit[orius] Bodo. – colleague of **302**
Curiously he bears the same *cognomen* as **302**
PB xli; and see **302**.

304 L. Q. Ul. f. – magistrate of an unknown town M[unicipium] C.F.; ca 47–44
BC
VM 71:14 = Gil 1366

305 Q. Isc. f. – colleague of **304**
The name is probably Iberian: cf Iskeratin (**191**), Iskerbeles (**686**)
See **304**.

306 L. Memmius Quir. Severus – aedilis, IIvir; Flavian or later; perhaps son of
L. Memmius Severus
The inscription is from an unknown town in the Singili valley (conv.
Astigitanus).
CIL II 2059 = ILER 1446; PB 240

307 Herennius ... – aidilis, IIvir, pon[tifex] ...scat[en]sis
The town ...scata or ...scatum is otherwise unknown, and the
provenance of the inscription is uncertain, but Spanish *pontifices* occur
almost exclusively in Baetica. The spelling 'aid.' suggests an early date.
C.M. del Rivero *El lapidario del Museo Arqueológico Nacional* (Madrid
1933) no. 336

308 ...s Fabianus – see **36**.

309 ...s Senecio – see **37**.

310 Anonymi – IIIIviri; AD 159; recipients of a rescript from Antoninus Pius concerning legacies
J. González *Stud. Doc. Hist. Iur.* 49 (1983) 400 = AE 1984, 511

2

Lusitania

Ammaia municipium (conv. Pacensis)

311 P. Cornelius Q. [f?] Macer – quaestor, IIvir: 1st century AD
He received the Roman citizenship from Claudius ('viritim a divo Claudio civitate donato') and since Claudius is referred to as *divus*, he must have died during a subsequent principate. A Q. Cornelius Macer, attested at Ilurco, perhaps under Commodus (**121**), is possibly related.
CIL II 159 = ILS 1978 = ILER 1523 = IRPac. 618; R. Etienne and G. Fabre *Conimbriga* 11 (1972) 201; J. Francisco Martín in *Estructuras sociales*, no. 34; L.A. Curchin ZPE 47 (1982) 105–6; R. Wiegels *Die Tribusinschriften des römischen Hispanien* (Berlin 1985) 72; G. Alföldy *Römisches Städtewesen auf der neukastilischen Hochebene* (Heidelberg 1987) 105

312 Proculus Pisiri f. – magistrate, probably IIvir; named on an honorific inscription to the emperor Claudius in AD 44–45
AE 1950, 217 = AE 1969/70, 238 = IRPac. 615; Alföldy *Fasti* 137

313 Omuncio Cilai f. – colleague of **312**
See **312**.

Aritium Vetus (conv. Pacensis)

314 Vegetus Taltici [f.] – magistratus; AD 37
Attested in the oath of allegiance to the new emperor, Gaius, the two magistrates (cf **315**) are given no more specific title.
CIL II 172 = ILS 190 = IRPac. 647

315 [V]ibius [M]arioni[s f.] – colleague of **314**
The restoration of the name is mine; the reported reading of the stone, with the magistrate's name in the ablative, is ' ...IBIONARIONI...'
CIL II 172 = ILS 190 = IRPac. 647

316 T. Aemilius Macrinus – aedilis, IIvir, flamen prov. Lusitaniae; of later date
than **314–15**; possibly a daughter T[ita?] Aemilia Macrina
M. de Figueiredo *Beira Alta* 12 (1953) 186

Baesuri (conv. Pacensis)

317 M. An. Ant. – magistrate; ca 47–44 BC
Hübner restores the name as 'M. An[nius] Ant[hius],' but a more likely
restoration for the *cognomen* is 'Ant[onianus].'
VM 104:1 = Gil 1174; A. Beltrán Martínez *Numismática antigua*
(Cartagena 1950) 445; *PB* iv
318 Anonymus – colleague of **317**
VM 104:1 = Gil 1174

Balsa (conv. Pacensis)

319 T. Manlius T. f. Quir. Faustinus – IIvir bis; late 2nd century AD; a native
of Balsa; sister Manlia T. f. Faustina
Although fairly common among the Baetican élite, the Manlii are rare in
Lusitania, the only other magistrate being T. Manlius T. f. of Brutobriga
(**321**).
CIL II 4990/5162 = *ILER* 5264 = *IRPac.* 79; *Estructuras sociales* no. 2; J. Encarnação *Conimbriga* 19 (1980) 193

Bretiande (ancient name unknown; conv. Scallabitanus)

320 Car[isius U]rsianus – curator rei publicae; civis Romanus
ILER 125

Brutobriga (conv. Scallabitanus)

321 T. Manlius T. f. Serg. – magistrate; ca 45–44 BC
Grant's attempt to make Manlius a *legatus pro praetore* of Hispania
Ulterior rather than a local magistrate is without foundation. Cf **319** for
another T. Manlius in Lusitania.
VM 118:1 = Gil 1181; Grant *FITA* 381; Galsterer *Untersuchungen* 15 n 67

Caesarobriga municipium (conv. Emeritensis)

322 L. Annius Quir. Placidus – quaestor, aedilis, IIvir ter; Flavian or later, given
the tribe Quirina; wife Domitia Attia
CIL II 896 = *ILER* 5271; *Estructuras sociales* no. 20

Capera (conv. Emeritensis)

323 M. Fidius Fidi f. Quir. [Macer] – mag[ister?] ter, IIvir bis, praefectus fabrum; Flavian period.

This magistrate apparently derived his *nomen* from his father's *cognomen*, Fidus. His own *cognomen* is lost, but a M. Fidius Macer, probably the same man, occurs in two other inscriptions from this town (*CIL* II 834–5 = *ILER* 3717, 6136). The title 'mag. III' is unusual, but this is clearly the reading on the stone (cf Blázquez's photograph). The inscription is dedicated to Augusta Trebaruna, a thinly disguised indigenous deity.

J.M. Blázquez *Caparra* (Madrid 1965) 59 and pl. XVI = *AE* 1967, 197 = *HAEp.* 2574 = A. García y Bellido *AEA* 45–7 (1972–4) 64–5 = *CPIL* 818; *Estructuras sociales* no. 24; L.A. Curchin *ZPE* 53 (1983) 114–15

324 P. Aufidius P. f. – held all offices in his town ('omnibus in re p. honoribus functus'); not earlier than AD 120; wife Martia C. f.

CIL II 815 = *CPIL* 184; *Estructuras sociales* no. 43

Caurium (conv. Emeritensis)

325 [Turius?] – magistrate.

The two *tesserae* in question read, 'tessera Cauriesis magistratu Turi[o?],' i.e., '*tessera* of Caurium, when Turi[us?] was magistrate.' Since the *tesserae* were both found at the site of Lumbrales (whose ancient name is unknown – but the site has pre-Roman walls), they appear to indicate an agreement of *hospitium* between Caurium and that town

HAEp. 1050–1 = *ILER* 5858

Collippo (conv. Scallabitanus)

326 Q. Allius Maximus – IIvir; AD 167

His *nomen* is non-Latin. Another Allius Maximus appears as legate of Tarraconensis in 280 (*CIL* II 3738 = *ILS* 597).

CIL II 5232 = *ILER* 1129 = D. de Pinho Brandão *Conimbriga* 11 (1972) 51–5; *Estructuras sociales* no. 33, cf no. 45

327 C. Sulpicius Silonianus – colleague of **326**

Estructuras sociales no. 32; and see **326**.

328 Q. Talotius Q. f. Allius Silonianus – evocatus cohortis VI praetoriae; AD 167

He was made a decurion by the *ordo Colliponensis* with exemption from *honorarium*, *munera*, and *onera*. He was perhaps a relative of the two duovirs whose names (Allius, Silonianus) he bears (cf. **326–7**).

CIL II 5232 = *ILER* 1129 = Brandão *Conimbriga* 11 (1972) 51–5; *Estructuras sociales* no. 45

sociales no. 45

329 C. Aurelius Quir. Cassianus – omnibus honoribus in re p. functus; not before AD 120; grandfather Cassianus, father Rufinus

Brandão *Conimbriga* 11 (1972) 56–60; *Estructuras sociales* no. 44

Conimbriga municipium Flavium (conv. Scallabitanus)

330 C. Turranius Quir. Rufus – member of a local romanized élite family, sporting a Latin *nomen*.

His receipt of Roman citizenship under the Flavians must have resulted from the holding of a municipal magistracy at Conimbriga. The Turranii were one of the most prominent families of this city, with numerous relatives attested.

R. Etienne and G. Fabre *Conimbriga* 11 (1972) 193–203 = AE 1971, 162 = *FC* II no. 70, cf p 99

Eburobrittium (conv. Scallabitanus)

331 ... Tolius Maximinus – IIvir; 2nd century or later

He was perhaps related to Tolia Maxima of nearby Collippo, whence Tolius' inscription, cf *CIL* II 349 = *ILER* 4411.

J. Leite de Vasconcellos *Revista de Arqueologia* 2 (1934) 194–5; *Estructuras sociales* no. 35

Emerita Augusta colonia (conv. Emeritensis)

332 Cn. Cornelius Cn. f. Pap. Severus – aedilis, IIvir, flamen Iuliae Augustae, praefectus fabrum; reign of Tiberius (before AD 29).

For another *flamen* of Julia Augusta cf **366**.

AE 1915, 95 = *ILER* 1558 = G. Forni in *Augusta Emerita* ed A. Blanco Freijeiro (Madrid 1976) 34 no. 14; Etienne *Culte* 199; *Estructuras sociales* no. 13

333 L. Pomponius M. f. Capito – IIvir, praefectus fabrum, flamen coloniae Augustae Emeritae, flamen prov. Lusitaniae divi Augusti divae Augustae; AD 48

AE 1966, 177 = *ILER* 5540

334 Anonymus – [IIII?]vir bis, IIvir, praefectus ..., flamen prov. Lusitaniae

The word after 'praefectus' is lost: the anonymous man might be a praefectus i.d. or praefectus fabrum. Alternatively, he might have been in charge of one of the *praefecturae* into which the territory of Emerita Augusta was divided.

CIL II 493; cf *Corpus agrimensorum Romanorum* 135–6

335 C. Pompeius L. f. Pap. Priscus – flamen coloniae, IIvir, flamen prov. Lusitaniae

The order of offices suggests that the local flaminate was held before the duovirate, an unusual *cursus*.

AE 1967, 187 = *ILER* 6404 = Forni in *Augusta Emerita* 34 no. 15; *Estructuras sociales* no. 14

336 L... Pompe[i]us ...nus – [aedilis?], IIvir, pontifex
J.R. Mélida *Catálogo monumental de España: Badajoz* (Madrid 1925) no. 907 = *ERAE* 600

337 L. G... Vetti... – decurio
His *cognomen* might be Vettinus, Vettidianus, or the like.
HAEp. 1845 = *ERAE* 543

338 Ummidius – IIvir, flamen
Cf C. Ummidius Durmius Quadratus, governor of Lusitania ca 31–9 (Alföldy *Fasti* 136–7) for a possible relative.
Unpublished inscription from the amphitheatre of Emerita; no inventory number

339 Anonymus – IIvir, p[ontifex? or praefectus?]
ERAE 626

340 Anonymus – aedilis, IIvir iterum
Inv. 622 = *ERAE* 592 (but the reading of the latter is incomplete.)

341 ... M. f. Pap. – IIvir, praefectus, pontifex
Inv. 8547 = *ERAE* 486 (but the reading of the latter is incomplete.)

342 Anonymus – IIvir
Inv. 18982, unpublished

343 Anonymus – [aedilis?] et IIvir
ERAE 658

344 Anonymus – q[uaestor], aedilis, [IIvir], praefectus
Inv. 10031 = *ERAE* 589 (but the reading of the latter is incomplete.)

345 ...nius C. f. Galba – [aedilis?], IIvir, [flamen?] divi Augusti
ERAE 103; *Estructuras sociales* no. 15

346 ... Vegetus – IIvir
ERAE 605

347 Ulpius Rufus – allectus (sc. decurio) Emeritae, excussatus, Traiani decurialis: a native of Tritium in conv. Cluniensis
HAEp. 677 = *ILER* 6398

348 ... Modestus M. f. Ser. – flamen divi Augusti, IIvir, praefectus fabrum
ERAE 108; *Estructuras sociales* no. 16

349 C. Titius C. f. Cl[audia tribu] Similis – procurator prov. Lusitaniae et Vettoniae, curator rei publicae Emeritensium, procurator prov. Moesiae Inferioris, eiusdem provinciae ius gladii, praepositus vexillationum expeditionis per Asiam Lyciam Pamphyliam et Phrygiam, primipilus legionis III Augustae Piae Vindicis, princeps peregrinorum, centurio frumentarius, cent-

urio legionis x…; early 3rd century; a native of Colonia Agrippensis in Germania Inferior

> CIL II 484 = ILS 1372 = ILER 1529; Pflaum Carrières no. 330

350 L. Antestius Pap. Persicus – IIviralis, pontifex perpetuus; mid-3rd century; children Antestius Antianus and Iulia Persica

> A. García y Bellido Esculturas romanas de España y Portugal (Madrid 1949) no. 285 = AE 1952, 117; Estructuras sociales no. 12

Igaeditani (conv. Scallabitanus)

351 Toutonus Arci f. – magistratus; 16 BC

The name is Celtic, with parallels in Gaul and Germany. The inscription is the oldest one from Lusitania.

> AE 1967, 144 = ILER 5846a; Palomar Lapesa Onomástica 105–6; J. Alarcão in The Princeton Encyclopedia of Classical Sites ed R. Stillwell (Princeton 1976) 293

352 Malgeinus Manli f. – colleague of 351

The Celtic name Malgeinus is found several times in Lusitania and Galicia.

> Palomar Lapesa Onomástica 83; and see 351.

353 Celtius Arantoni f. – colleague of 351

The Celtic name Celtius is very common in Lusitania.

> Palomar Lapesa Onomástica 38, 63; and see 351.

354 Amminus Ati f. – colleague of 351

The Celtic name Amminus occurs only in Lusitania, Gaul and Britain.

> Palomar Lapesa Onomástica 33; and see 351.

Metellinum colonia Caecilia (conv. Emeritensis)

355 Q. Licinius Saturninus – IIvir; reign of Domitian; inscription dedicated to Domitia Augusta (on whom cf Suet. Dom. 3).

> CIL II 610 = ILER 1262; Estructuras sociales no. 19

356 L. Mummius Pomponianus – colleague of 355

> Estructuras sociales no. 18; see 355.

Mirobriga municipium Flavium (conv. Pacensis)

357 M. Iulius Marcellus – aedilis et IIvir; 1st century AD

He is possibly a cod[icarius] (shipper).

> CIL II 25 = ILER 1518 = IRPac. 150; Estructuras sociales no. 11; J.C. Edmondson Two Industries in Roman Lusitania (Oxford 1987) 155

Myrtilis municipium (conv. Pacensis)

358 L. Ap. Dec.(?) – magistrate; 1st century BC

The name as presented here is a composite reconstruction, based on the assumption that the readings of various local coins (Ap. D.; L. A. Dec.; Ap. De.; L. Ap.) all refer to a single monetal magistrate. Grant's supposition that he is the same L. Ap. Dec. attested as quaestor at Urso in Baetica is doubtful.

VM 109:1, 3, 4, 6 = Gil 1451–2, 1454, 1456; Grant *FITA* 24

359 L. Ac[ilius?] – magistrate ca 47–44 BC

VM 109:2 = Gil 1455

360 C. Iulius Marinus – IIvir; reign of Marcus Aurelius

CIL II 15 = *ILER* 1515 = *IRPac.* 96; *Estructuras sociales* no. 3

361 C. Marcius Optatus – colleague of **360**

Estructuras sociales no. 4; and see **360**.

Norba colonia Caesarina (conv. Emeritensis)

362 P. Norbanus Serg. Flaccinus – aedilis.

His name reflects that of the founder of the colony, C. Norbanus Flaccus, cos. 38 BC, proconsul prov. Hispaniae 36–34 BC. The epitaph was found at Abertura near the site of Norba; its rural provenance suggests that Norbanus may have owned an estate in the vicinity.

HAEp. 761 = *ILER* 5551 = *CPIL* 785; *Estructuras sociales* no. 37

363 Q. Norbanus Q. f. Capito – aedilis, IIvir; 1st century AD; another namesake of the colonial founder; wife Iulia Quintilla and mother-in-law Sulpicia Fausta

CIL II 695 = *ILER* 4869 = *CPIL* 119; *Estructuras sociales* no. 23

364 D. Iulius Celsus – IIvir, AD 194–5; dedicated a silver statue to Septimius Severus.

This is the only Iulius attested among the élite of the conventus Emeritensis. A certain C. Iulius Celsus is recorded as a procurator of Lusitania earlier in the century, but was not of Spanish origin (*HAEp.* 1217; cf H.-G. Pflaum *Les procurateurs équestres sous le Haut-Empire romain* [Paris 1950] no. 106 bis).

CIL II 693 = *AE* 1919, 88 = *ILER* 1153 = *CPIL* 118; *Estructuras sociales* no. 22

365 L. Petronius Niger – colleague of **364**

Estructuras sociales no. 21; and see **364**.

Olisipo municipium Felicitas Iulia, et vicinia (conv. Scallabitanus)

366 Q. Iulius Q. f. Gal. Plotus – aedilis, IIvir, flamen Germanici Caesaris, flamen Iuliae Augustae in perpetu[u]m.

Since Germanicus died in AD 19 (Tac. *Ann.* 2.72) and Livia did not become Iulia Augusta until AD 14 (Suet. *Aug* 101) we may confidently date the career of Q. Iulius Plotus to the early years of Tiberius's reign. Francisco Martin's claim that Livia could have been Augusta prior to AD 14 contradicts the terms of Augustus' will.

CIL II 194 = *ILS* 6896 = *ILER* 5534; *Estructuras sociales* no. 29

367 Q. Antonius Gallus – IIvir under Trajan (before 107)
CIL II 4993 = *ILS* 326 = *ILER* 1265;
Estructuras sociales no. 31

368 T. Marcius Marcianus – colleague of 367.
Estructuras sociales no. 30; and see 367.

369 M. Gellius Rutilianus – IIvir; AD 121–2; wife Caelia Vegeta, flaminica
He was possibly flamen later, for his wife was flaminica (*CIL* II 197 and 5218 = *ILER* 4453).
CIL II 186 and p 692 = *ILER* 1104; *CIL* II 4992/5221 = *ILER* 1268; *Estructuras sociales* no. 25

370 L. Iulius Avitus – colleague of 369
Estructuras sociales, no. 26; and see 369.

371 Q. Coelius Cassianus – IIvir ca 178–80
CIL II 187 and p 692 = *ILER* 1144; *Estructuras sociales*, no. 28)

372 M. Fabricius Tuscus – colleague of 371
Estructuras sociales no. 27; and see 371.

373 C. Gavius C. f. Gal. Rectus – aedilis: died at age twenty-nine
The minimum age for holding municipal office was twenty-five (*Mal.* 54).
CIL II 262 = *ILER* 5549; *Estructuras sociales* no. 42

374 C. Iulius C. f. Gal. Rufinus – aedilis designatus
CIL II 225 = *ILER* 6381; *Estructuras sociales* no. 40

375 C. Caecilius Q. f. Gal. Gallus – aedilis.
CIL II 192 = *ILER* 5548; *Estructuras sociales* no. 38

376 Q. Caecilius Q. f. Gal. Caecilianus – aedilis; brother perhaps of 375, wife Iunia M. f. Marcella, son M. Caecilius Avitus
CIL II 261 = *ILER* 5550; *Estructuras sociales* no. 41

377 L. Cantius L. f. Gal. Marinus – aedilis; grandmother Vibia Maxima and mother Maria Procula
CIL II 193 = *ILER* 5547; *Estructuras sociales* no. 39

Ossonoba (conv. Pacensis)

378 ...us L. f. Felicior – flamen et IIvir Ossonobensis
He is designated as 'Vi...ensi,' and therefore is probably a native of Vipasca. Francisco Martín's attempt to make this man a relative of C. Iulius Felix at Olisipo (*CIL* II 224) is hopeless, since we do not know Felicior's *nomen*.

CIL II 5141 = *ILER* 1514 = *IRPac.* 8; *Estructuras sociales* no. 1

Pax Iulia colonia (conv. Pacensis)

379 M. Aurelius C. f. Gal. – IIvir, flamen Ti. Caesaris Augusti, praefectus
fabrum; early 1st century AD, the flaminate obviously falling between 14
and 37
Doubts as to the authenticity of this inscription now appear to be
groundless.
CIL II 49 = *ILER* 1557 = *IRPac.* 236; Etienne *Culte* 199 n 2; *Estructuras
sociales* no. 7

380 C. Iulius C. f. ... – IIvir bis., praefectus [fabrum?]
CIL II 52 = *ILER* 1516 = *IRPac.* 233; *Estructuras sociales* no. 8; J.
d'Encarnação *Conimbriga* 19 (1980) 193

381 C. Iulius C. f. Gal. Pedo – IIvir, flamen divorum
He was an efficient administrator and a financial contributor to the
annona. As Francisco Martín remarks, he was in all likelihood a man of
substance. The mark 'L. I[ulius?] Ped[o]' occurs on amphora stamps of ca
1st century AD.
CIL II 53 = *ILS* 6897 = *ILER* 1559 = *IRPac.* 239; *Estructuras sociales* no. 9;
Callender *Roman Amphorae* no. 875

382 ... Clodius M. f. Gal. Quadratus – aedilis; 1st century AD
CIL II 50 = *ILER* 5552 = *IRPac.* 237; *Estructuras sociales* no. 36

383 Q. Petronius Maternus – IIvir; reign of Antoninus Pius
The inscription is dedicated to Antoninus's adoptive son, L. Aelius
Aurelius Commodus, viz L. Verus. Vives erroneously dates it to the reign
of Commodus. The same Petronius reappears in *CIL* II 48, which may be,
as Hübner reasonably conjectures, an inscription to the other imperial
son, Marcus Aurelius. An inscription from the vicinity of Pax Iulia (*CIL* II
5187) mentions a Q. P. Ma...er, son of Iulia Q. f. Quintilla of Ebora;
d'Encarnação thinks this may refer to Q. P[etronius] Ma[t]er[nus]. The
amphora stamp 'QPM' could conceivably refer to Petronius Maternus or
his family.
CIL II 47 = *ILS* 6899 = *ILER* 1145 = *IRPac.* 291; *Estructuras sociales* no. 5;
Callender *Roman Amphorae* no. 1490; J. d'Encarnação *Conimbriga* 19
(1980) 193

384 C. Iulius Iulianus – colleague of 383; also mentioned separately as a
IIviralis
CIL II 47 = *ILS* 6899 = *ILER* 1145 = *IRPac.* 291; *IRPac* 305; *Estructuras
sociales* no. 6

Salacia municipium Imperatoria (conv. Pacensis)

385 Sisbe A. [S?] – magistrate ca 47–44 BC
VM 84:3 = Gil 1399

386 Conil. Siscr. f. – magistrate ca 47–44 BC
VM 84:4 = Gil 1403; Palomar Lapesa *Onomástica* 67, 98

387 Sisuc. – magistrate ca 47–44 BC
VM 84:6 = Gil 1402; Palomar Lapesa *Onomástica* 98

388 Cor[nelius?] – magistrate ca 47–44 BC
VM 84:8 = Gil 1400

389 L. Cornelius [C?] f. Bocchus – praefectus Caesarum bis, flamen provinciae, pontifex perpetuus, flamen perpetuus, praefectus fabrum, tribunus militum legionis III Augustae; 1st century AD; also honoured by Scallabis 'ob merita in coloniam.'

He must have seen military service in Africa, where the Third Legion was permanently stationed. He is almost certainly the Spanish writer Cornelius Bocchus cited by the elder Pliny (NH 16.216; 37.24, 97, 127; indexes of books 33 and 34), and possibly also the Bocchus named by Solinus (27.3, 37.8, 38.22), in which case he should date to the reign of Claudius. Some confusion has arisen from the filiation 'L. f.' in CIL II 5184. Etienne recognizes two separate men, making L. Cornelius L. f. the son of L. Cornelius C. f. Against this argument we must weigh the extreme unlikelihood of two synonymous men holding both the provincial flaminate and legionary tribunate, the latter office in particular being rare among the Lusitanian élite.

CIL II 35 = ILS 2920 = AE 1967, 195 = ILER 1562 = IRPac. 185; CIL II 2497/5617 = Eph. Epigr. VIII 4 = ILER 1546 = IRPac. 189; CIL II 5184 = ILS 2921 = ILER 1561; PW 77; PIR² C 1333; Etienne Culte 123–4; EREsp. 93; R. Syme Harv. Stud. 73 (1969) 220–1 = RP 759–60; Wiegels no. 249; PME C 228–9

390 L. Co... – IIvir, flamen; possibly a Cornelius, and conceivably related to **389**
IRPac 188 = J.C. Lázaro Faria *Ficheiro Epigráfico* 9 (1984) 14–15 = AE 1985, 499

391 L. Porcius L. f. Gal. Himerus – IIvir, praefectus pro IIviro, flamen divorum bis; 1st century AD.

Francisco Martín insists that this man is a relative of L. Porcius Maternus, IIvir of Iliturgicola (**118**), and of L. Porcius Stilo, IIvir of Obulco (**221**). However, Porcius (and especially L. Porcius) is a very common name in Spain among both élite and non-élite and there is no compelling reason to link L. Porcius Himerus with the various L. Porcii in Baetica.

CIL II 34 = ILS 6894 = ILER 1585 = IRPac. 187; *Estructuras sociales* no. 10

392 (L?) Iunius L. f. Gal. Philo – IIvir, flamen divi Augusti perpetuus; 1st century AD

> J. d'Encarnação *Ficheiro Epigráfico* 4 (1982) 8–10 = AE 1982, 461 = *IRPac*. 186

Uncertain Town

393 C. Allius Quadratus – quaestor, VIIIvir; Augustan; father C. Allius Syriacus, mother Allia Serani f. Maxuma.

> This is the only octovir attested in Spain. The inscription was found at Alburquerque, equidistant from Emerita and Norba; therefore Allius might have been octovir at either city. Also of interest is the title 'quaestor,' which by example disproves Langhammer's conjecture that, although quaestors might exist in Latin colonies, there were none in Roman colonies such as Emerita or Norba. A Q. Allius Maximus appears at Collippo (**326**).
>
> *Eph. Epigr.* IX 119 = *ILER* 5561 = V. Carrasco Llanez *Revista de estudios extremeños* 32 (1976) 160–1; *Estructuras sociales* no. 46; Galsterer *Untersuchungen* 24 and n 75; Langhammer *Magistratus* 157; Mackie *Administration* 37 n 20

3

Tarraconensis
(Hispania Citerior)

Aeso (conv. Tarraconensis)

394 L. Aemilius Maternus – iivir; late 1st or early 2nd century AD; dedicated an inscription to the moon goddess (Luna Augusta) in memory of his deceased daughter Aemilia Materna; wife Fabia Fusca
  F. Fita *BRAH* 32 (1898) 532 = *ERLérida* 86 = *IRC* II 19, replacing *CIL* II 4458 = *ILER* 640

395 M. Licinius L. f. Quir. Celtiber – aedilis, iivir; 2nd century; grandson Q. Fabius Licinianus
  CIL II 4464 = *ILER* 1380 = *ERLérida* 89 = *IRC* II 28 *ERLérida* 91 = *IRC* II 27

396 Q. Fabius Q. f. Gal. Maternus – aedilis; late 1st, or 2nd century; mother Licinia M. f. Numantina (probably the daughter of **395**)
  J. Pons i Sala *Faventia* 1 (1979) 99 = *AE* 1979, 375 = *IRC* II 26

397 M. Licinius Celtiber Fabius Licinianus – iivir; 2nd century; brother of **396**
  ERLérida 78 = A. Jimeno *Epigrafía romana de la provincia de Soria* (Soria 1980) 170 = *IRC* II 29

398 C. Antonius C. f. Gal. Verecundus – iivir bis, tribunus militum legionis III Augustae bis (in Africa); 2nd century; mother Porcia Serana
  HAEp. 498 = *AE* 1957, 313 = *AE* 1972, 311 = *ERLérida* 81 = *IRC* II 24; *PME* A 146

399 L. Marcius – see **744**.

400 M. Porcius M. f. Gal. Catullus – iivir bis; late 2nd century; daughter Porcia Catulla, who married C. Licinius Silvanus, perhaps a member of the same house as **395–7**
  R. Pita Mercé *Ampurias* 30 (1968) 339–40 = *AE* 1972, 312–13 = *ERLérida* 82–3; A. d'Ors *Emerita* 40 (1972) 66

401 L. Porcius L. f. Quir. Serenus – iiiivir, iivir; Flavian or later; perhaps

related to **400** or to the mother of **398**, son L. Porcius Priscus and daughter
Porcia Procula
>   *CIL* II 4466–7 = *ILER* 5679, 4735 = *ERLérida* 74, 106 = *IRC* II 31, 53; A.
>   d'Ors *Emerita* 40 (1972) 66

402 L. Valerius L. f. Gal. Faventinus – IIviralis; 2nd century; 'assisted the
people by purchasing grain.'
>   *CIL* II 4468 = *ILER* 1379 = *ERLérida* 95 = *IRC* II 32; J. Pons in *Memorias de
>   Historia Antigua* III (Oviedo 1979) 119–20

Alaba (conv. Carthaginiensis)

403 L. Caecilius L. f. Gal. [M?]aecianus – eques (sc. Romanus), omnibus
honoribus in re p. sua functus, flamen p.H.c. between 150 and 180; father
L. Caecilius Charito
>   *CIL* II 4200 = *ILER* 1595 = *RIT* 263; Wiegels no. 230; Alföldy *Flamines* no.
>   11

Alcalá (ancient name unknown; conv. Carthaginiensis)

404 [C?] Cornelius C. f. Gal. Vetulus – IIvir, pontifex Caesaris primus; 1st
century, possibly in reign of Tiberius; wife perhaps Cornelia L. f. Silliboris
Possibly *CIL* II 3350 is a fake or reworked inscription, as Galsterer notes.
>   *CIL* II 3350–1 = *ILER* 6368, 1426; Etienne *Culte* 206; Galsterer *Untersu-
>   chungen* 59 n 92

Alcora (ancient name unknown; conv. Tarraconensis)

405 ...nius C. f. ...nanus – aedilis ...; son ... Rufus
>   *CIL* II 4041

Amallobriga (conv. Cluniensis)

406 Granius Silo Elaesi f. – mag[istratus?]
>   He delivered a pact of *hospitium* to the town of Cauca in AD 134
>   G. Bravo Castañeda *Gerión* 3 (1985) 312 = *AE* 1985, 581

407 Aemilius Sapienus Ottae f. – colleague of **406**
>   See **406**.

408 Iulius Proculus Aii f. – colleague of **406**
>   See **406**.

Aquae Calidae (ancient name uncertain; *Caldes de Montbui*; conv.
Tarraconensis)

409 L. Caecilius Gal. Serenus (or Seranus) – aedilis, IIvir; flamen; late 1st or
2nd century

2nd century
On the problem of the ancient toponym, see next entry.
IRC I 42 = *AE* 1984, 611

Aquae Calidae vel Voconiae (*Caldes de Malavella*; conv. Tarraconensis)

410 L. Aemilius L. f. Quir. Probus – aedilis, IIvir; Flavian or later given the tribe Quirina; parents L. Aemilius Celatus and Porcia Proba.
The site matches the location of 'Aquis Voconiis' in the Itineraries. However, since Aemilius Probus is called Aquicaldus, it is possible that Caldes de Malavella rather than Caldes de Montbui is the ancient Aquae Calidae (see discussion in Pallí Aguilera). But there might have been two places with the same name, especially since both sites have hot springs.
AE 1985, 634 = R. Wiegels *Die Tribusinschriften des römischen Hispanien* (Berlin 1985) 91; cf F. Pallí Aguilera *La Vía Augusta en Cataluña* (Bellaterra 1985) 44, 152

Aquae Flaviae (conv. Bracaraugustanus)

411 C. Ceraecius C. f. Quir. Fuscus – omnibus honoribus in re p. sua functus, flamen p.H.c. between 120 and 180
The *nomen* beginning with '*Cer*' is a common Celtic formation.
CIL II 4204 = *ILER* 1607 = *RIT* 266; *CIL* II 2473 = *ILER* 661; Albertos *OPP* 85; Alföldy *Flamines* no. 15

Archena (ancient name unknown; conv. Carthaginiensis)

412 C. Cornelius Capito – IIvir; principate of Augustus; repaired the local aqueduct
CIL II 3541 and p 955 = *ILER* 2043
413 L. Heius Labeo – colleague of **412**
See **412**.

Asturica Augusta (conv. Asturum)

414 L. Domitius Silo – [magistrate?], AD 152
The *cognomen* Silo is common in Spain, although whether it is of Latin or Celtic origin is unclear.
CIL II 2633 = *ILS* 6101 = T. Mañanes Pérez *Epigrafía y numismática de Astorga romana y su entorno* (León and Salamanca 1982) no. 86; Albertos *OPP* 207–8; A. Tranoy *La Galice romaine* (Paris 1981) 204
415 L. Flavius Serenus – colleague of **414**
CIL II 2633 = *ILS* 6101 = Mañanes Pérez (see **414**) no. 86

Attaccum (conv. Carthaginiensis)

416 L. Aemilius L. f. Paulus – flamen p.H.c., omnibus in re p. sua honoribus functus, tribunus militum legionis III Cyrenaicae (in Egypt), praefectus cohortis I...; probably Flavian or Trajanic

The *cursus* is apparently in retrograde order; therefore Aemilius held magistracies following military service, and finally the flaminate.

CIL II 4189 = ILER 1601 = RIT 253; Etienne *Culte* 137; Wiegels no. 209; Alföldy *Flamines* no. 2; PME A 84

Avobriga (conv. Bracaraugustanus)

417 L. Sulpicius Q. f. Gal. Niger Gibbianus – omnibus in re p. sua honoribus functus, flamen Romae divorum et Augustorum p.H.c. between 150 and 180.

The *agnomen* Gibbianus is very rare, the only other possible example being a Sempro[nius] Gib[bianus] at Palantia.

CIL II 4247 = ILER 6025 = RIT 307; Alföldy *Flamines* no. 64; Kajanto *Cognomina* 246; cf L.A. Curchin ZPE 53 (1983) 114 no. 7

Baetulo oppidum civium Romanorum (conv. Tarraconensis)

418 Q. Caecilius Tertullus – legatus, AD 98

He is named in a hospitality agreement between Baetulo and Q. Licinius Silvanus Granianus of Tarraco, cos. suff. 106.

AE 1936, 66 = EJER no. 23 = HAEp. 548 = ILER 5829

419 M. Fabius Gal. Nepos – aedilis, IIvir bis, flamen Romae et Augustorum, curator balnei novi; early to mid-2nd century.

He was a native of Iesso, but appears to have held his offices at Baetulo, whence the inscription.

CIL II 4610 = ILER 1571 = IRC I 141

Barcino colonia Faventia Iulia Augusta Paterna (conv. Tarraconensis)

420 C. Coelius Atisi f. – IIvir quinquennalis; built walls, towers, and gates; Augustan period

L. Wickert SPAW 1929, 5 = ILER 2090 = IRB 51; Alföldy *Gerión* 2 (1984) 232; cf Albertos OPP 39

421 Q. Salvius T. f. Gal. – aedilis, duovir et duovir quinquennalis; Augustan period

CIL II 4530 = IRB 65; Alföldy *Gerión* 2 (1984) 232

422 L. Cornelius C. f. Gal. Secundus – aedilis, IIvir; Augustan or slightly later; father C. Aemilius L. f. Gal., mother Cornelia, brother Q. Cornelius C. f. Gal. Niger, grandmother Numitoria L. f.

Cornelius Secundus seems to have taken his *nomen* from his mother, which is unusual, unless his father was also a Cornelius and C. Aemilius is really a step-father.

AE 1966, 208 = *ILER* 6848 = *IRB* 52; Alföldy *Gerión* 2 (1984) 232

423 Q. ... Nigellio – aedilis, flamen; 1st century AD

CIL II 6321 = *ILER* 5531 = *IRB* 69; Alföldy *Gerión* 2 (1984) 233

424 T. Iulius T. f. Gal. Placidus – aedilis, IIvir, flamen; 1st century AD

CIL II 6151 = *ILER* 5559 = *IRB* 56; Alföldy *Gerión* 2 (1984) 233

425 C. Aemilius C. f. Gal. Antonianus – aedilis, IIvir, flamen; 1st century AD; daughter Aemilia Optata

CIL II 4521 = *IRB* 46; Alföldy *Gerión* 2 (1984) 232

426 L. Calpurnius ... f. Gal. Iuncus – aedilis, IIvir, flamen; 1st century AD; wife Valeria L. lib.

CIL II 4524 = *ILER* 5557 = *IRB* 50; Alföldy *Gerión* 2 (1984) 233

427 L. Calpurnius L. f. Gal. Iuncus – aedilis, IIvir bis, flamen; 1st century AD; son of **426**, daughter Calpurnia L. f. Severa

CIL II 4524 = *ILER* 5557 = *IRB* 50; Alföldy *Gerión* 2 (1984) 234

428 ...us M. f. Ani. ... – aedilis, IIvir; 1st to 2nd century; wife ... Montana Aniensis, the tribe of Caesaraugusta, suggests a connection with that city.

CIL II 4532 = *IRB* 68; Alföldy *Gerión* 2 (1984) 234

429 ... Mandulius ... f. Ter. Crescens – [aedilis?], IIvir, flamen [Romae divorum?] et Aug[ustorum], praefectus fabrum; ca AD 70–150

CIL II 4516/6147 = *ILER* 1575 = *IRB* 38; Etienne *Culte* 206; Wiegels no. 294a; Alföldy *Gerión* 2 (1984) 234

430 L. Pedanius L. f. Pal. Aemilianus – aedilis, IIvir bis, flamen divorum et Augustorum; AD 70–180; mother Aemilia Furiana

The tribe Palatina, unusual for Barcino, reappears in **444**.

AE 1957, 33 = *HAEp.* 559 = *ILER* 1576 = *IRB* 60; I. Rodá *Hisp. Ant.* 5 (1975) 238–40; Alföldy *Gerión* 2 (1984) 233

431 [L.?] Pedanius L. f. Atilianus – aedilis; AD 70–180; father L. Pedanius Paternus, mother Pomponia Philete

CIL II 4529 = *ILER* 1704 = *IRB* 61; Rodá *Hisp. Ant.* 5 (1975) 246–8; Alföldy *Gerión* 2 (1984) 233

432 Q. Calpurnius Q. f. Gal. Flavus – aedilis, IIvir; honores flaminales (posthumous); ca AD 70–180

CIL II 4523 and p XLVIII = *ILER* 5555 = *IRB* 49; Alföldy *Gerión* 2 (1984) 233

433 M. Herennius C. f. Gal. Severus – aedilis, IIvir, flamen, aug[ur] (or flamen Augusti); early 2nd century; sister: Herennia C. f. Optata

He is possibly related to the Hadrianic consul P. Herennius Severus of Valentia (*PIR²* H 130). C. Herennius Optatus, friend and perhaps fellow freedman of a sevir at Barcino (*IRB* 94) is possibly a relative; but the tribe Galeria tells against a servile origin.

CIL II 4525 = *ILER* 5558 = *IRB* 54; *HAEp.* 565 = *AE* 1957, 36 = *IRB* 47; Etienne *Culte* 210; Alföldy *Gerión* 2 (1984) 233

434 M. Aemilius L. f. Gal. Optatus – aedilicii et IIvirales honores granted by decree of the decurions; early 2nd century AD

He died at age fourteen, therefore he received an honorary (and posthumous) magistracy only.

HAEp. 565 = *IRB* 47; Alföldy *Gerión* 2 (1984) 233

435 Q. Cornelius Seranus – aedilis, IIvir; first half of 2nd century; parents Q. Cornelius Spurii f. Secundus of Carthage and Geminia Optata, grandmother Cornelia Quarta, sisters Cornelia Tertullina, Cornelia Quartilla, Cornelia Dubisima

His father is perhaps related to L. Cornelius Secundus, **422**.

AE 1966, 207 = *HAEp.* 1949 = *ILER* 5498 = *IRB* 121; Alföldy *Gerión* 2 (1984) 234

436 C. Iulius Gal. Lepidus – primipilus, centurio legionis x... Geminae Piae Felicis, centurio legionis I Adiutricis, centurio legionis x Geminae Piae Felicis, centurio legionis xx Ulpiae Victricis, centurio legionis VII Geminae Piae Felicis, adlectus in numerum decurionum ab ordine Barcinonensium; perhaps reign of Trajan, a native of Iesso in conv. Caesaraugustanus (as is **419**)

The military offices appear to be in retrograde order, suggesting that Iulius Lepidus was originally enrolled in the Spanish Seventh Legion.

CIL II 4463 and p 981 = *ILER* 1685 = *ERLérida* no. 94 = *IRC* II 25

437 C. Iulius C. f. Ani. Seneca Licinianus – aedilis, IIvir, flamen, praefectus fabrum, tribunus militum legionis VI Victricis Piae Fidelis (in Germany or Britain), tribunus militum legionis xv Apollinaris, flamen p.H.c. under Trajan or Hadrian

His tribe Aniensis is that of Caesaraugusta, which suggests that his family originated there.

CIL II 6150 = *ILER* 1639 = *IRB* 37; Etienne *Culte* 137–8; Alföldy *Flamines* no. 34; Wiegels no. 275; *PME* I 121; *CIC* 99; Alföldy *Gerión* 2 (1984) 234

438 C. Marius L. f. Ani. Aemilianus – omnibus honoribus in re p. sua functus, IIvir ter, flamen Romae et Divi Augusti, iudex ex quinque decuriis; not earlier than AD 120; wife Vibia Liviana

Like **437** he appears to have family origins in Caesaraugusta.

CIL II 4617 = *HAEp.* 2579 = *ILER* 1377; *AE* 1969–70, 281 = *ILER* 6031 = *IRB* 59 = *IRC* I 103; I. Rodá *Hisp. Ant.* 5 (1975) 254; Wiegels no. 300; Alföldy *Gerión* 2 (1984) 234

439 C. Iulius C. f. Gal. Paulinus – omnibus honoribus in re p. sua perfunctus; not earlier than AD 120; wife Sergia Fulvianilla

CIL II 4522/4526 = *ILER* 5265 = *IRB* 55; Alföldy *Gerión* 2 (1984) 233

440 L. Pedanius L. f. Ursus – decurio coloniae Barcinonis; 2nd century AD; mother Pedania Dionysia

AE 1957, 30 = *HAEp.* 555 = *ILER* 1358 = *IRB* 63; Rodá *Hisp. Ant.* 5 (1975) 241–4

441 M. Ac[ilius] Gal. Firma[nus] – [IIvir, IIvir quinquen]n. ter, flamen R[omae et Augusti]; 2nd century AD

The restoration is that of Hübner, followed by Etienne, although the first office might be [aedilis].

CIL II 4520 = *IRB* 45; Etienne *Culte* 210, 227

442 L. Porcius L. f. Gal. Celer – aedilis; 2nd century; died at age seventeen; mother Domitia Lucilla

ILER 1368 = *AE* 1972, 297 = *IRB* 64; Alföldy *Gerión* 2 (1984) 233

443 Anonymi – aedilicii et IIvirales; 2nd century

The same inscription mentions **433**.

AE 1957, 36 = *IRB* 47

444 L. Pedanius L. f. Pal. Clemens Senior – omnibus honoribus in re p. sua functus; quinquennalis (Q.Q.) at Tarraco; second half of 2nd century AD

He is another member of the urban tribe Palatina (cf **430**).

AE 1957, 27 = *ILER* 1357 = *IRB* 62; Rodá *Hisp. Ant.* 5 (1975) 252–3; Alföldy *Gerión* 2 (1984) 233

445 L. Caecilius L. f. Pap. Optatus – centurio legionis VII Geminae Felicis et centurio legionis XV Apollinaris; missus honeste missione ab Imp. M. Aurelio Antonino et Aurelio Vero Augustis (AD 161–9); atlectus a Barcinonensibus inter immunes, consecutus in honores aedilicios, IIvir ter, flamen Romae divorum et Augustorum.

He provides a good example of a retired centurion attaining municipal offices. He left seventy-five hundred denarii to the city, the interest from which was to pay for boxing matches on June 10th of each year and for a distribution of oil in the baths on the same day. On the *immunes* of Barcino cf *Dig.* 50.15.8 Paul. June 10th was the birthday of the centurion's first regiment, the Legio VII Gemina; cf *CIL* 2552, 2554 = *ILER* 24, 26. The tribe Papiria possibly indicates an origin at Emerita Augusta, which was enrolled in that tribe.

CIL II 4514 = *ILER* 5838 = *IRB* 35; Etienne *Culte* 209, 292; E.M. Schtajerman *Die Krise der Sklavenhalterordnung im Westen des römisches Reiches* (Berlin 1964) 144; I. Rodá *El origen de la vida municipal y la prosopografía romana de Barcino* (Barcelona 1974) 18–26; I. Rodá *Quaderns d'Arqueologia i Història de la Ciutat* 18 (1980) 5–49; Alföldy *Gerión* 2 (1984) 234

446 C. Iulius C. f. Pal. Silvanus – aedilis; ca 160–200; died at age eighteen; father, C. Publicius Melissus, mother Aurelia Nigella

To judge by the different *nomina*, his father is rather a stepfather; Publicius also has a son C. Publicius Hermes who is only a sevir Augustalis. The tribe Palatina belongs to Rome (cf **444**) and is appropriate for the Publicii, a freedman family.

CIL II 4527 = ILER 5587 = IRB 57; Alföldy *Gerión* 2 (1984) 234

447 L. Valerius L. f. Gal. Terentianus – decurio Barcinonis; died at age twenty-four; brother L. Valerius L. f. Cornelianus

CIL II 4531 = ILER 6327; IRB 67

448 C. Domitius L. f. Maternus – honor decurionatus

He was perhaps a native of Aquincum in Pannonia Inferior, since he bears the epithet 'Acucensis,' i.e., possibly Aqui[n]censis.

CIL II 6153 = ILER 1375 = IRB 53

Baria (conv. Carthaginiensis)

449 Anonymus – [flamen?], tr[ibunus militum?], IIvir, p[raefectus fabrum?]. 1st or 2nd century AD

C. Dubois *Bulletin hispanique* 3 (1901) 219 = L.A. Curchin ZPE 49 (1982) 186 and ZPE 53 (1983) 116 = AE 1982, 632 = H. Devijver ZPE 59 (1985) 218

Bergidum Flavium (conv. Asturum)

450 C. Valerius Flaviani f. Arabinus – omnibus honoribus in re p. sua functus, sacerdos Romae et Aug.; 2nd century.

Although the text reads 'sacerdoti Romae et Aug. p.H.c.,' it appears that *p.H.c.* is in the nominative case as the dedicant of the inscription, rather than in the genitive as part of the title. Nonetheless, as the recipient of such a dedication, Valerius Arabinus may well have been a provincial priest.

CIL II 4248 and p 973 = ILS 6937 = ILER 1705 = RIT 333; Etienne *Culte* 183 n 5; Pastor *Los Astures* 173

Bilbilis municipium Augusta (conv. Caesaraugustanus)

451 M. Sempronius Tiberi[anus?] – IIvir; ca 1 BC

VM 139:1–3 = Gil 1584–6; CIC 187

452 L. Licinius Varus – colleague of **451**

CIC 111; and see **451**.

453 L. Cornelius Caldus – IIvir; ca AD 1

VM 139:4–5 = Gil 1587–8; CIC 58

454 L. Sempronius Rutilus – colleague of **453**

CIC 185; and see **453**.

455 C. Pom[peius] Capell[a] – IIvir; reign of Tiberius
Gómez-Pantoja reads 'Pom[ponius] Capell[ianus],' but Pompeius is a
much commoner *nomen*, and the longer *cognomen* is hardly suggested by
the abbreviation.
VM 139:6 = Gil 1761; *CIC* 153

456 C. Valerius Tranquillus – colleague of **455**
CIC 217; and see **455**.

457 C. Cornelius Refectus – IIvir; reign of Gaius
VM 139:10 = Gil 2000; *CIC* 62

458 M. Helvius Front[o] – colleague of **457**
CIC 93; and see **457**.

Bocchoris (Balearis Maior, conv. Carthaginiensis)

459 C. Coelius C. f. – legatus, 10 BC
He is named on a *tessera hospitalis* with the town's patron, M. Crassus
Frugi, cos. 14 BC.
EJER no. 16 = *HAEp.* 545 = *AE* 1957, 317 = Veny *Corpus* 21 = *ILER* 5827

460 C. Caecilius T. f. – colleague of **459**
See **459**.

461 Q. Caecilius Quinctus – praetor; AD 6
He is named on a *tessera hospitalis* with the town's patron, M. Atilius
Vernus (otherwise unknown). The title 'praetor' is possibly the Latin
translation of a Punic title, e.g., *sufes*.
CIL II 3695 = *ILS* 6098 = Veny *Corpus* 22 = *ILER* 5828; J.B. Reid *The*
Municipalities of the Roman Empire (Cambridge 1913) 246

462 C. Valerius Icesta – colleague of **461**
He has a non-Latin *cognomen*, otherwise unknown but with an Illyrian
ending.
CIL II 3695 = *ILS* 6098 = Veny *Corpus* 22 = *ILER* 5828; cf Albertos
OPP 123

Bracara Augusta (conv. Bracaraugustanus)

463 Q. Pontius Q. f. Quir. Severus – omnibus honoribus in re p. functus,
flamen p.H.c. between 120 and 180
CIL II 4237 = *ILER* 1614 = *RIT* 299; Alföldy *Flamines* no. 53

Brigaecium (conv. Asturum)

464 L. Fabius L. f. Quir. Silo – IIvir, sacerdos Romae et Aug. conventus
Asturum, adlectus in decurias quinque iudicum Romae, flamen p.H.c.
between 140 and 180

Adlection to the panels of judges was the prerogative of the emperor: cf below on **769**. On the *cognomen* Silo, see above on **414**.
CIL II 6094 = *ILER* 1664 = *RIT* 275 = T. Mañanes Pérez *Epigrafía y numismática de Astorga romana y su entorno* (León and Salamanca 1982) no. 96; Alföldy *Flamines* no. 24; Pastor *Los Astures* 173–4

Caesaraugusta colonia immunis (conv. Caesaraugustanus)

465 Q. Lutatius – IIvir; ca 23–13 BC
VM 147:1–2 = Gil 1589–90; J. Arce *Caesaraugusta, ciudad romana* (Zaragoza 1979) 56–7; *CIC* 116

466 M. Fabius – colleague of **465**
CIC 69; see **465**.

467 C. Alsanus – IIvir; ca 23–13 BC
VM 147:3–5 = Gil 1591–4; Arce *Caesaraugusta* 57; *CIC* 7

468 T. Cervius – colleague of **467**
CIC 50; and see **467**.

469 C. Sabinus – IIvir; ca 23–13 BC
VM 147:6; Arce *Caesaraugusta* 57; *CIC* 173

470 P. Varus – colleague of **469**
VM 147:6; *CIC* 223

471 L. Cassius – IIvir; ca 23–13 BC
VM 147:7–11 = Gil 1595–1601; *CIC* 623

472 C. Valerius Fen[estella?] – colleague of **471**
Cf **933** for the rare name Fenestella.
VM 147:7–11 = Gil 1595–1601; Arce *Caesaraugusta* 57; *CIC* 211

473 M'. Kaninius – IIvir iterum; ca 12 BC
VM 148:1–4 = Gil 1602–5; J.M. de Navascués *BRAH* 168 (1971) 633–4; Arce *Caesaraugusta* 57; *CIC* 45

474 L. Titius – colleague of **473**
VM 148:1–4 = Gil 1602–5; *CIC* 201

475 M. Porcius – IIvir; 8 BC
VM 148:7–9 = Gil 1606–8; Navascués *BRAH* 168 (1971) 633; *CIC* 162

476 Cn. Fadius – colleague of **475**
VM 148:7–9 = Gil 1606–8; Arce *Caesaraugusta* 57; *CIC* 75

477 T. Verrius – IIvir; 6 BC
VM 148:5–6 = Gil 1609–10; Navascués *BRAH* 168 (1971) 633; *CIC* 218

478 C. Alliarius – colleague of **477**
VM 148:5–6 = Gil 1609–10; Arce *Caesaraugusta* 57; *CIC* 8

479 Cn. Domitius Ampian[us] – IIvir; 4 and 2 BC
VM 148:10–12 = Gil 1611–14; Navascués *BRAH* 168 (1971) 632–3; *CIC* 67

480 C. Vettius Lancia[nus] – colleague of **479**
Arce sees him as a native of Lancia, perhaps rightly.
VM 148:10–12 = Gil 1611–14; Arce *Caesaraugusta* 57; *CIC* 220

481 Ti. Clodius Flavus – IIvir, praefectus Germ[anici Caesaris]; perhaps ca AD 4
VM 149:1–5 = Gil 1615–19; *CIC* 54

482 L. Iu[v]entius Lupercus – IIvir with **481**
CIC 103; see **481**.

483 M. Cato – IIvir; AD 31
VM 150:10–12, 151:1–4 = Gil 1776–81; *CIC* 48

484 L. Vettiacus – colleague of **483**
CIC 224; see **483**.

485 Iunianus Lupus – [IIvir?], praefectus G[aii] Caesaris; AD 34
VM 151:8–10 = Gil 1791–3; *CIC* 100

486 C. Pomponius Parra – IIvir with **485**
CIC 156; see **485**.

487 L. Lucretius – IIvir; AD 14–37
VM 150:4–5 = Gil 1782–3; *CIC* 113

488 Sex. Aebutius – colleague of **487**.
His *nomen* may indicate Italian origin.
VM 150:4–5 = Gil 1782–3; Arce *Caesaraugusta* 57; *CIC* 1

489 Clemens – IIvir; AD 14–37
VM 150:7–9 = Gil 1784–7

490 Lucretius – colleague of **489**
Cf **487** for a likely relative.
CIC 114; see **489**.

491 Fulvianus – [IIvir?], praefectus G[aii Caesaris]; AD 14–37
VM 151:5–6 = Gil 1789–90; *CIC* 81

492 Lupus – IIvir with **491**. Cf **485** for a homonymous, possibly identical,
magistrate.
CIC 115; and see **491**.

493 C. Carri[nas] Aquil[a? -us?] – IIvir; AD 14–37
For the *cognomen* Aquila, cf **506**.
VM 151:7 = Gil 1794; A. Beltrán *Numisma* 20 (1956) 24; *CIC* 46

494 L. Funi[sulanus] Vete[ranus?] – colleague of **493**
Gil, less plausibly, reads 'Funi[us].' Syme notes the existence of a senator
L. Funisulanus Vettonianus (suff. 78) of the tribe Aniensis, in which
Caesaraugusta was enrolled, as well as two apparent descendants. Our
duovir presumably belongs to the same family.
VM 151:7 = Gil 1794; Beltrán *Numisma* 20 (1956) 24; *CIC* 87; R. Syme
Ktema 6 (1981) 277

495 M'. Flavius Festus – IIvir; AD 14–37
Cf **625** for a duovir of the same name at Celsa under Augustus.
VM 152:7–8 = Gil 1795–6; *CIC* 77

496 M. Ofillius Silvanus – IIvir iterum, colleague of **495**
    CIC 143; and see **495**.
497 T. Caecilius Lepidus – IIvir; AD 14–37
    VM 152:4–6, 9 = Gil 1797–1800; *CIC* 39
498 C. Aufidius Gemellus – colleague of **497**
    CIC 23; and see **497**.
499 Licinianus – IIvir; AD 37
    VM 154:4–8 = Gil 2001–5; *CIC* 105
500 Germanus – colleague of **499**
    CIC 90; and see **499**.
501 Scipio – IIvir; AD 38 or 39
    VM 153:5–9, 154:1–3 = Gil 2006–13
502 Montanus – colleague of **501**
    VM 153:1–9, 154:1–3 = Gil 2006–17
503 Titullus – IIvir colleague of **502**; AD 38 or 39
    VM 153:1–4 = Gil 2014–17; *CIC* 202
504 M. Iulius Antonianus – aedilis
    He is named on a lead pipe together with 'Artemas c[oloniae] C[aesaraugus-
    tae] s[ervus].'
    CIL II 2992 = *ILER* 5082 = *ERZaragoza* 71; *CIC* 96; Mackie *Administration*
    166
505 M. Porcius M. f. Ani. Aper – IIvir, praefectus fabrum, tribunus militum
    legionis VI Ferratae, procurator Augusti ab alimentis, flamen p.H.c. between
    105 and 110
    CIL II 4238 = *ILER* 1615 = *RIT* 300; Etienne *Culte* 139; Pflaum *Carrières* no.
    187; *EREsp.* 107; Wiegels no. 315; Alföldy *Flamines* no. 54; *PME* P 94;
    CIC 163
506 Q. Herennius Q. f. Ani. Aquila – omnibus honoribus in re p. sua functus,
    inter decurias iudicum Romae adlectus, flamen p.H.c.; 2nd century AD,
    perhaps after 120
    CIL II 6096 = *ILER* 1632 = *RIT* 283; Etienne *Culte* 137; Wiegels no. 269;
    Alföldy *Flamines* no. 31; *CIC* 94
507 M. Valerius M. f. Gal. Ani. Capellianus – see **671**
508 M. Sempronius M. f. Quir. Capito – see **739**.

Calagurris municipium Iulia Nassica (conv. Caesaraugustanus)

509 C. Sextius – aedilis; ca 34 BC
    VM 157:2 = Gil 1026; *CIC* 191
510 C. Valerius – aedilis, IIvir; colleague of **509**
    VM 157:2–3 = Gil 1026, 1031; *CIC* 205–6

511 L. Granius – IIvir; ca 33–28 BC; colleague of **510**
VM 157:3 = Gil 1031; *CIC* 91

512 Q. Antonius – IIvir; ca 33–28 BC
VM 158:2 = Gil 1027; *CIC* 11

513 L. Fabius – IIvir; colleague of **512**
CIC 68; and see **512**.

514 C. Mar[ius] Cap[ito] – IIvir; ca 33–28 BC
VM 157:4 = Gil 1030; *CIC* 126

515 Q. Urso[nius?] – IIvir; colleague of **514**
Gómez-Pantoja reads Q. Ursus, but since all the other magistrates in this series have *nomina*, 'Urso.' seems likelier to represent a *nomen* than a *cognomen*.
VM 157:4–5 = Gil 1030, 1032; *CIC* 203–4

516 M. Plaet[orius] Tran[quillus?] – IIvir iterum; ca 33–28 BC; colleague of **515**
VM 157:5 = Gil 1032; *CIC* 146

517 M'. Memmius – IIvir; ca 33–28 BC
VM 157:6 = Gil 1029; *CIC* 135

518 L. Iunius – colleague of **517**
CIC 101; and see **517**.

519 Q. Aemilius – IIvir; ca 33–28 BC
VM 157:7 = Gil 1028; *CIC* 5

520 C. Postumius Mil[o] – colleague of **519**
CIC 166; and see **519**.

521 L. Baebius – IIvir; ca 27–5 BC
VM 158:3 = Gil 1033; *CIC* 27

522 P. Antestius – colleague of **521**
CIC 10; and see **521**.

523 C. Marius – pr., IIvir; ca 27–5 BC
He is perhaps the same man as **514**
VM 158:4–6 = Gil 1034–6; *CIC* 123

524 M. Valerius Quad[ratus] – colleague of **523**
A duovir of the same name appears at Turiaso under Tiberius (**938**) and may be related.
See **523**.

525 L. Baebius Priscus – IIvir; ca 27–5 BC
He is perhaps the same man as **521**.
VM 158:8–12 = Gil 1037–41; *CIC* 29

526 C. Granius Brocchus – colleague of **525**
CIC 92; and see **525**.

527 C. Sempronius Barbatus – IIvir; perhaps ca 2 BC
VM 159:4 = Gil 1621; *CIC* 179

528 Q. Baebius Flavus – colleague of 527; perhaps a relative of 525
   CIC 28; and see 527.

529 M. Licinius Capella – IIvir; ca 1 BC
   VM 159:1 = Gil 1622; CIC 106

530 C. Fulvius Rutil. – colleague of 529
   CIC 84; and see 529.

531 L. Valentinus – IIvir; ca AD 1
   VM 159:2–3 = Gil 1623–4; CIC 222

532 L. Novus – colleague of 531
   CIC 142; and see 531.

533 L. Fulvius Sparsus – IIvir; AD 14–37
   He is perhaps a relative of 530
   VM 159:5 = Gil 1801; CIC 85

534 L. Saturninus – colleague of 533
   CIC 176; and see 533.

535 C. Celer – IIvir; AD 14–37
   VM 159:6, 8 = Gil 1802–3; CIC 49

536 C. Rectus – colleague of 535
   CIC 171; and see 535.

537 L. Valerius Flavus – aedilis; AD 14–37
   VM 159:7 = Gil 1804; CIC 212

538 T. Valerius Merula – colleague of 537
   CIC 215; AND SEE 537.

Carthago Nova colonia Urbs Iulia (conv. Carthaginiensis)

539 L. Fabricius – magistrate; perhaps early 40s BC
   VM 173:8 = Gil 1042

540 P. Atelius – colleague of 539
   See 539.

541 Helvius Pollio – IIvir quinquennalis; 46–45 BC
   VM 130:12–14 = Gil 1043–5

542 Albinus – colleague of 541
   See 541.

543 Conducius – IIvir quinquennalis; 42–23 BC
   VM 130:3–4 = Gil 1047–8; Grant FITA 216

544 Malleolus – colleague of 543
   See 543.

545 C. Caedius – IIvir quinquennalis; 42–23 BC
   VM 130:2 = Gil 1049

546 T. Popilius – colleague of 545
   See 545.

547 L. Appuleius – IIvir quinquennalis; 42–23 BC (32 BC according to Beltrán)
VM 130:10–11 = Gil 1050–1; F. Beltrán Lloris *Numisma* 28 (1978) 174

548 C. Maecius – colleague of **547**
VM 130:9–11 = Gil 1050–2

549 Q. Acilius – IIvir quinquennalis; colleague of **548**; 42–23 BC (32 BC according to Beltrán)
VM 130:9 = Gil 1052; Beltrán Lloris *Numisma* 28 (1978) 174

550 P. Baebius Pollio – IIvir quinquennalis; 42–23 BC
VM 130:5–6 = Gil 1053

551 C. Aquinus Mela – colleague of **550**
A certain C. Aquinus M. f., attested on lead ingots from this city, is presumably related or identical to this magistrate.
VM 130:5–6 = Gil 1053; C. Domergue *MCV* 1 (1965) 19 n 1; Domergue *AEA* 39 (1966) 54–7

552 Cn. Cornelius L. f. Gal. Cinna – IIvir; second half of 1st century BC; built two walls, one of them 102 feet in length.
CIL II 3425 = *ILS* 5332 = *ILER* 2088; *Eph. Epigr.* IX 331; C. Beldá Navarro *El proceso de romanización de la provincia de Murcia* (Murcia 1975) 32; M. Koch *MM* 17 (1976) 294

553 ... Maecius C. f. Vetus – augur, aedilis; second half of 1st century BC; built a wall sixty feet in length. The magistrate C. Maecius (**548**) may be an ancestor.
AE 1975, 525; Koch *MM* 17 (1976) 292–4

554 M. Cornelius M. f. Gal. Marcellus – augur, quinquennalis; second half of 1st century BC; built a wall from the Popilian Gate to the nearest tower and beyond.
Blázquez erroneously believes that the inscription mentions two gates. Cf **569** for another quinquennalis serving as augur.
CIL II 3426 = *ILS* 5333/4; Koch *MM* 17 (1976) 294; J.M. Blázquez in *Symposion de ciudades augusteas* I (Zaragoza 1976) 112

555 Hiberus – IIvir quinquennalis, perhaps 23 BC
Blázquez dates him to 7 BC on the assumption that this is Q. Varius Hiberus (see commentary on **560**).
VM 130:16 = Gil 1628; Blázquez in *Symposion de ciudades augusteas* I 114–15

556 C. Lucius P. f. – colleague of **555**
See **555**.

557 Cn. Atelius Ponti[anus?] – IIvir quinquennalis; perhaps 19 BC; colleague of King Juba, patron of Carthago Nova
VM 130:15 = Gil 1629; on Juba as IIvir quinquennalis see also *ILS* 840

558 Hiberus – praefectus M. Agrippae quinquennalis; between 18 and 12 BC (or 17 BC according to Beltrán).

He is perhaps the same as, or a relative of **555**. When a member of the imperial family was a duovir (here quinquennalis), his municipal duties were discharged by a prefect.

VM 131:1–3 = Gil 1630–2; Beltrán Lloris *Numisma* 28 (1978) 175

559 L. Bennius – praefectus Imperatoris Caesaris quinquennalis; colleague of **558**

VM 131:1–4 = Gil 1630–3

560 Q. Varius – magistrate; perhaps between 18 and 12 BC; colleague of **559**

Q. Varius Hiberus, attested on lead ingots from Carthago Nova, is very probably a relative of this man, and possibly also of **555** and **558**, who likewise bear the uncommon *cognomen* Hiberus.

VM 131:4 = Gil 1633; C. Domergue *MCV* 1 (1965) 24 n 3

561 Cn. Statius Libo – praefectus, sacerdos; perhaps between 18 and 12 BC

VM 131:7, 173:9 = Gil 1634–5

562 M. Postumius Albinus – IIvir quinquennalis; perhaps 12 BC

VM 131:8–9 = Gil 1636–7; Blázquez in *Symposion de ciudades augusteas* I 113

563 L. Porcius Capito – colleague of **562**

See **562**.

564 C. Varius Rufus – IIvir quinquennalis; perhaps after 12 BC

VM 131:10–12 = Gil 1638–40

565 Sex. Iulius Pollio – colleague of **564**

See **564**.

566 Helvius Pollio – praefectus; perhaps AD 4; a possible relative of **541**

The future emperor Tiberius, who was adopted by Augustus in AD 4, was honorary quinquennalis of Carthago Nova in this year.

VM 130:17 = Gil 1641

567 Hiberus – colleague of **566**; perhaps son of **555**

See **566**.

568 C. Laetilius M. f. Apalus – IIvir quinquennalis; perhaps AD 5; colleague of King Ptolemy; honoured by the college of piscatores et propolae

Two other members of the Laetilius family appear in *CIL* II 3473–4, and the mark 'Laetili Ferm' is found on lead ingots.

VM 131:5–6 = Gil 1642–3; *CIL* II 5929 = *ILS* 3624 = *ILER* 1414; Domergue *MCV* 1 (1965) 17 n 7

569 L. Iunius – IIvir quinquennalis, augur; perhaps after AD 5

VM 130:7–8 = Gil 1644–5; Beltrán Lloris *Numisma* 28 (1978) 174

570 L. Acilius – colleague of **569**

See **569**.

571 C. Sediato P. f. Rufus – aedilis; reign of Augustus
  Koch MM 19 (1978) 261–2 = AE 1977, 460

572 Anonymus – IIvir, IIvir quinquennalis; reign of Augustus. The same double title occurs at **581**
  CIL II 3435

573 P. Turul[l]ius – IIvir quinquennalis; ca AD 18
  P. Turullius M. f. Mai., attested on lead ingots from this city, is presumably a relative; his Italian tribe Maecia, furthermore, suggests a family connection with the senatorial Turullii from Lanuvium in Italy.
  VM 131:13–17 = Gil 1823–7; R. Syme *Hist.* 13 (1964) 123–4 = RP 602–3; Domergue MCV 1 (1965) 17 n 7, 19 n 1

574 M. Postumius Albinus – IIvir quinquennalis iterum; colleague of **573** and presumably a descendant of **562**
  VM 131: 13–17 = Gil 1823–7

575 Cn. Atellius Flaccus – IIvir quinquennalis, ca 37–9
  VM 132:1, 7–10 = Gil 2018–19

576 Cn. Pompeius Flaccus – colleague of **575**
  See **575**.

577 ... Pollio – IIvir
  He is perhaps a Helvius Pollio, like **541** and **566**.
  CIL II 3429 = ILER 6605

578 L. Aemilius M. f. M. n. Quir. Rectus – scriba quaestorius or aedilicius at Carthago Nova, Sicellis (location unknown), Asso (in the conventus Carthaginiensis), Sparta, and Argos, civis adlectus, aedilis (under Trajan), equo publico donatus ab Imperatore Caesare Traiano Hadriano, patronus rei publicae Assotanorum
  In honour of his election as aedile he dedicated a silver statue to the Concordia Decurionum. He was a native of Rome.
  CIL II 3423 and p 952 = ILER 6081; CIL II 3424 = ILS 6953 = ILER 1411; CIL II 5941 = ILS 6954 = ILER 1413; CIL II 5942)

579 Cn. Numisius Cn. f. Serg. Modestus – omnibus honoribus in re p. sua functus, electus a concilio provinciae ad statuas aurandas Divi Hadriani, flamen p.H.c. between 140 and 160
  Garzetti, citing this inscription, claims that the number of statues of Hadrian at Tarraco was so great that 'a special magistracy had to be created to look after them'; but the inscription attests neither the number of statues nor a special magistracy.
  CIL II 4230 and p 973 = ILS 6930 = ILER 1611 = RIT 294; Etienne *Culte* 140 no. 4; Alföldy *Flamines* no. 47; A. Garzetti *From Tiberius to the Antonines* (London 1974) 389

580 L. Magius Cn. f. Fab. Sabellus – aedilis, IIvir

The tribe, rare in Spain, suggests a non-local family.
Eph. Epigr. IX 332

581 L. Numisius Cn. f. Serg. Laetus – aedilis, IIvir et IIvir quinquennalis,
flamen Augustorum, pontifex, praefectus cohortis Musulamiorum, flamen
p.H.c. bis; probably son or brother of **579**

Etienne and Devijver support a date in the reign of Marcus Aurelius;
Alföldy prefers the first half of the 2nd century.

AE 1908, 149 = P. Paris *Bulletin Hispanique* 13 (1911) 121 = *ILER* 1643;
Etienne *Culte* 141; Wiegels no. 303; Alföldy *Flamines* no. 46

582 C. Antonius P. f. Col. Balbus – aedilis

Collina is one of the four urban tribes at Rome; Balbus' family may
therefore have been of servile origin. Beltrán Lloris identifies him with C.
Antonius Balbus, attested in painted amphora inscriptions as an exporter
of Spanish oil.

HAEp. 42 = *ILER* 6318; M. Beltrán Lloris *Las ánforas romanas en España*
(Zaragoza 1970) 220

Castulo municipium Caesarini(?) Iuvenales (conv. Carthaginiensis)

583 Sacaliscer – magistrate; ca 120–90 BC

The name contains a modified form of the Celtiberian onomastic element
'Sacar-,' but is written in Latin characters.

VM 70:13 = Gil 392; J. Untermann *Elementos de un atlas antroponímico
de la Hispania antigua* (Madrid 1975) 117; Albertos *OPP* 195

584 Soced. – colleague of **583**

A possible female relative, Socedeiaunin Istamiuris f., is mentioned in
Eph. Epigr. IX 329.

VM 70:13 = Gil 392; Albertos *OPP* 210

585 C. N... L. f. – magistrate; ca 120–90 BC
VM 70:14 = Gil 393

586 M. Fulvius – magistrate; ca 120–90 BC
VM 71:1 = Gil 394

587 C. Aelius – colleague of **585** and **586**
VM 70:14, 71:1 = Gil 393–4

588 M. Isc[er.?] – colleague of **585, 586**, and **587**(bis)

Cognomina beginning with 'Isc-' (e.g., Iscerbeles, and cf Sacaliscer, **583**)
are well attested in Tarraconensis.

VM 70:14, 71:1 = Gil 393–4; cf Albertos *OPP* 125

589 Cn. Voconius St. f. – magistrate; ca 120–90 BC
VM 71:2–3 = Gil 395–7

590 Cn. Fulvius Cn. f. – colleague of **589**
See **589**.

591 M. Valerius – magistrate ca 120–90 BC
   VM 71:7 = Gil 398
592 C. Cornelius – colleague of **591**
   See **591**.
593 M. Popillius M. f. – magistrate; before 49 BC
   VM 71:6 = Gil 1248
594 P. Coe[lius?] Star.[f?] – colleague of **593**
   See **593**.
595 M. Ba[dius?] L. f. – magistrate; before 49 BC
   VM 71:8–10, 12, 173:1 = Gil 1249–53
596 M. Virillius Q. f[?] – colleague of 595
   See **595**.
597 Ap. Clo[dius?] – magistrate; before 49 BC
   VM 71:5 = Gil 1254
598 A. Postumius Cn. [f ?] – colleague of **597**
   See **597**.
599 M. Iunius C. f. Gal. Paternus – IIvir, flamen Romae et Augusti; reign of
   Trajan or Hadrian; wife Cornelia P. f. Severa
   HAEp. 1464 = *ILER* 1716; Etienne *Culte* 205
600 L. Cornelius L. f. Gal. Agricola – IIvir, flamen Romae et Augusti; reign of
   Trajan or Hadrian
   ILER 1581; Etienne *Culte* 205
601 P. Cornelius M. f. Gal. Verecundus – omnibus honoribus functus, flamen
   p.H.c. between 120 and 180
   CIL II 4209 = *ILER* 1610 = *RIT* 270; A. d'Ors *Emerita* 40 (1972) 66; Alföldy
   Flamines no. 19
602 C. Cornelius C. f. Gal. Valentinus – IIvir, flamen Romae et Augusti; wife
   Cornelia L. f. Verecundina (perhaps a relative of **601**)
   Etienne misreads Cornelius's *cognomen* as 'Valens.'
   CIL II 3276 = *ILER* 5677; Etienne *Culte* 211
603 Anonymus – IIvir, perhaps f[lamen perpe]tuus
   CIL II 3277

Cauca (conv. Cluniensis)

604 M. Valerius Lentulus – IIvir
   He witnessed a pact of *hospitium* with Amallobriga in AD 134.
   G. Bravo Castañeda *Gerión* 3 (1985) 312 = *AE* 1985, 581
605 L. Sempronius Quadratus – colleague of **604**
   See **604**.

Celsa colonia Victrix Iulia Lepida (conv. Caesaraugustanus)

Grant *FITA* 212 and F. Beltrán Lloris *Numisma* 28 (1978) 175 think that some of the coins attributed to Celsa are actually from an otherwise unknown town called Lepida. But it is clear, both from the magistrates' titles ('pr. IIvir') and the coin types (Heiss *Monnaies* pl XI, 15–16 – one 'Lep.,' one 'Celsa' – have identical designs on the reverse) that Celsa and Lepida are the same town. See Gil p 248 on a likely reason for the apparent change of name.

606 M. Ful[vius] – pr. quin[quennalis]; ca 45–44 BC
(VM 160:5 = Gil 1054; *CIC* 82; cf. Galsterer *Untersuchungen* 25)

607 C. Otac[ilius] – colleague of **606**
VM 160:5 = Gil 1054; *CIC* 144

608 L. Nep[os] – pr., IIvir; ca 39–37 BC
Gómez-Pantoja restores the *nomen* as 'Nep[ius],' but Nepos is a much commoner name.
VM 160:4 = Gil 1055; *CIC* 138

609 L. Sura – colleague of **608**
Gómez-Pantoja reads 'Sur[ius]' but the coin reads 'SVRA.'
CIC 197; and see **608**.

610 P. Sal[vius?] Pa[ternus?] – pr., IIvir; ca 39–37 BC
VM 160:1–2 = Gil 1056–7; *CIC* 175

611 M. Fulvius – colleague of **610**; perhaps son of **606**
CIC 83; and see **610**.

612 C. Balbus – pr., IIvir; ca 39–37 BC
VM 160:3 = Gil 1058; *CIC* 30

613 L. Porcius – colleague of **612**
CIC 161; and see **612**.

614 L. Sempronius Maximus – aedilis; ca 39–37 BC
VM 160:6 = Gil 1059; *CIC* 183

615 M. Caed[ius?] – colleague of **614**
CIC 34; and see **614**.

616 L. Cal[purnius] – aedilis; ca 39–37 BC
VM 160:7 = Gil 1060; *CIC* 43

617 Sex. Niger – colleague of **616**
CIC 139; and see **616**.

618 L. Pompeius Bucco – IIvir; ca 28 BC
VM 160:9 = Gil 1062; *CIC* 148

619 L. Cornelius Front[o] – colleague of **618**
CIC 60; and see **618**.

620 M. Iunius Hispanus – IIvir; ca 27–25 BC
VM 160:10–11, 173:11 = Gil 1063–6; *CIC* 102

621 L. Cornelius Terre[nus?] – colleague of **620**
    VM 160:10–11, 173:11 = Gil 1063–6; *CIC* 64; cf Kajanto *Cognomina* 341

622 L. Sura – IIvir; ca 27–25 BC; perhaps son of **609**
    (VM 160:12 = Gil 1067; *CIC* 196)

623 L. Bucco – colleague of **622**; perhaps the same as **618**
    CIC 32; and see **622**.

624 L. Baccius – IIvir; ca 27–25 BC
    His *nomen* is Etruscan.
    VM 161:1–4 = Gil 1068–71; A. Balil *Hispania* 25 (1965) 362; *CIC* 25

625 M'. Flavius Festus – colleague of **624**
    A duovir of the same name appears at Caesaraugusta (**495**) and is possibly
    related.
    VM 161:1–4 = Gil 1068–71; *CIC* 77

626 L. Aufidius Pansa – aedilis; ca 27–25 BC
    VM 161:5–6 = Gil 1072–3; *CIC* 24

627 Sex. Pomp[eius] Niger – colleague of **626**; perhaps son of **617**
    Gómez-Pantoja restores the *nomen* as 'Pomp[onius].'
    CIC 155; and see **626**.

628 Cn. Domitius – IIvir; ca 5 BC
    VM 161:8 = Gil 1646; *CIC* 66

629 C. Pompeius – colleague of **628**
    CIC 147; and see **628**.

630 Bacc[ius] Front[o] – IIvir bis; reign of Tiberius; perhaps a relative of **624**
    VM 161:9 = Gil 1838; *CIC* 26

631 Cn. Bucco – colleague of **630**
    CIC 31; and see **630**.

632 Vetilius Bucco – aedilis; reign of Tiberius
    VM 161:7 = Gil 1839; *CIC* 219

633 C. Fufius – colleague of **632**
    CIC 80; and see **632**.

Clunia probably municipium; later colonia Sulpicia (conv. Cluniensis)

See also Addenda **977**

634 Cn. Pompeius – IIIIvir; AD 14–37
    VM 163:2 = Gil 1840

635 M. Antonius – colleague of **634**
    See **634**.

636 T. Antonius – colleague of **634**; AD 14–37; perhaps a relative of **635**
    See **634**.

637 M. Iulius Seranus – colleague of **634**
    See **634**.

638 C. Aemilius Met[ellus?] – IIIIvir; AD 14–37
   VM 163:3 = Gil 1841

639 T. Cornelius Maternus – colleague of **638**
   See **638**.

640 L. Caecilius Pres[sus?] – colleague of **638**
   The *cognomen* might also be restored as 'Pres[ens],' i.e., Praesens.
   See **638**.

641 C. Aelius Caud[inus] – colleague of **638**
   See **638**.

642 L. Iulius Rufus – IIIIvir; AD 14–37
   VM 163:4 = Gil 1842

643 T. Calpurnius Con. – colleague of **642**
   See **642**.

644 T. Pomp[eius] Lon[gus?] – colleague of **642**
   See **642**.

645 P. Iulius Nep[os?] – colleague of **642**
   See **642**.

646 L. Rufinius – IIIIvir; AD 14–37
   VM 163:5 = Gil 1843

647 T. Consi. – colleague of **646**
   See **646**.

648 T. Longius – colleague of **646**
   See **646**.

649 P. Antonius – colleague of **646**
   See **646**.

650 L. Domitius Robustus – aedilis; AD 14–37
   VM 163:6 = Gil 1844

651 T. Octavius Metal. – colleague of **650**
   See **650**.

652 M. Lucretius Ter. – aedilis; AD 14–37
   VM 163:7 = Gil 1845

653 C. Calpurnius Varus – colleague of **652**
   See **652**.

654 L. Sempronius Rufus – aedilis; AD 14–37
   VM 163:8 = Gil 1846

655 Cn. Ar[rius?] Gracilis – colleague of **654**
   See **654**.

656 C. Calvisius Aeonis f. Gal. Sabinus – mag[ister or magistratus], flamen
   Romae et Divi Augusti; reign of Tiberius
   He distributed grain to the people when the official price was high
   (*annona cara*). Calvisius also received a dedication from the decurions of
   Uxama for his good deeds there.
   CIL II 2782, 2822 = *ILER* 1580, 6385; Etienne *Culte* 206–7

657 C. Magius L. f. Gal. Silo – legatus; AD 40
He and **658** arranged *hospitium* between Clunia and her patron, a certain
C. Terentius Bassus.
CIL II 5792 = *ILS* 6102

658 T. Aemilius Fuscus – colleague of **657**
See **657**.

659 ... Caelius Clouti f. – IIIIvir I ...
The date is uncertain, although the indigenous filiation suggests 1st
century. Hübner restores 'i[ure dic.],' but 'I[I]' (i.e., 'bis') is equally
possible and perhaps more likely since there is no other IIIIvir i.d. in
Spain.
CIL II 2781

660 Valerius Marcellus – legatus; AD 222
He is named on a hospitality pact between the *concilium conventus
Cluniensis* and C. Marius Pudens, commander of Legio VII Gemina. The
Trajanic duovir Valerius Marcellus of Aurgi, **22**, is possibly a relative.
CIL VI 1454 = *ILS* 6109

Coelerni (conv. Bracaraugustanus)

661 P. Campanius Geminus – legatus; AD 132
He arranged *hospitium* between Coelerni and C. Antonius Aquilus, prae-
fectus cohortis I Celtiberorum.
J. Ferro Couselo and J. Lorenzo Fernández *Bol. Aur.* 1 (1971) 9–15 = C.
Castillo *Emerita* 41 (1973) 115 = *AE* 1972, 282

Complutum (conv. Caesaraugustanus)

662 Cn. Nonius C. f. Quir. Crescens – mag[ister or magistratus], flamen Romae
et Aug; a Flavian or later date is indicated by the tribe Quirina; son C.
Nonius Sincerus
CIL II 3033 = *ILER* 1579; cf Etienne Culte 228; *CIC* 140

663 L. Caecilius L. f. Quir. Caecilianus – duovir ter, flamen divorum et
Augustorum p.H.c. between 70 and 150; son Q. Caecilius Campanus
CIL II 4199 = *ILER* 1596 = *RIT* 262; Alföldy *Flamines* no. 10; *CIC* 38

Consabura municipium (conv. Carthaginiensis)

664 L. Domitius M. f. Serg. Dentonianus – iudex decuriarum V, equo publico
per Traianum, IIvir, flamen perpetuus, tribunus militum cohortis Asturum
et Callaecorum (in Mauretania Tingitana), flamen p.H.c. between 105 and
117
CIL II 4211 = *ILS* 6936 = *ILER* 1586 = *RIT* 271; Etienne *Culte* 136; Wiegels
no. 256; Alföldy *Flamines* no. 20; *PME* D 20

Contrebia Balaisca (conv. Caesaraugustanus)

665 Lubbus Urdinocum Letondonis f. – praetor; 87 BC

'Lub-' is a frequent element in indigenous names. The father's name, Letondo, has parallels in Celtiberia.

G. Fatás *BRAH* 167 (1979) 424 = *AE* 1979, 377; cf Fatás *Contrebia Balaisca* II (Zaragoza 1980) 12, 90–99; A. d'Ors *Anuario de Historia del Derecho Español* 50 (1980) 1–20

666 Lesso Siriscum Lubbi f. – magistratus; 87 BC

The indigenous name Lesso is found also at Saguntum (*CIL* II 3852).

Fatás *BRAH* 167 (1979) 424 = *AE* 1979, 377

667 Babbus Bolgondiscum Ablonis f. – colleague of **666**

The name Babbus is otherwise unknown. His father's name, Ablo, is borne also by **670**.

See **666**.

668 Segilus Annicum Lubbi f. – colleague of **666**

The indigenous name Segilus is attested twice at Tarraco (*CIL* II 4338, 6118).

See **666**.

669 ...atu[s] ...ulovicum Uxenti f. – colleague of **666**

See **666**.

670 Ablo Tindilicum Lubbi f. – colleague of **666**

'Abl-' is a frequent element in indigenous nomenclature.

See **666**.

Damania (conv. Caesaraugustanus)

671 M. Valerius M. f. Gal. Ani. Capellianus – adlectus in coloniam Caesaraugustanam ex beneficio Divi Hadriani, omnibus honoribus in utraque re p. functus, flamen Romae divorum et Augustorum p.H.c. between 140 and 160

Evidently he not only moved to Caesaraugusta but was re-enrolled in Aniensis, the tribe of that colony. He then proceeded to Tarraco to exercise the provincial priesthood.

CIL II 4249 = *ILS* 6933 = *ILER* 1591 = *RIT* 309; Etienne *Culte* 139; Alföldy *Flamines* no. 66; *CIC* 209

Dertosa municipium Hibera Iulia Ilercavonia; later colonia (conv. Tarraconensis)

672 C. Cassius C. f. Gal. Niger – omnibus honoribus functus; after AD 120; son C. Cassius Avitus

CIL II 4059 = *ILER* 3926

673 L. Munnius L. f. Gal. Placidus – IIvir, flamen Romae et Aug.; 1st or early 2nd century; wife: Porcia L. f. Placida, son L. Munnius Placidus

   Eph. Epigr. IX 386–7 = *ILER* 1567, 1574; Etienne *Culte* 207

674 M. Baebius Crassus – legatus; AD 138

   He performed a *legatio* (probably of congratulations and loyalty) at his own expense, to the emperor Antoninus Pius upon the accession of the latter.

   CIL II 4057 = *ILER* 1115

675 Anonymus (or Anonymi) – legatus (or legati), honoured 'ob legationes in concilio p.H.c. [et?] aput Antoninum Augustum prospere gestas.' If this is a single man, he might be the same as **674**.

   CIL II 4055 = *ILS* 6925 = *ILER* 490

676 M. Porcius Theopompus – sevir Augustalis primus; honoured with 'aedilicium ius in perpetuum.'

   He was a freedman, as both his *cognomen* and appointment suggest. Mommsen (in *CIL*) considers *aedilicium ius* to be the same as *aedilicii honores*.

   CIL II 4061 = *ILER* 5573; Etienne *Culte* 258, 279

677 M. Porcius M. f. Terentianus – son of **676**, who dedicated the monument

   He was granted 'aedilicii et duovirales honores' by the local *ordo*.

   CIL II 4060 = *ILER* 1383

678 P. Valerius Dionysius – sevir Augustalis

   He received 'aedilicii honores' from the *ordo* 'ob merita eius.' Like **676** he was probably a freedman and so not entitled to hold an actual magistracy.

   CIL II 4062 = *ILS* 6955 = *ILER* 1382

Dianium municipium (conv. Carthaginiensis)

679 Q. Granius Q. f. Gal. Clemens – omnibus honoribus in re p. functus; mid-2nd century AD; nephews: Iunius Festus and [Iunius] Severus (the latter perhaps the same as **682**)

   CIL II 5962 = M.A. Rabanal Alonso and J.M. Abascal Palazón *Lucentum* 4 (1985) 206–7 no. 28

680 L. Valerius L. f. Gal. Propinquus – omnibus honoribus in re p. sua functus, adlectus in quinque decurias, flamen p.H.c. between 120 and 180

   Etienne's dating to the reign of Antoninus Pius is rather speculative. Also, in *CIL* II 4250 Valerius calls himself 'flamen Romae divorum et Augustorum p.H.c.'; the two flaminal titles are probably equivalent.

   CIL II 3584–5 = *ILER* 1641–2 = Rabanal and Abascal (see **679**) 204–5 no. 25–6; *CIL* II 4250 = *ILER* 1589 = *RIT* 310; Etienne *Culte* 163, 486; Wiegels no. 339; Alföldy *Flamines* no. 67

681 ... Cornelius Q. f. Gal. Placidus – omnibus honoribus in re p. sua functus; mid-2nd century AD; wife Aemilia L. f. Severina.

A certain Q. L. Corneli Placidi named on an amphora seal (*CIL* II 6254.11) is possibly related.

CIL II 3582 = *ILER* 1405 = Rabanal and Abascal (see **679**) 208 no. 30

682 T. Iunius T. f. Gal. Severus – omnibus honoribus in re p. sua functus, praefectus cohortis IIII Dalmatarum (in Germania Superior), tribunus legionis xx Valeriae Victricis (in Britain); perhaps nephew of **679** and father or uncle of T. Iunius Severus, cos. suff. 154

CIL II 3583 = *ILER* 1406 = Rabanal and Abascal (see **679**) 207–8 no. 29; Wiegels no. 283; *PME* I 153

683 Q. Sempronius Q. f. Gal. Taurus – d[ecurio] m[unicipii], according to G. Alföldy (cited by Rabanal and Abascal); 2nd century AD

The abbreviation D.M. normally stands for 'Dis manibus,' but appears to have a different meaning in this inscription, since it occurs after the man's name, where one expects his titles to be listed.

CIL II 3592 = Rabanal and Abascal (see **679**) 210 no. 34

Ebusus municipium Flavium (conv. Carthaginiensis)

684 L. Oculatius L. f. Quir. Rectus – aedilis, IIvir, flamen; 2nd century AD; son L. Oculatius L. f. Rectus

CIL II 3662 = *ILER* 5530 = Veny *Corpus* 179, cf 176

Egara municipium Flavium (conv. Tarraconensis)

685 Q. Granius Q. f. Gal. Optatus – IIvir, tribunus militum; first half of 2nd century (probably between 120 and 140); wife Grania Anthusa

CIL II 4495 = *ILER* 1690 = G. Fabre et al., *Epigrafia romana de Terrassa* (Terrassa 1981) no. 6 = *IRC* I 69; Wiegels no. 268; *PME* G 26

Emporiae municipium (conv. Tarraconensis)

686 Iskerbeles – magistrate; 2nd century BC

The name, written in Iberian script, comprises the common Iberian elements 'Isker-' and '-beles.'

Villaronga *Aes Coinage* 35 no. 16; J. Untermann *Elementos de un atlas antroponímico de la Hispania antigua* (Madrid 1965) 71

687 Iltirarker – magistrate; 2nd century BC

The element 'Iltir-/Ildir-' is common in Iberian names (cf **201**).

Villaronga *Aes Coinage* no. 17; Albertos *OPP* 123

688 Atabels – magistrate; 2nd century BC

The name and script are Iberian. The suffix '-bels' is equivalent to '-beles,' the latter seen in **686**.

Villaronga *Aes Coinage* no. 18; Untermann *Elementos* 71

689 Tiberius – magistrate; 2nd century BC
This is an instance of a Latin name written in Iberian script, indicating a transitional phase of romanization.
Villaronga *Aes Coinage* no. 19; J. Siles *Faventia* 3 (1981) 109

690 Lucius – magistrate; 2nd century BC
This is another Latin name written in Iberian script.
Villaronga *Aes Coinage* no. 20 and pp 12–13; Siles *Faventia* 3 (1981) 109

691 C. Ca. T. – quaestor; 27 BC–AD 14
The coins naming **691–720** are dated by Gil to the period 45–23 BC and by Villaronga to 'after 27 BC.' These dates are conjectural, but Villaronga's demonstration that the coin weights follow the system introduced by Augustus seems convincing.
VM 122:3 = Gil 1079 = Villaronga *Aes Coinage* issues 99–100

692 C. O. Ca[r.] – colleague of **691**
See **691**.

693 C. I. Nicom[edes] – quaestor; 27 BC–AD 14
VM 121:9–10 = Gil 1081–2 = Villaronga *Aes Coinage* issues 85–6; Grant *FITA* 156

694 P. Fl[avius?] – perhaps colleague of **693**
The restoration of the abbreviation 'P. Fl.' is uncertain; Villaronga interprets it as 'p[rimus] fl[amen].'
VM 121:9–10 = Gil 1081–2 = Villaronga *Aes Coinage* issues 85–6 and p 14

695 C. I. – quaestor; 27 BC–AD 14; possibly the same man as **693**
VM 121:7–8 = Gil 1080, 1100 = Villaronga *Aes Coinage* issues 73–4

696 L. C. – colleague of **695**
VM 121:7–8, 122:9 = Gil 1080, 1100, 1090 = Villaronga *Aes Coinage* issues 73–4, 80

697 C. R. – quaestor; colleague of **696**
(VM 122:9 = Gil 1090 = Villaronga *Aes Coinage* issue 80

698 C. P. C. – quaestor; 27 BC–AD 14
VM 122:7 = Gil 1083 = Villaronga *Aes Coinage* issue 88

699 M. S. R. – colleague of **698**
See **698**.

700 C. S. B. – quaestor; 27 BC–AD 14
VM 122:1 = Gil 1084 = Villaronga *Aes Coinage* issue 94

701 L. C. M. – colleague of **700**
See **700**.

702 Cn. C. Gr. – quaestor; 27 BC–AD 14
VM 122:2, 4 = Gil 1086 = Villaronga *Aes Coinage* issues 97–8

703 L. C. Fa. – colleague of **702**
See **702**.

704 Cn. C. P. – quaestor; 27 BC–AD 14
VM 123:3–4 = Gil 1087–8 = Villaronga *Aes Coinage* issues 95–6

705 C. M. A. – colleague of **704**
VM 123:3–4, 122:5 = Gil 1087–9 = Villaronga *Aes Coinage* issues 95–6, 102–3

706 C. O. C. – quaestor, colleague of **705**
VM 122:5 = Gil 1089 = Villaronga *Aes Coinage* issues 102–3

707 C. T. C. – quaestor; 27 BC–AD 14
VM 121:4 = Gil 1085 = Villaronga *Aes Coinage* issue 101

708 Q. C. Ca. – colleague of **707**
See **707**.

709 L. M. Ruf[us?] – quaestor; 27 BC–AD 14
VM 122:10 = Gil 1091 = Villaronga *Aes Coinage* issue 89

710 P. C. – perhaps colleague of **709**
But Villaronga interprets the initials as 'p[raefectus] C[aesaris].'
Villaronga *Aes Coinage* p 14; see **709**.

711 M. A. B. – quaestor; 27 BC–AD 14
VM 121:5–6 = Gil 1092–3 = Villaronga *Aes Coinage* issues 104–6

712 M. F. M. – colleague of **711**
See **711**.

713 M. O. H. – quaestor; 27 BC–AD 14
VM 122:6, 123:1 = Gil 1094–5 = Villaronga *Aes Coinage* issues 90–2

714 L. A. F. – colleague of **713**
See **713**.

715 P. C. Pu. – quaestor; 27 BC–AD 14
VM 123:2 = Gil 1096 = Villaronga *Aes Coinage* issue 93

716 Q. C. C. – colleague of **715**
See **715**.

717 P. I. P. – quaestor; 27 BC–AD 14
VM 122:8 = Gil 1097 = Villaronga *Aes Coinage* issues 83–4

718 C. S. M. – colleague of **717**
See **717**.

719 P. L. – perhaps quaestor; 27 BC–AD 14
Gil 1098 = Villaronga *Aes Coinage* issues 75–6

720 L. L. – colleague of **719**
See **719**.

721 [L?] Caecilius L. f. Gal. Macer – aedilis, IIvir; end of the Republic
He provided a *campus* at his own expense. He is possibly identical with **701**.
M.J. Pena Gimeno *Epigrafía ampuritana, 1953–1980* (Barcelona 1981) no. 6 = AE 1981, 563

722 [C? M]ini[cius G]al. Am[phio?] – aedilis, ɪɪvir, quaestor bis, flamen divi
Augusti; reign of Tiberius; possibly identical with or related to **705**
Pena Gimeno *Epigrafía ampuritana* no. 3 = AE 1981, 562

723 L. Minicius L. f. Rufus – aedilis, ɪɪvir, quaestor, flamen Romae et Aug.; 1st
century AD; possibly identical with or descended from **709**, perhaps a
relative of **722**
M.J. Pena et al., *Información arqueológica* 27–8 (1978) 65–7 = Pena
Gimeno *Epigrafía ampuritana* no. 2 = AE 1981, 561

724 Anonymi – legati [et] atvocati of the Indicetani, ca AD 75–8
These *legati* represented the Indicetani (the Iberian inhabitants of
Emporiae, Strabo 3.4.8) in a lawsuit. The case is recorded on three
tabulae defixionis, which also name the provincial governor T. Aurelius
Fulvus, the *iuridicus* Q. Pomponius Rufus and the imperial procurator
Marius Maturus.
M. Almagro *Las inscripciones ampuritanas griegas, ibéricas y latinas*
(Barcelona 1952) 163–8 = Alföldy *Fasti* 19–20 = ʃLER 5917–19

725 C. Aemilius C. f. Gal. Montanus – aedilis, ɪɪvir
He built a shrine and statue to Tutela at his own expense. This shrine is
one of eight on the north side of the forum, all built, it would seem, by
wealthy citizens.
Pena Gimeno *Epigrafía ampuritana* no. 7 = AE 1981, 564; cf E. Ripoll
Perelló *Ampurias: Description of the Ruins and Monographic Museum*
(Barcelona 1976) 71

726 M'. Cornelius M'. f. Gal. Saturninus Paternus – aedilis, ɪɪvir, flamen;
dedicated by the cultores Larum
AE 1900, 118 = Almagro *Las inscripciones ampuritanas* 90–2 = ILER 1566

727 L. Rosius L. f. Ser. Rufus – aedilis, ɪɪvir, q[uaestor]; father L. Rosius,
mother Rosia
Previous editors restore 'q[uinquennalis]' because 'q.' follows 'ɪɪvir'; but
we now know from **723** that the quaestorship can be listed after the
duovirate.
Eph. Epigr. IX 399 = Almagro *Las inscripciones ampuritanas* 107–8 = ILER
6800

Ercavica municipium (conv. Caesaraugustanus)

728 C. Cornelius Florus – ɪɪvir; reign of Tiberius
VM 162:5–6 = Gil 1918–19; CIC 59

729 L. Caelius Alegris – colleague of **728**
CIC 36; and see **728**.

730 C. Terentius Sura – ɪɪvir; AD 38
VM 162:8–11 = Gil 2021–5; CIC 200

731 L. Licinius Gracilis – colleague of **730**
CIC 108; and see **730**.

732 M. Calpurnius M. f. Lupus – omnibus honoribus in re p. sua functus, praefectus cohortis I Biturgium, flamen p.H.c. between 120 and 180
CIL II 4203 = *ILER* 1310 = *RIT* 265; Alföldy *Flamines* no. 14; Wiegels no. 235; *PME* C 58; *CIC* 44

733 Aelius ...ctalis – see **38***.

734 Anonymus – see **38***.

735 ... Turellius Gal. Avitus – flamen, IIvir
Rodríguez Colmenero (see **733**) 231 no. 80 = *AE* 1982, 618; G. Alföldy *Römisches Städtewesen auf der neukastilischen Hochebene* (Heidelberg 1987) 68

Gandía (ancient name unknown; conv. Carthaginiensis)

736 Minicius M. f. Gal. Marcellus – decurio, omnibus honoribus in re p. sua functus; 2nd century or later; mother perhaps Pompeia
CIL II 3606 = *ILER* 6410

Gerunda (conv. Tarraconensis)

737 L. Plotius L. f. Gal. Asprenas – aedilis, IIvir, flamen, tribunus legionis III Gallicae (in Syria); late 1st or 2nd century; wife Iulia C. f. Marcia
CIL II 4622 = *ILER* 5533; Wiegels no. 309; *PME* P 46

738 C. Marius C. f. Pal. Verus – omnibus honoribus in re p. sua functus, flamen p.H.c. between 120 and 180
The urban tribe Palatina suggests servile descent.
CIL II 4229 = *ILER* 1627 = *RIT* 293; Alföldy *Flamines* no. 44

Grallia (conv. Caesaraugustanus)

739 M. Sempronius M. f. Quir. Capito – a native of Grallia, adlectus in ordine Caesaraugustano, omnibus honoribus in utraque re p. functus, flamen p.H.c. ca 120–80
CIL II 4244 = *ILER* 1612 = *RIT* 304; Alföldy *Flamines* no. 61; *CIC* 180

Guiuntum (Balearis Maior, conv. Carthaginiensis)

740 Cn. Gavius Cn. f. Quir. Amethystus – omnibus honoribus in rebus publicis suis functus, flamen p.H.c. between 120 and 180
He is a citizen of both Palma and Guium, but probably a native of the latter, since he is not in the tribe Velina (to which Palma belonged) and

since he is unlikely to have gone from a large town to a small one in the course of what was obviously an ascending career.

CIL II 4218 = *ILS* 6935 = *ILER* 1622 = *RIT* 280; Etienne *Culte* 147 n 8; Alföldy *Flamines* no. 28

Iacca (conv. Caesaraugustanus)

741 L. Valerius Ser. Veraius – IIvir bis

He repaired the road leading from Iacca into Aquitania, presumably at his own expense rather than as executive officer of the city, since Iacca is not mentioned in the inscription. For another duovir involved in road construction see **802**.

HAEp. 971; cf R.P. Duncan-Jones *JRS* 64 (1974) 82 n 28

Ilerda municipium (conv. Caesaraugustanus)

742 C. Licinius C. f. Gal. Saturninus – aedilis, IIvir, flamen; mid-2nd century; wife Porcia P. f. Nigrina

A certain Q. Licinius Saturninus, attested as a duovir at Metellinum in Lusitania (**355**), is perhaps related.

CIL II 3010 = *ILER* 5529 = *ERLérida* 1 = *IRC* II 2; *CIC* 109

743 Ti. Manlius Ti. f. Gal. Silvanus – aedilis, IIvir, flamen; late 1st or early 2nd century; wife: Cornelia Faventina, who was possibly from Iesso (cf *CIL* II 4453–4)

CIL 5848 = *ILER* 5527 = *ERLérida* 2 = *IRC* II 13*; *CIC* 119

744 C. Marcius Gal. Masclus – aedilis, IIvir, flamen; 2nd century; mother Marcia Tempestiva

The inscription is sometimes wrongly reported as coming from Aeso, with the reading 'L. Marcius.'

AE 1938, 21 = *HAEp.* 497 = *AE* 1957, 312 = *ILER* 5528 = *ERLérida* 5 = *IRC* II 3; *CIC* 121

745 M. Cornelius L. f. Gal. Arrianus – aedilis, IIvir, flamen, aug[ur] [Augusti?]; 2nd century; wife Licinia L. f. Nigrina

An inscription in his memory was discovered near the Roman villa of Els Viláns (Aytona), a large rural establishment covering some two hectares, of which he was presumably the owner.

R. Pita Mercé *Ampurias* 30 (1968) 332 = *ERLérida* 32 = *AE* 1972, 315 = *IRC* II 11; Gorges *Villas* 282–3; *CIC* 57

746 ... Atilius Commodus – omnibus honoribus in re p. sua functus ...; mid-2nd century

J. Vives *Anuari del Institut d'Estudis Catalans* 8 (1927–31) 374 = *ERLérida* 7 = *IRC* II 1; *CIC* 17

Ilici colonia Iulia Augusta (conv. Carthaginiensis)

747 Q. Terentius Montanus – IIvir; second half of 1st century BC
Gil 1116–17

748 C. Salvius – colleague of **747**
See **747**.

749 L. Manlius – IIvir; ca 27–26 BC
VM 133:1–3 = Gil 1118–20

750 T. Petronius – colleague of **749**
See **749**.

751 Q. Papirius Car. – IIvir q.; ca 27–26 BC according to Gil (13–12 BC according to Blázquez
The coin is Augustan, but cannot be closely dated.
VM 134:4 = Gil 1121; J.M. Blázquez in *Symposion de ciudades augusteas*
I (Zaragoza 1976) 113

752 Q. Terentius Montanus – colleague of **751**; perhaps the same as, or the son of **747**
VM 134:4 = Gil 1121

753 L. Terentius Lon[gus?] – IIvir q.; before AD 19
VM 133:12–13 = Gil 1923–4

754 L. Papirius Avitus – colleague of **753**
See **753**.

755 M. Iulius Setal. – IIvir, AD 22
The *cognomen* is Celtic.
VM 133:9–11 = Gil 1925–7; Albertos OPP 206

756 L. Sestius Celer – colleague of **755**
See **755**.

757 T. Coelius Proculus – magistrate; reign of Tiberius
VM 133:6–8 = Gil 1928–30

758 M. Aemilius Severus – colleague of **757**
See **757**.

759 ...ius Q. f. C... – aedilis, IIvir et q.; end of 1st century AD
HAEp. 1969 = E. Ramos Fernández *La ciudad romana de Ilici* (Alicante 1975) 274 no. 1 = M.A. Rabanal Alonso and J.M. Abascal Palazón *Lucentum* 4 (1985) 225 no. 66

760 Anonymus – [a]edil[is?]
CIL II 5952 = Rabanal and Abascal (see **759**) 225 no. 67; A. Degrassi *Scritti vari di antichità* I (Roma 1962) 125 n 190

761 L. Porcius ... – IIIIvir, IIIIv[ir...], aug[ur?] or [flamen] Aug[usti]
Local triumvirs are rare but not unknown. Another possible restoration might be: [I]IIIvir, IIIIv[ir quinq.].
CIL II 5950 = *ILER* 201; Degrassi *Scritti vari* I 125; G. Alföldy *AEA* 45–7 (1972–4) 411 n 3

Iluro oppidum civium Romanorum (conv. Tarraconensis)

762 L. Marcius Q. f. Gal. Optatus – aedilis at Tarraco, IIvir at Iluro, IIvir quinquennalis primus, praefectus Asturiae, tribunus militum legionis II Augustae (in Britain); reign of Nero or Vespasian; died in Phrygia
CIL II 4616 = ILS 6948 = ILER 3436 = IRC I 101; Pflaum *EREsp*. 92; Wiegels no. 298; *PME* M 30; P. Le Roux *ZPE* 43 (1981) 203–4

763 Anonymus – [aedilis?], [IIvir?], flamen Romae et Augusti, [praefectus fabrum?] in Germany, [praefectus cohortis?] Gallorum Equitatae, [tribunus militum?] legionis IV Macedonicae at Mainz; 60s AD
The inscription is heavily, if plausibly, restored, and the local magistracies are conjectural.
AE 1983, 626 = IRC I 102

764 M. M...ius ... f. Celer – IIvir
The inscription is fragmentary and it is uncertain whether we have here a single name, or the first and last parts of the names of two duovirs.
M. Prevosti i Monclús *Cronologia i poblament a l'àrea rural d'Iluro* (Mataró 1981) 209–10 = IRC I 88

765 P. Manlius Cn. f. Gal. – aedilis, IIvir; Augustan or slightly later
The inscription is ascribed to Barcino in CIL, but the earliest manuscript and several later authorities locate it near Iluro.
CIL II 4528 = ILER 1372 = IRB 58 = IRC I 126; G. Alföldy *Gerión* 2 (1984) 232

766 Cn. Manlius P. f. Gal. Secundus – aedilis; Augustan or slightly later; son of **765**
CIL II 4528 = ILER 1372 = IRB 58 = IRC I 126; Alföldy Gerión 2 (1984) 232

Intercatia (conv. Cluniensis)

767 L. Antonius Paterni f. Quir. Modestus – omnibus honoribus in re p. sua functus, sacerdos Romae et Augusti ararum Augustanarum, flamen p.H.c.; second half of 2nd century; wife Paetinia Paterna of Amoca (CIL II 4233)
CIL II 6093 = ILER 1606 = RIT 256; Etienne *Culte* 191; Alföldy *Flamines* no. 5

Labitolosa (conv. Caesaraugustanus)

768 M. Clodius M. f. Gal. Flaccus – IIvir bis, flamen, tribunus militum legionis IIII Flaviae in Moesia Superior, vir praestantissimus et civis optimus; late 1st or early 2nd century
CIL II 5837 = ILER 1378; Wiegels no. 240; *PME* C 199; CIC 53

Lancia (conv. Asturum)

769 L. Iunius Blaesi f. Quir. Maro Aemilius Paternus – omnibus in re p. sua honoribus functus, IIvir bis, sacerdos Romae et Aug. conventus Asturum, adlectus in quinque decurias legitume Romae iudicantium, flamen Augustalis p.H.c. between 110 and 140

His adlection to the five *decuriae* was done by act of the emperor, whose name is not given here.

CIL II 4223 and p 365 = *ILS* 6932 = *ILER* 1550 = *RIT* 287 = T. Mañanes Pérez *Epigrafía y numismática de Astorga romana y su entorno* (León and Salamanca 1982) no. 97; Etienne *Culte* 136–7 and n 1; Alföldy *Flamines* no. 36; Pastor *Los Astures* 174

Lara de los Infantes municipium? (ancient name unknown; conv. Cluniensis)

770 C. Terentius ... f. Reburrinus – veteranus legionis VII Geminae Felicis, IIvir; late 1st or early 2nd century

CIL II 2853 = *ILER* 5671 = J.A. Abásolo Alvarez *Epigrafía romana de la región de Lara de los Infantes* (Burgos 1974) 216 = G. Alföldy *ZPE* 41 (1981) 249 = *AE* 1981, 551; P. Le Roux *L'armée romaine et l'organisation des provinces ibériques* (Paris 1982) 201–2

771 L. Antonius ... f. Quir. ... – aedilis, II [vir?]

The fragmentary inscription reads 'AED II...,' which allows the alternative interpretation 'aedilis bis.'

A. García y Bellido *Esculturas romanas de España y Portugal* (Madrid 1949) no. 358 = Abásolo (see **770**) 127 = F. Marco Simón *Caesaraugusta* 43–4 (1978) 144 no. 132 = Alföldy *ZPE* 41 (1981) 248–9 = *AE* 1981, 550

772 L. Antonius C. f. Quir. Aquilus – IIvir, tribunus militum cohortis ...; 1st century AD; perhaps related to **771**

The inscription comes from Barbadillo del Pez, eighteen km east of Lara, but the latter is the nearest known Roman town.

J.A. Abásolo Alvarez *Boletín del Seminario de Estudios de Arte y Arqueología* 50 (1984) 199 = *AE* 1984, 568

773 C. Moenius Nigrini f. Quir. Fronto – II[vir]

Abásolo (see **770**) 215 = Alföldy *ZPE* 41 (1981) 245–7 = *ZPE* 44 (1981) 113, 117 = *AE* 1981, 548

774 Valerius Cres[cens?] – [II?]vir; 2nd or early 3rd century

Abásolo (see **770**) 195 = Marco Simón (see **771**) 159 no. 224 = Alföldy *ZPE* 41 (1981) 250, 252 = *AE* 1981, 552

775 Valerius St... – IIvir; a relative of **774**

Abásolo (see **770**) 195 = Marco Simón (see **771**) 159 no. 224 = Alföldy *ZPE* 41 (1981) 250, 252 = *AE* 1981, 552

776 Anonymus – xvir
The reading is uncertain, based on a copy made in the 17th(?) century.
CIL II 2883 = Abásolo (see **770**) 200 = Marco Simón (see **771**) 159 no. 228

777 [M?] Popidius Celsinus – decurio; 2nd or early 3rd century
Abásolo (see **770**) 10 = Marco Simón (see **771**) 122 no. 16 = Alföldy *ZPE*
41 (1981) 250–2 = *AE* 1981, 553

Libisosa colonia Forum Augustum (conv. Carthaginiensis)

778 C. Vibius C. f. Gal. Porcianus Quintius Italicianus – equo publico donatus a
Divo Hadriano, omnibus honoribus in re p. sua functus, flamen p.H.c.
between 140 and 160
CIL II 4254 = *ILER* 1617 = *RIT* 313; Etienne *Culte* 139; Wiegels no. 346;
Alföldy *Flamines* no. 70

Limici (conv. Bracaraugustanus)

779 M. Flavius M. f. Quir. Sabinus – IIvir, sacerdos conventus Bracaraugustani,
flamen p.H.c. between 140 and 180
CIL II 4215 = *ILS* 6931 = *ILER* 1621a = *RIT* 276; Alföldy *Flamines* no. 25

Liria civitas Edetanorum (conv. Tarraconensis)
See also Addenda **978**

780 M. Valerius M. f. Gal. Propinquus Grattius Cerealis – flamen p.H.c., cui
honores civitatis suae res publica [indul?]sit, adlectus in equite[s] a Tito
Imperatore, praefectus fabrum bis, praefectus cohortis II Asturum in
Germania [Inferiore ca 82–5], tribunus legionis V Macedonicae in Moesia
[Inferiore], praefectus alae Phrygum, item praefectus alae III Thracum in
Syria.
Although the rest of his *cursus* appears to be in chronological order, the
prestigious provincial priesthood has been moved to the head of the list of
honours; a similar displacement occurs in *CIL* II 6150. Alföldy dates
Valerius' flaminate to ca 100 – reasonably, if we accept Pflaum's thesis
that the flaminate was the last post held.
CIL II 4251 = *ILS* 2711 = *ILER* 1618 = *RIT* 311; Etienne *Culte* 134; Pflaum
EREsp. 93; Wiegels no. 340; Alföldy *Flamines* no. 68; Alföldy *Chiron* 3
(1973) 369–73; *PME* V 30

781 L. Caecilius L. f. Gal. Cassianus – omnibus honoribus functus; wife Licinia
C. f. Celerina, son L. Caecilius Crassus
CIL II 3790 = *ILER* 6030

782 ... Baebius M. f. Gal. Baebianus Severus – IIvir, flamen
CIL II 3789 = *ILER* 5678

783 L. Fabius Fabullus – q[uaestor], iiiivir bis
  L. Martí Ferrando *Archivo de prehistoria levantina* 13 (1972) 178 no.
  XXIX
784 L. Iunius Iusti f. Gal. Severus – iivir bis, flamen bis; 3rd century; wife
  Iunia Apronia
  Apronia had apparently been a slave of Iunius (whom she calls 'patron
  and husband') and was later manumitted by and married to him.
  CIL II 6014 = *ILER* 6029

Lougei (conv. Lucensis)

785 Silvanus Clouti (f.) – legatus
  He arranged *hospitium* with C. Asinius Gallus (cos. 8 BC and son of the
  historian Asinius Pollio) in AD 1.
  G. Pereira Menaut *Veleia* 1 (1984) 282 = *AE* 1984, 553 = M.D. Dopico
  Caínzos *Gerión* 4 (1986) 268
786 Nollius Andami [f.] – colleague of **785**
  See **785**.

Lucentum (conv. Carthaginiensis)

787 P. Fabricius Respectus – iivir; 2nd century AD
  CIL II 3557 = *ILER* 2072 = M.A. Rabanal Alonso and J.M. Abascal Palazón
  Lucentum 4 (1985) 195 no. 4
788 P. Fabricius Iustus – colleague (and presumably relative) of **787**
  See **787**.
789 ... Tadius M. f. Rufus – praefectus; attended to the construction of a tower
  or towers
  CIL II 3561 = *ILER* 2091 = Rabanal and Abascal *Lucentum* 4 [1985] 197 no.
  8

Lucus Augusti (conv. Lucensis)

790 [Vecc]o Veci f. – princeps Co[pororum?]; perhaps 1st century AD
  The text is poorly preserved. Lucus Augusti was located in the territory
  of the Copori tribe, according to Ptolemy (2.6.23). Vecco (or whatever his
  true name is) appears to have been their chief. For another *princeps* of
  this *conventus* cf **967**.
  CIL II 2585 = *HAEp.* 307 = *ILER* 6393 = F. Arias Vilas et al. *Inscriptions
  romaines de la province de Lugo* (Paris 1979) 34
791 [Vec?]ius Verobli f. – princeps ...; perhaps 1st century AD
  (*CIL* II 2585 = *HAEp.* 307 = *ILER* 6393 = Arias Vilas (see **790**)34

Luzaga (ancient name unknown; conv. Caesaraugustanus)

792 Deivorix – magistrate; 1st century BC
He witnessed a *tessera hospitalis* between two tribes. The name is a Celtic
formation similar to types found in Gaul. The tessera is written in
indigenous language and script.
F. Fita BRAH 2 (1881) 35–44; Albertos OPP 104; M. Vigil in *Historia de
España Alfaguara* I (Madrid 1973) 415; J.M. Blázquez *La romanización* II
(Madrid 1975) 362

Maggava (conv. Cluniensis)

793 Caraegius – mag[istratus?]; AD 14
He is named on a *tessera hospitalis* and his name bears the common
Celtic prefix 'Car-'.
AE 1967, 239 = ILER 5823–4 = CIP 9

794 Aburnus – colleague of **793**
His name is apparently a variant of the indigenous name 'Abrunus.'
See **793**; cf Albertos OPP 4.

795 Caelius – colleague of **793**
See **793**.

Mago municipium Flavium (Balearis Minor, conv. Carthaginiensis)

796 [Q. Caecilius] Q. f. Labeo – aedilis, IIvir; 2nd century AD; parents Q.
Caecilius Philistio and Iulia Severa
The father, a freedman of Caecilia Q. f. Severa, appears also in CIL II
3714–5, 3717.
CIL II 3708 and p 963 = ILER 1384 = Veny *Corpus* 128

797 Q. Cornelius Q. f. Quir. Secundus – aedilis, IIvir, flamen divorum et
Augustorum; 2nd century; son-in-law L. Cornelius Satur, grandson Q. Corne-
lius Satur
CIL II 3709 and p 963 = ILER 1572 = Veny *Corpus* 121

798 L. Fabius L. f. Quir. Fabullus – aedilis, IIvir ter, flamen divorum
Augustorum; Flavian or later.
L. Fabius Fabullus of Liria (**783**) and the senatorial Fabii Fabulli (PIR² F
30–2) are possible relatives.
CIL II 3710 = ILS 6958 = ILER 1573 = Veny *Corpus* 122

799 ... Maecius Quir. Maecianus – aedilicius ter, IIviratu in insula functus,
etiam flaminatu p.H.c.; between 160 and 180; a native of Iamo, a Flavian
municipium not far from Mago
Maecius' wife is the priestess Serena, attested in CIL II 3712–3.

CIL II 3711 and p 963 = *ILS* 6959 = *ILER* 1640 = Veny *Corpus* 123; Alföldy *Corpus* no. 41; J.-N. Bonneville *MCV* 18 (1982) 27

Mascarell (ancient name unknown; conv. Tarraconensis)

800 M. Tettienus M. f. Gal. Pollio – aedilis, iivir, flamen, aug[ur] (or flamen Augusti), quaestor; 1st century AD; wife: Baebia L. f. Lepida.
He was possibly a magistrate at Saguntum (as suggested by the late position of 'quaestor' in the *cursus*); his wife comes almost certainly from there, for she is of the *gens Baebia*.
CIL II 4028 = *ILER* 5535 = *ELSaguntum* p 301 no. xv; G. Alföldy *Res Publica Leserensis* (Valencia 1977) 41 n 2; G. Alföldy *Gerión* 2 (1984) 236

Murcia (ancient name unknown; conv. Carthaginiensis)

801 M. Postumius ... – pontifex, aedilis; 1st century AD
CIL II 5945

Numantia (conv. Cluniensis)

802 L. Lucretius Densus – iivir; perhaps 2nd century AD; built a via Aug[usta]
The rock-carved inscription recording this construction stands on the north bank of the river Duero. The density of Roman remains on this bank suggests the likelihood of a local road running westward from Numantia, and this would be the ambitiously named *via Augusta*.
CIL II 2886 = *ILER* 1966 = A. Jimeno *Epigrafía romana de la provincia de Soria* (Soria 1980) 136; B. Taracena *Carta arqueológica de España: Soria* (Madrid 1941) 22, 99; G. Alföldy *ZPE* 44 (1981) 118 n 18

Osca municipium Urbs Victrix (conv. Caesaraugustanus)

803 M. Quinctius – iivir; ca 26 BC
VM 136:6 = Gil 1126; *CIC* 170
804 Q. Aelius – colleague of 803
CIC 2; and see 803.
805 Compostus – iivir; ca 1 BC
VM 136:9–10 = Gil 1697–8; *CIC* 56
806 Marullus – colleague of 805
CIC 132; and see 805.
807 Sparsus – iivir; ca AD 1
VM 136:7–8 = Gil 1699–1700; *CIC* 192
808 Caecilianus – colleague of 807
CIC 42; and see 807.

809 Hospes – IIvir; reign of Tiberius
VM 137:3–4 = Gil 1940–1; *CIC* 95
810 Florus – colleague of **809**
CIC 79; and see **809**.
811 Quietus – IIvir; reign of Tiberius
VM 137:1 = Gil 1944; *CIC* 169
812 Peregrinus – colleague of **811**
CIC 145; and see **811**.
813 M. Aelius Maxumus – IIvir; reign of Tiberius
VM 137:2 = Gil 1945; *CIC* 3
814 Q. Ae[lius?] Proculus – colleague of **813**
CIC 4; and see **813**.
815 C. Tarracina – IIvir; reign of Gaius
The name is Oscan.
VM 137:7–11; Gil 2026–30; A. Balil *Hispania* 25 (1965) 362; *CIC* 198
816 P. Priscus – colleague of **815**
VM 137:7–11 = Gil 2026–30; *CIC* 168
817 M. Marius M. f. Gal. Nepos – IIvir, flamen; daughter Maria Materna
HAEp. 2211 = *AE* 1966, 185; *CIC* 128

Osicerda (conv. Caesaraugustanus)

818 L. Cornelius C. f. Gal. Romanus – flamen, IIvir at Osicerda, IIvir at
Tarraco; late 1st or early 2nd century; wife: Aemilia Kara
CIL II 4267 = *ILS* 6944 = *ILER* 1564 = *RIT* 341; *CIC* 63

Palantia (conv. Cluniensis)

819 Caisaros Cecciq[um] – princeps Argailorum
In indigenous nomenclature a gentilic is given in the genitive plural (cf
examples s.v. Contrebia). The Cecciqes had their home near Palantia. The
cognomen Caisaros is common in Celtic and need not suggest any
connection with a Caesar. Although the inscription is in Latin, Caisaros
retains the ancestral title of tribal chieftain (as does **967**).
CIL II 5762 = *ILER* 5929 = *CIP* 85; Albertos *OPP* 70
820 Anonymus – mag[istratus] Elaisicum; 2 BC
He witnessed a *tessera hospitalis* between the *civitas Palantina* and one
Acces Licirni [f.] of the Vaccaean city Intercatia. Elaisicum is a gentilic
designation.
CIL II 5763 = *ILS* 6096 = *CIP* 86; Albertos *OPP* 112

Palma colonia; later municipium (Balearis Maior, conv. Carthaginiensis)

821 L. Aufidius Q. f. Vel. Secundus – omnibus honoribus in re p. sua functus, flamen p.H.c. between 120 and 180

    CIL II 4197 and p. 972 = Veny *Corpus* 5 = *ILER* 1605 = *RIT* 260; Alföldy *Flamines* no. 9

822 L. Clodius M. f. Vel. Ingenuus – omnibus honoribus in re p. sua perfunctus, praefectus fabrum, flamen Romae divorum et Augustorum p.H.c. between 120 and 180

    CIL II 4205 = *ILS* 6929 = Veny *Corpus* 4 = *ILER* 1597 = *RIT* 267; Alföldy *Flamines* no. 16

823 ...us P. f. Vel. ...s – IIvir

    HAEp. 1457/2733 = Veny *Corpus* 2; *AE* 1957, 38

824 Cn. Gavius Cn. f. Quir. Amethystus – see **740**.

Peñalba de Villastar (ancient name unknown; conv. Carthaginiensis)

825 Eniorosis – possible magistrate, named in a Celtiberian inscription

    A. Tovar *Ampurias* 17–18 (1955–6) 168 = Tovar *Emerita* 27 (1959) 353–4 = *HAEp.* 792

826 Equaesius – colleague of **825**

    See **825**.

Pollentia colonia; later municipium (Balearis Maior, conv. Carthaginiensis)

827 L. Dentilius L. f. Vel. Modestus – aedilis, IIvir, flamen; perhaps reign of Trajan; nephew L. Favonius ...

    CIL II 3697 and p 962 = Veny *Corpus* 26 = *ILER* 6373

828 Q. Caecilius Q. f. Vel. Catullus – aedilis, IIvir, [flamen] Romae et Aug.; perhaps reign of Hadrian

    Caecilii are very common at Pollentia and apparently designate natives who originally took their *nomen* from Q. Caecilius Metellus, who founded the colony in 123/2 BC.

    CIL II 3696 and p 962 = Veny *Corpus* 25 = *ILER* 6371; cf Knapp *Roman Experience* 132

829 L. Vibius L. f. Vel. Nigellio – aedilis, IIvir bis; wife Manlia Fabiana, son Vibius Manlianus

    CIL II 3698 = Veny *Corpus* 27 = *ILER* 6028

Pompaelo (conv. Caesaraugustanus)

830 Sex. Pompeius Nepos – legatus; AD 57

    He is named on a *tessera hospitalis* between Pompaelo and one L. Pompeius Primianus

    CIL II 2958 = *ILER* 5832; *CIC* 149

831 Sergius Crescens – colleague of **830**
CIL II 2958 = ILER 5832; CIC 189

832 Cn. Pompeius Cn. f. [Pompaelonensis] – IIvir, flamen p.H.c. between 70 and 180
Even if Pompaelonensis is a *cognomen*, as Alföldy believes, a connection with Pompaelo seems likely.
CIL II 4234 = ILER 1630 = RIT 297; Etienne *Culte* 142; Alföldy *Flamines* no. 51; CIC 150

833 Anonymi – IIviri
They are addressees of a rescript from the provincial governor in 119, advising them to use the power of their office against *contumaces* and those 'qui cautionibus accipiendis desunt.'
CIL II 2959 = ILER 5826 = Alföldy *Fasti* 79; Mackie *Administration* 104, 136, 164–5

834 T. Antonius Paternus – [legatus?]; AD 185
He is named on a *tessera* enacting hospitality between Pompaelo and P. Sempronius Taurinus of Damania.
CIL II 2960; CIC 12

835 L. Caecilius Aestivus – colleague of **834**
CIC 35; see **834**.

Rubielos (ancient name unknown; conv. Carthaginiensis)

836 C. Marius C. f. Gal. Marianus – aedilis, flamen, IIvir; late 1st or 2nd century; mother: Valeria C. f. Severa
Alföldy considers him a possible magistrate of Lesera – which is, however, some sixty km distant.
CIL II 3174 = ILER 5532; G. Alföldy *Res Publica Leserensis* (Valencia 1977) 18–19

Saetabis municipium Augustum (conv. Carthaginiensis)

837 Q. Iunius Q. f. Gal. Iustus – IIvir, flamen divi Augusti; reign of Tiberius
CIL II 3620 = ILER 1578 = A. Ventura Conejero *Játiva romana* (Valencia 1972) 40–1; Etienne *Culte* 207

838 [L. or M.] Fulvius L. f. Gal. Marcianus – IIvir, flamen Romae et Augusti; reign of Tiberius; mother Fulvia M. f. Marcella
CIL II 3623 and p 960 = ILER 5536 = Ventura Conejero *Játiva romana* 43–4

839 Q. Fabius ... f. Gal. M... – omnibus honoribus in re p. sua functus, equo publico donatus ab Imperatore Hadriano, allectus in v decurias ab eodem, praefectus cohortis primae ..., flamen p.H.c. between 125 and 138
Several other Fabii are attested at Saetabis (CIL II 3618, 3652, 3658).

CIL II 4213 = *ILER* 1636 = *RIT* 273; Wiegels no. 259; Alföldy *Flamines* no. 22; *PME* F 9

Saguntum municipium (conv. Tarraconensis)

840 Icorbeles – magistrate; ca 120–90 BC
The name is Iberian, paralleled at Ilerda.
VM 17:2 = Gil 327; Albertos *OPP* 123

841 Balcacaldur – colleague of 840
'Balce-' is a common Iberian anthroponymic element.
VM 17:2, 7 = Gil 327, 332; cf Albertos *OPP* 48

842 Biulacos – magistrate, colleague of 841
Although written in Iberian script, this name appears to be a common Indo-European one, with parallels in northern Italy.
VM 17:7 = Gil 332; Albertos *OPP* 54–5

843 Valerius – magistrate; ca 120–90 BC
VM 173:6 = Gil 328

844 L. Calpurnius – aedilis; ca 120–90 BC
VM 18:1–2 = Gil 329–30, 335

845 Cn. Baebius Glab[rio?] – colleague of 844
VM 18:2–3 = Gil 330, 335–6

846 M. Aemilius Ercol[es?] – ae[dilis], colleague of 845
The *cognomen* is apparently a variant of 'Hercules' (cf Kajanto *Cognomina* index s.v. 'Erc-').
VM 18:3, 5 = Gil 333, 336

847 C. Popilius – magistrate; ca 120–90 BC
VM 18:4 = Gil 334

848 M. Acilius – colleague of 847
See 847.

849 L. Sempronius Vetto – magistrate; ca 120–90 BC
VM 18:6 = Gil 337

850 L. Fabius Postumus – colleague of 849
See 849.

851 C. Lucilius L. f. – IIvir; second half of 1st century BC
He rebuilt the city walls and towers.
CIL II 6021 = *ILER* 1396 = *ELSaguntum* 57

852 ... Fulvius ... f. Titianus – colleague of 851
See 851.

853 L. Sempronius Geminus – IIvir; reign of Tiberius
VM 124:1, 3 = Gil 1952–4

854 L. Valerius Sura – colleague of 853
See 853.

855 L. Aemilius Maxumus – aedilis; reign of Tiberius
VM 124:2, 4 = Gil 1955–6
856 M. Baebius Sobrinus – colleague of 855
See 855.
857 M. Baebius M. f. Gal. Crispus – aedilis, pontifex, Salius; Julio-Claudian
period; perhaps a relative of 856
CIL II 3853 = ILS 6950 = ILER 1540 = ELSaguntum 51; G. Alföldy Gerión 2
(1984) 235
858 Cn. Baebius Cn. f. Gal. Geminus – pontifex, aedilis, Salius; Julio-Claudian
period; perhaps a descendant of 845
Note that although Baebius Geminus holds the same appointments as his
presumed relative 857, the order is different.
CIL II 3854–5 = ILER 1541, 1390 = ELSaguntum 52, 66
859 C. Licinius Q. f. Gal. Campanus – aedilis, IIvir, flamen; Julio-Claudian
period
The cognomen suggests a possible Italian origin.
CIL II 3860 = ILER 1563 = ELSaguntum 58
860 M. Calpurnius M. f. Gal. Lupercus – aedilis, IIvir, pontifex; Julio-Claudian
period
CIL II 3858 = ILER 5537 = ELSaguntum 54
861 L. Manlius C. f. Fabianus – IIvir; Julio-Claudian period
CIL II 3862 = ILER 1393 = ELSaguntum 59; Alföldy Gerión 2 (1984) 235
862 C. Voconius C. f. Gal. Placidus – aedilis, IIvir bis, flamen bis, quaestor,
Saliorum magister, eques Romanus; reign of Vespasian; father of Pliny's
friend C. Licinius Marinus Voconius Romanus (PIR² L 210)
CIL II 3865 = ILS 6951 = ILER 1570 = ELSaguntum 63; Pliny Ep. 2.13.4;
Etienne Culte 208
863 C. Cornelius Maximus Valentinus – aedilis, IIvir; 1st century AD; wife Fabia
Marcellina
HAEp. 510 = AE 1955, 162 = ILER 6374 = ELSaguntum 55
864 ... Q. f. Niger – [IIvi?]r, pontifex; 1st century AD
Niger is a common cognomen and there is no need to follow Alföldy in
making this man a relative of the Q. Fabius Niger in ELSaguntum 46.
CIL II 3863 = ELSaguntum 60; Alföldy Gerión 2 (1984) 235
865 C. Aemilius C. f. Gal. Nepos – aedilis, IIvir; 1st century AD
CIL II 6025 = ILER 1395 = ELSaguntum 299
866 Valerius L. f. Mar[cell?]us – aedilis; died after thirty days in office; 1st
century AD
CIL II 6064 = ELSaguntum 284; Alföldy Gerión 2 (1984) 236
867 P. Baebius L. f. Gal. Maximus Iulianus – aedilis, flamen; ca 70–150

He is another member of the *gens Baebia* (cf also *CIL* II 3880–91).

CIL II 3856 = *ILER* 5539 = *ELSaguntum* 53; Alföldy *Gerión* 2 (1984) 236

868 Q. Varvius Q. f. Gal. Celer – aedilis, IIvir, flamen bis, Saliorum magister, quaestor; ca 70–150

CIL II 3864 = *ILER* 1569 = *ELSaguntum* 62; Alföldy *Gerión* 2 (1984) 236

869 L. Aemilius L. f. Gal. Gallus – aedilis, IIvir, flamen bis, Saliorum magister, quaestor, pontifex; ca 70–150 AD; mother Aemilia L. f. Severa

He is probably related to 875.

HAEp. 512 = *AE* 1957, 314 = *ILER* 6409 = *ELSaguntum* 49; Alföldy *Gerión* 2 (1984) 236

870 L. Aemilius L. f. Gal. Veranus – aedilis, IIvir, flamen bis, quaestor; ca 70–150

AE 1955, 163 = *ILER* 1568 = *ELSaguntum* 50; cf G. Alföldy *AEA* 54 (1981) 127; Alföldy *Gerión* 2 (1984) 236

871 ... Valerius L. f. Gal. Optatus – aedilis, flamen, IIvir, Saliorum magister; ca 70–150

CIL II 6055 = *ILER* 6022–3 = *ELSaguntum* 319; Alföldy *Gerión* 2 (1984) 236

872 ... Valerius ... f. Gal. Sp... – aedilis, [IIvir?]; 1st to 2nd century AD

ELSaguntum 61; Alföldy *Gerión* 2 (1984) 236

873 Q. Caecilius ... f. Gal. Valerianus – aedilis, IIvir bis, quaestor, flamen, pontifex; early 2nd century; father of 874; probably the son of P. Caecilius Rufus and Valeria (*CIL* II 3960 = *ILER* 3854), his mother's name forming the basis of his *cognomen*

HAEp. 2414 = *ELSaguntum* 291; G. Alföldy *ZPE* 41 (1981) 225–8; Alföldy *Gerión* 2 (1984) 236

874 Q. Caecilius Q. f. Gal. Rufinus – aedilis, [IIvir], pontifex, legatus; equo publico donatus; son of 873

He undertook at his own expense a mission to the emperor Hadrian in Rome, for which he was honoured by the p.H.c. His *cognomen* appears to be derived from his presumed grandfather, P. Caecilius Rufus.

CIL II 3857 = *ILER* 1394 = *ELSaguntum* 44; *CIL* II 4201 = *ILS* 6927 = *ILER* 1304 = *RIT* 331; Alföldy *ZPE* 41 (1981) 226–8

875 L. Aemilius Ga... – omnibus honoribus functus; not before AD 120; probably related to, and possibly identical with, 869

ELSaguntum 307 bis

876 [Geminius] ...mus – omnibus honoribus in re p. sua functus; not before AD 120

His *nomen* is restored on the evidence of the name of his freedwoman, Geminia Barbara

CIL II 6056 = *ILER* 4955 = *ELSaguntum* 329

877 Anonymus – omnibus honoribus in re p. sua functus; not before AD 120

D. Fletcher Valls and J. Alcacer Grau *Boletín de la Sociedad Castellonense de Cultura* 31 (1955) 349 no. LXXXV; Alföldy *Gerión* 2 (1984) 237

878 ... Fabius Felix – IIvir; 2nd to 3rd century
ELSaguntum 308
879 ... Fabius Fabianus – colleague of **878**
See **878**.
880 Anonymus – [II?]vir
ELSaguntum 28

Salaria colonia (conv. Carthaginiensis)

881 L. Postumius Q. f. Serg. Fabullus – flamen Augustorum p.H.c., tribunus militum legionis VII, IIvir
The flaminate dates to the period 70–90. Etienne confusingly dates his flaminate to Vespasian (*Culte* 131), then assigns his subsequent (*Culte* 153) tribunate to the first half of the 1st century (*Culte* 133). Alföldy correctly divines that the *cursus* is in retrograde order.
CIL II 3329 = *ILER* 1658; Wiegels no. 320; Alföldy *Flamines* no. 58; PME P 103

Segobriga (conv. Carthaginiensis)

See also Addenda **980**

882 L. Turellius L. f. Geminus – aedilis; AD 12
He erected inscriptions to Germanicus and the younger Drusus.
CIL II 3103–4 = *ILER* 1056, 1050 = A. Rodríguez Colmenero *Lucentum* 1 (1982) 231–2 no. 81–2 = M. Almagro Basch *Segobriga* II (Madrid 1984) no. 24–6
883 L. Annius L. f. Gal. Cantaber – flamen Romae et divorum Augustorum p.H.c. between 120 and 180; omnibus honoribus gestis
The *cognomen* suggests an origin in northern Cluniensis (Cantabria). The *cursus* is evidently in reverse order.
CIL II 4191 = *ILER* 1598 = *RIT* 254; Alföldy *Flamines* no. 3

Segontia (conv. Cluniensis)

884 C. Atilius C. f. Quir. Crassus – omnibus honoribus in re p. sua functus, flamen p.H.c. probably between 120 and 200
CIL II 4195 = *ILER* 1604 = *RIT* 258; Alföldy *Flamines* no. 7

Sigarra municipium (conv. Tarraconensis)

885 C. Vibius Lupercus – IIIIvir; second half of 1st century AD; wife Iunia

Severina, son C. Vibius Latro, who re-appears as a magistrate at Tarraco,
891

    CIL II 4479 = *ILER* 5415; *CIL* II 4480 = *IRC* I 19

Sofuentes (ancient name unknown; conv. Caesaraugustanus)

886 Bucco Sadansis f. – IIV[ir?]; 1st century AD

His origin is given as 'Arsitanus,' possibly referring to Arse (Saguntum)
or to Arsaos (a coin-issuing town of the Vascones). The names of both
father and son are non-Latin.

ERZaragoza 34; *CIC* 33; cf J. Galiay Sarañana *La dominación romana en
Aragón* (Zaragoza 1946) 213

Tarraco colonia Iulia Urbs Triumphalis (conv. Tarraconensis)

887 ... [Calpu]rnius Tiro – aedilis; 1st century AD

The restoration is virtually certain, for the *gens Calpurnia* is heavily
represented among the élite of Spain.

RIT 340

888 L. Marcius Q. f. Gal. Optatus – see **762**

889 ...rius Q. f. [Gal?] Fuscus – IIvir, flamen Divi Claudi, praefectus orae maritimae, flamen divorum et Augustorum p.H.c.; Flavian

The priesthood of the deified Claudius is plausibly but not necessarily of
Vespasianic date.

CIL II 4217 = *ILER* 1594 = *RIT* 316; Alföldy *Flamines* no. 73; Wiegels no.
353; *PME* F 113

890 M. Clodius M. f. Gal. Martialis – IIvir, quaestor, flamen, aug[ur] (or
Augusti), praefectus fabrum, praefectus ins[ularum Baliarum orae
maritimae?]; Flavian or early 2nd century

HAEp. 176 = *ILER* 6050 = *RIT* 168; Wiegels no. 242; cf. *PME* p 281

891 C. Vibius C. f. Gal. Latro – quaestor, IIvir, item IIvir quinquennalis, flamen
p.H.c.; end of 1st or beginning of 2nd century

The monument to him is erected 'ex testamento Fulviae Celerae' (possibly
the local and provincial *flaminica* Fulvia Celera, who may then be his
wife, *CIL* II 4270, 4276). Latro was the son of a municipal magistrate of
Sigarra, C. Vibius Lupercus (**885**).

CIL II 4253 = *ILER* 1616 = *RIT* 312; Alföldy *Flamines* no. 69

892 Q. Caecilius L. f. Gal. Fronto – quaestor, IIvir, procurator Augusti; end of
1st century or Trajanic/Hadrianic

C. Caecilius Fronto, named in *RIT* 159 as an heir of an equestrian official,
is presumably a relative.

CIL II 4139 = *ILER* 1317 = *RIT* 157; *PIR²* C 46; Pflaum *Carrières* no. 1011;
EREsp. 107–8; Wiegels no. 229

893 L. Caecina C. f. Gal. Severus – IIvir, quaestor, praefectus fabrum, praefectus cohortis I et orae maritimae; between AD 70 and 150

CIL II 4264 = *ILS* 2716 = *ILER* 1565 = *RIT* 165; *AE* 1929, 230, 234 = *ILER* 6362, 6369 = *RIT* 164, 166; Wiegels no. 234; *PME* C 29

894 Ti. Claudius L. f. Quir. Paullinus – IIvir, quaestor, praefectus insularum Baliarum et orae maritimae; Flavian or first half of 2nd century

HAEp. 862 = *ILER* 5629 = *RIT* 167; Wiegels no. 239

895 L. Cornelius C. f. Gal. Celsus – IIvir, praefectus orae maritimae, praefectus cohortis I et II; Flavian or first half of 2nd century; wife Pompeia Donace

CIL II 4266 = *ILS* 2717 = *ILER* 1325 = *RIT* 169; Wiegels no. 250; *PME* C 231

896 P. Licinius L. f. Gal. Laevinus – aedilis, quaestor, flamen Romae et Aug., IIvir, praefectus cohortis novae tironum orae maritimae; Flavian or first half of 2nd century; mother Iulia Q. f. Ingenua

CIL II 4224 = *ILER* 1582 = *RIT* 171; Wiegels no. 286; *PME* L 10

897 C. Egnatuleius C. f. Gal. Seneca – aedilis, quaestor, IIvir, flamen Divi Titi, equo publico donatus, praefectus cohortis IIII Thracum equitatae (in Germany), flamen p.H.c. between 85 and 150

Evidently he was already an *eques* before receiving the provincial flaminate.

CIL II 2227/4212 = *ILER* 1633/1455 = *RIT* 272; Wiegels no. 257; Alföldy *Flamines* no. 21; *PME* E 6; R.C. Knapp *ZPE* 36 (1979) 137

898 L. Caecilius Porcianus – decurio adlectus in colonia Tarraconensi, itemque aedilis, [IIvir?]; 1st or 2nd century

He was an immigrant from Africa, who seems to have settled and flourished at Tarraco and was provided with a monument and burial plot by the local *ordo*. Another man of the same name appears at Segobriga (*CIL* II 4252).

CIL II 4263 = *ILER* 1314 = *RIT* 339

899 L. Fonteius M. f. Gal. Maternus Novitianus – aediliciis honoribus ab ordine datus; IIvir, quaestor, iudex decuriae III, flamen Divi Vespasiani; equo publico donatus ab Imperatore Nerva Augusto, flamen p.H.c. (end of 1st century); possibly the son of M. Fonteius Novitianus of Aquae Calidae (*CIL* II 4487)

Previous editors read 'iudic[i] dec[uriarum] III,' on the grounds that the first three *decuriae* were composed of knights. However, the normal title, even for knights holding the *equus publicus*, is 'iudex decuriarum V' or 'adlectus in V decurias.' I therefore restore 'dec[uriae],' which finds exact parallels in **907** ('iudex decuriae I') and **910** ('iudex decuriae IIII').

CIL II 4216, 6095 = *ILER* 1634, 1587 = *RIT* 278–9; *EREsp.* 98; Wiegels no. 265; Alföldy *Flamines* no. 27

900 P. Fabius P. f. Serg. Lepidus – ornamentis aediliciis; end of 1st century or first half of 2nd; mother Iulia Sex. f. Reburrina, who repaid the cost of the statue erected by the decurions

    CIL II 4268 = *ILER* 1328 = *RIT* 343

901 L. Cornelius C. f. Gal. Romanus – see **818**

902 L. Pedanius L. f. Pal. Clemens Senior – see **444**

903 M. Voconius M. f. Gal. Vaccula – aedilis, flamen Divi Augusti, quaestor; between 70 and 150

    CIL II 4279 = *ILER* 1577 = *RIT* 356

904 Anonymus – [IIvi?]r, aedilis, Lu[percus?]; early Empire

The restoration is dubious, since no other Luperci are known in Spain.

RIT 357

905 L. Antonius L. f. Gal. Saturninus – aedilis, IIvir, flamen p.H.c. between 70 and 180

He is perhaps related to L. Antonius Saturninus, cos. suff. 83, but the *nomen* and *cognomen* are too common to prove Syme's suggestion that the local magistrate may be the consul's father.

CIL II 4194 = *ILER* 1635 = *RIT* 257; R. Syme *Tacitus* (Oxford 1958) 596 and n 6; Syme *Harv. Stud.* 73 (1969) 230 = *RP* 768; Syme *JRS* 68 (1978) 15 = *RP* 1075; Alföldy *Flamines* no. 6

906 C. Calpurnius P. f. Quir. Flaccus – flamen p.H.c. between 100 and 125, curator templi, praefectus murorum

He was perhaps in charge of repairing the temple and walls of Tarraco in preparation for Hadrian's visit in 122–3; we know at least that the temple of Augustus was repaired on this occasion (S.H.A. *Hadr.* 12.3). He is probably the father of C. Calpurnius Flaccus, cos. suff. 124, in which case he may be the Calpurnius Flaccus to whom Pliny writes.

CIL II 4202 = *ILS* 6946 = *ILER* 1631 = *RIT* 264; Pliny *Ep.* 5.2; *PIR*² C 265; Alföldy *Flamines* no. 13; Syme *Harv. Stud.* 73 (1969) 231 = *RP* 769

907 L. Numisius L. f. Pal. Montanus – omnibus honoribus in re p. sua functus; aedilis, quaestor, IIvir, item quinquennalis IIvir, equo publico donatus ab Imperatore Hadriano, iudex decuriae I, flamen p.H.c. between 120 and 140; sister Numisia Victorina, wife Porcia Materna, flaminica p.H.c. et postea Osicerdensi, Caesaraugustae, Tarraconensi perpetua

His wife's religious success probably aided his own career, since the tribe Palatina suggests low social origin.

CIL II 4231, 4241, 4275 = *ILER* 1628, 1656, 1327 = *RIT* 295, 325, 349; Wiegels no. 305; Alföldy *Flamines* no. 48; M.M. Alves Dias *MM* 19 (1978) 268–71

908 L. Numisius L. f. Pal. Ovinianus – omnibus honoribus in re p. sua functus, tribunus cohortis I Macedonicae, flamen p.H.c. between 120 and 140; brother of **907**

CIL II 4232 = *ILER* 1629 = *RIT* 296; Wiegels no. 306; Alföldy *Flamines* no. 49; *PME* N 21

909 L. Minicius L. f. Gal. Apronianus – aedilis, quaestor, IIvir, IIvir quinquennalis, flamen Divi Traiani Parthici; reign of Hadrian; a native of Tarraco
He dedicated a silver statue to the Genius of the colony. He may be related to the senatorial family L. Minicii of Barcino.
CIL II 4071, 4274 = *ILER* 558, 1552 = *RIT* 23, 918; *CIL* II 4488 = *ILER* 170; J.-N. Bonneville *MCV* 18 (1982) 21

910 L. Aemilius ... f. Pal. Sempronius Clemens Silvanianus – aedilis, quaestor, IIvir, flamen, curator Capitoli, iudex decuriae IIII; 2nd century
As a member of the fourth *decuria* he would be a *ducenarius* (man meeting one-half of the equestrian census). The Capitol referred to is surely that of Tarraco; on curators of local temples, 906.
AE 1946, 2 = *ILER* 6388–9 = *RIT* 922; cf Th. Mommsen *Römisches Staatsrecht* III (Leipzig 1887) 535–6

911 M. Lucretius Quir. Peregrinus – centurio legionis I Minerviae Piae Fidelis (in Germania Inferior), item legionis III Cyrenaicae (in Arabia), praefectus cohortis IIII Lingonum (in Britain), decurio Tarraconensi adlectus; 2nd century; a retired centurion and equestrian who entered municipal politics
AE 1961, 330 = *HAEp*. 809 = *ILER* 5601 = *RIT* 172; Wiegels no. 291; *PME* L 37

912 Q. Anthracius Q. f. Vel. Ingenuus – adlectus in ordine Tarraconensi, aedilis, IIvir; 2nd century; native of Majorca; wife Didia Amabilis
CIL II 4262 = *ILER* 1322 = *RIT* 338

913 Anonymus – legatus; sent to purchase grain (in Africa?) to assist the plebs; 2nd century
RIT 364

914 ...cianus – adlectus inter quinquennales, iudex Romae; 2nd century; wife Fabia Lepida who was possibly related to 900
AE 1928, 195 = *ILER* 5564 = *RIT* 342

915 ... Pollentinus – [omnibus honoribus functus?], flamen p.H.c.; early Empire
RIT 317; Alföldy *Flamines* no. 75

916 M. Granius Probus – decurio, pontifex, aediliciis honoribus functus; perhaps second half of 2nd century; mother Caecilia Galla, sister Herennia Aphrodite
The Granii, Caecilii and Herennii are all attested elsewhere at Tarraco.
CIL II 4272 = *ILER* 1535 = *RIT* 345

917 C. Valerius Avitus – IIvir; reigns of Antoninus Pius and Marcus Aurelius
A native of Augustobriga in the conv. Cluniensis, he was removed by

Antoninus Pius to Tarraco, where he later became a magistrate. He must also have been well-to-do, for he owned the Els Munts villa, twelve km N.E. of Tarraco, one of the most magnificent villas on the east coast. He was not however the original owner: it was built in the 1st century and continued to be occupied into the 5th.

CIL II 4277–8 = ILS 6943, 5485 = ILER 1330–1 = RIT 352 – 4; RIT 923; Gorges *Villas* 407–8

918 M. Valerius Vindex – omnibus honoribus in re p. sua functus; end of 2nd or first third of 3rd century

AE 1928, 198 = ILER 5106 = RIT 355

919 Aemilius Valerius Chorintus – honores aedilicii (posthumous); second half of 2nd century, or 3rd century; wife Antonia Frontonia

He was possibly of manumitted extraction, or a descendant of a local (or immigrant) Greek family. Cf **676–8** for similar honours bestowed on known freedmen.

CIL II 4261 = ILER 3882 = RIT 336

920 ... M. f. Serg. ... – [IIvir?] designatus bis; uncertain date

CIL II 6099 = RIT 358

921 Messius Marianus – curator rei publicae Tarraconensis; 4th century

This is the only attested curator r.p. in the province.

CIL II 4112 = ILER 1306 = RIT 155

Termes perhaps a municipium (conv. Cluniensis)

922 L. Licinius Pilus – IIIIvir; 2nd century AD

He was witness of a *tessera hospitalis* with the Dercinoassedenses, *vicani* of Clunia.

EJER no. 25 = AE 1953, 267 = HAEp. 549 = A. Jimeno *Epigrafía romana de la provincia de Soria* (Soria 1980) no. 133

923 M. Terentius Celsus – colleague of **922**

See **922**.

924 L. Pompeius Vitulus – colleague of **922**

See **922**.

925 T. Pompeius Rarus – colleague of **922**

See **922**.

Toletum (conv. Carthaginiensis)

926 Celtamb. – magistrate; perhaps ca 80 BC

VM 134:1 = Gil 819; Gil 933

927 C. Viccius C. f. – magistrate; perhaps ca 80–72 BC

VM 134:4–5 = Gil 932, 934

Tritium Magallum (conv. Caesaraugustanus)

928 T. Mamilius Silonis [f.] Quir. Praesens – omnibus honoribus in re p. sua
functus, decurialis allectus Italicam, excusatus a Divo Pio, flamen p.H.c. ca
165–70
A relative, T. Mamilius Martialis, emigrated to Saguntum, perhaps in the
1st century (cf *ELSaguntum* 282).
CIL II 4227 = *ILS* 6934 = *ILER* 1626 = *RIT* 291; Etienne *Culte* 140; J. Gagé
Rev. Et. Anc. 71 (1969) 71–5; Alföldy *Flamines* no. 42; *CIC* 118

Turiaso municipium (conv. Caesaraugustanus)

929 M. Caecilius Severus – IIvir; ca AD 1
VM 155:9, 156:1 = Gil 1740–1; *CIC* 41
930 C. Valerius Aquilus – colleague of **929**
CIC 208; and see **929**.
931 L. Marius – IIvir; ca AD 2
VM 155:10–11 = Gil 1742–3; *CIC* 124
932 L. Novius – colleague of **931**
CIC 141; and see **931**.
933 L. Fenest[ella] – IIvir; ca AD 3
The name is Etruscan and very rare; hence this Fenestella may be related
to the historian Fenestella (indeed, Weinrib makes them identical). Cf **472**
for a possible homonym.
VM 155:12 = Gil 1744; *CIC* 76; E.J. Weinrib *The Spaniards in Rome from
Marius to Domitian* [diss. Harvard University 1968] 168–9; cf Plut. *Cras.* 5
934 L. Seranus – colleague of **933**
VM 155:12 = Gil 1744; *CIC* 188
935 M'. Sulpicius Lucanus – IIvir; AD 14–37
VM 156:6–7 = Gil 1983–4; *CIC* 194
936 M. Sempronius Front[o] – colleague of **935**
CIC 182; and see **935**.
937 C. Caecilius Ser[enus] – IIvir; AD 14–37
VM 157:1 = Gil 1985; *CIC* 40
938 M. Valerius Quad[ratus] – colleague of **937**; perhaps related to **524**
CIC 216; and see **937**.
939 M. Pontius Marsus – IIvir; AD 14–37
VM 156:10–11 = Gil 1986–7; *CIC* 159
940 C. Marius Vegetus — colleague of **939**
CIC 130; and see **939**.

941 L. Caecilius Aquin[us] – IIvir; AD 14–37
    VM 156:12 = Gil 1988; *CIC* 37

942 M. Cel. Palud[ius?] – colleague of **941**
    'Cel.' might be Caelius or Celtius. Gómez-Pantoja suggests Gel[lius].
    VM 156:12 = Gil 1988; *CIC* 89; cf Kajanto *Cognomina* 117, 310

943 T. Sulpicius – aedilis; AD 14–37
    VM 156:8 = Gil 1989; *CIC* 195

944 Q. Pontius Pla[cidus?] – colleague of **943**
    CIC 160; and see **943**.

945 Marius Vegetus – aedilis; AD 14–37; perhaps the same as **940**
    VM 156:9 = Gil 1990; *CIC* 129

946 Licinius Crescens – colleague of **945**
    CIC 107; and see **945**.

947 Rectus – aedilis; AD 14–37
    VM 157:2 = Gil 1991; *CIC* 172

948 Macrinus – colleague of **947**
    CIC 117; and see **947**.

Tutugi (conv. Carthaginiensis)

949 P. Atelliu[s Ser.] Chanus[ius Pa]ul[i]n[us] – IIvir; ca AD 200
    He dedicates an inscription to Caracalla by decree of the decurions. His last name and tribe Sergia are restored on the basis of *CIL* II 5834, from Huéscar (only seven km north of Tutugi), which names a certain P. Atellius Ser. Paulinus, perhaps his father. The *cognomen* Chanusius is uncommon.
    J. González *Mainake* 2 (1980) 138 = *AE* 1983, 609 = *ILGranada* 28

Valentia colonia Latina (conv. Tarraconensis)

950 C. Lucienus – q[uaestor]; ca 120–90 BC
    The nomen is Umbrian.
    VM 125:1 = Gil 366; A. Balil *Hispania* 25 (1965) 362

951 C. Munius – colleague of **950**
    See **950**.

952 L. Coranius – q[uaestor]; ca 120–90 BC
    VM 125:2 = Gil 367

953 C. Numi[sius?] – colleague of **952**
    See **952**.

954 T. Ahi[us] T. f. – q[uaestor]; ca 120–90 BC
    VM 125:3–4 = Gil 368–9

955 L. Trinius L. f. – colleague of **954**

His *nomen* is native to Picenum, suggesting an immigrant from Italy.
Balil *Hispania* 25 (1965) 362; see **954**.

956 C. Iulius C. f. Gal. Niger – aedilis, decurio; 1st century AD; daughter Iulia
C. f. Maxima, mother of **957**
   AE 1938, 22 = G. Pereira Menaut *Inscripciones romanas de Valentia*
   (Valencia 1979) 22

957 L. Antonius L. f. Gal. Crescens – aedilis, IIvir, flamen; reign of Trajan;
grandson of **956**
   AE 1933, 5–6 = Pereira Menaut *Inscripciones romanas de Valentia* 23

958 ...nianus – omnibus honoribus functus; mother: Eutychia
   Pereira Menaut *Inscripciones romanas de Valentia* 26

Valeria probably municipium (conv. Carthaginiensis)
See also Addenda **984**

959 ... Valerius [Av]itus – IIIIvir, flamen Romae et Aug[usti].
   The *cognomen* is amply attested in Spain, unlike Rodríguez Colmenero's
   suggested '[Tac]itus.'
   CIL II 3179 = A. Rodríguez Colmenero *Lucentum* 1 (1982) 213 no. 28;
   G. Alföldy *Römisches Städtewesen auf der neukastilischen Hochebene*
   (Heidelberg 1987) 87

960 C. Grattius Nigrinus – IIIIvir, flamen, aug[ur] (or flamen Augusti?); 1st
century AD
   Alföldy (see **959**) 87

Vergilia municipium (conv. Carthaginiensis)

961 P. Clodius P. f. Secundus – IIvir
   P. Clodius Secundinus in *ILER* 1442, also from Vergilia, is presumably his
   son, since Secundinus is a diminutive form of Secundus.
   AE 1915, 14 = *ILER* 1424

962 M. Cornelius Marcius M. f. Quir. Severus – omnibus honoribus in re p.
sua functus, flamen p.H.c. between 120 and 180
   CIL II 4207 = *ILER* 1609 = *RIT* 269; Alföldy *Flamines* no. 18

Villajoyosa (ancient name unknown; conv. Carthaginiensis)

963 Q. Manlius Q. f. Quir. Celsinus – IIvir ter, flamen ter; first half of 2nd
century AD; wife Manilia Chrysis
   CIL II 3571 = *ILER* 5212 = M.A. Rabanal Alonso and J.M. Abascal Palazón
   Lucentum 4 (1985) 218 no. 54

Zoelae (conv. Asturum)

964 Abienus Pentili [f.] – magistratus; AD 27

He witnessed a *tessera hospitalis* between two *gentilitates* of the Zoelaean people. The name and filiation are indigenous. 'Abienus' (variant Abianus) is apparently derived from the Celtic or Ligurian name 'Abia,' while 'Pentilius' is found in Aquitania and Britain.

CIL II 2633 = *ILS* 6101 = T. Mañanes Pérez *Epigrafía y numismática de Astorga romana y su entorno* (León and Salamanca 1982) no. 86; Albertos *OPP* 3, 180; A. Tranoy *La Galice romaine* (Paris 1981) 379

Uncertain Towns

965 C. Pullius Dionysi f. Quir. Mercurialis – II[vir]; son L. Pullius Cani...

The inscription comes from Alcubilla de Avellaneda near Clunia, but it seems unlikely that Pullius was duovir there: Clunia belongs to the tribe Galeria, and her magistrates are quattuorvirs. Pullius might have been duovir at Lara de los Infantes or Numantia (both apparently represented in tribe Quirina and both with duovirs).

CIL II 2802 = *ILER* 3919 = G. Alföldy *ZPE* 44 (1981) 113–18 = *AE* 1981, 554

966 C. Lutatius ... f. Vel. Cerealis – IIvir ter, pontifex perpetuus, iudex Romae inter selectos decuriarum v, equo publico honoratus, flamen p.H.c. between AD 70 and 150

The tribe Velina suggests an origin at Palma or Pollentia.

RIT 290; Alföldy *Flamines* no. 40

967 Nicer Clutosi [f.] – principis Albionum; a member of the Cariaca clan

The Albiones were a tribe in the conv. Lucensis. It is unclear whether 'principis' is a grammatical error for 'princeps,' or whether the title refers to his father, Clutosus. The crude lettering of this text may indicate semi-romanization rather than the late (3rd century) date favoured by Blázquez. For another *princeps* from this region cf **790**

A. García y Bellido *Emerita* 11 (1943) 418–30 = *AE* 1946, 121 = *HAEp.* 1663 = *ILER* 5630 = M. Escortell Ponsoda *Guía-catálogo del Museo Arqueológico Provincial* (Oviedo 1983) pl 70; J.M. Blázquez in *Actas del III Congreso español de estudios clásicos* II (Madrid 1968) 139; J. Caro Baroja in *Legio VII Gemina* (León 1970) 45; J.M. Vázquez Varela and F. Acuña Castroviejo in *La romanización de Galicia* (Sada and La Coruña 1976) 82; A. Tranoy *La Galice romaine* (Paris 1981) 54

968 C. Lep[idius?] M. f. – IIvir

He is named on three terracotta plaques listing road distances between various towns of the conv. Lucensis, Bracaraugustanus, and Asturum. The abbreviation 'Lep.' is usually interpreted as the *cognomen* Lepidus, but the *nomen* Lepidius seems likelier, since the combination *praenomen–*

nomen is far commoner than *praenomen–cognomen* in the nomenclature
of Spanish magistrates.

AE 1921, 6–7, 9 = *ILER* 1778 = F. Diego Santos *Inscripciones romanas de la
provincia de León* (León 1986) 328; G. Arias Bonet *El miliario
extravagante* 1 (1963) 4–12; J.M. Roldán Hervás *Itineraria hispana*
(Valladolid and Granada 1975) 167

969 Latinus Ari [f.] – mag[istratus?], AD 28; possibly from conv. Lucensis.
Despite the indigenous filiation, the *cognomen* Latinus may indicate a
certain degree of romanization.

AE 1961, 96 = *ILER* 5835 = F. Arias Vilas et al., *Inscriptions romaines de la
province de Lugo* (Paris 1979) 55; Tranoy *La Galice romaine* 204 n 97

970 Aius Temari [f.] – colleague of **969**
The name Aius is common in Celtiberia.
See **969**.

971 M. Ulpius C. f. Quir. Reburrus – omnibus honoribus in re p. sua functus,
flamen p.H.c. between 150 and 180; from the conv. Bracaraugustanus; wife
Pompeia Maximina in *CIL* II 4236.

The *res publica* in question might be Bracara. The *cognomen* is a Celtic
loan-word.

CIL II 4257 = *ILER* 1621 = *RIT* 308; Etienne *Culte* 145 n 5; Kajanto
Cognomina 236; Alföldy *Flamines* no. 65

972 M. Iulius Q. f. Serenianus Adoptivus – omnibus honoribus in re p. sua
functus, sacerdos Romae et Augusti, adlectus in quinque decurias equitum
Romanorum a[b Imp.?] Commodo, flamen p.H.c., patronus; a knight from
the conv. Lucensis, possibly from Lucus itself; son M. Iulius Adoptivus

Eph. Epigr. VIII 199 = *AE* 1897, 100 = *RIT* 284; *CIL* II 4221 = *ILER* 1665 = *RIT*
285; Etienne *Culte* 141, 145 n 9; Wiegels no. 276; Alföldy *Flamines* no.
35

973 Potamius – principalis; between 367 and 375
He and his colleague (**974**) are mentioned on a bronze *modius* found at
Ponte Puñide (La Coruña). The two were evidently in charge of
controlling weights and measures in the community, and d'Ors believes
they held the local *cura annonae*.

R. Ureña *BRAH* 66 (1915) 485 = *AE* 1915, 75 = *EJER* 65–7 = *HAEp.*
542 = *ILER* 5836; R. Gil Miquel 'Modio romano, de bronce, hallado en
Ponte Puñide,' *Museo Arqueológico Nacional, Adquisiciones en 1930*
(Madrid 1932) 5–6

974 Quentianus – colleague of **973**
The substitution of 'e' for 'i' (the name should be Quintianus) is a
common practice in provincial Latin, especially in the late period.
Ureña *BRAH* 66 (1915) 485 = *AE* 1915, 75 = *EJER* 65–7 = *HAEp.* 542 = *ILER*
5836

4

Addenda

The following new magistrates reached my attention too late to be assigned consecutive numbers under the listings for their respective cities. However, the indexes and tables have been revised to include the new data.

BAETICA

Italica

975 M. Trahius C. f. – pr[aefectus, or possibly praetor]; 1st century BC; donated an unidentified building as well as 'caulae' (perhaps signifying the doors of a temple)

His *nomen*, a form of Traius, is significant in that it may indicate an ancestor of the emperor Trajan (Traianus being a *cognomen* derived from Traius).

A. Caballos Rufino *Habis* 18–19 (1987–8) 299–317

Singilia Barba

976 M. Hirrius M. f. Quir. Annianus – IIvir; given a statue by order of the decurions; relative M. Hirrius ... olixus

R. Atencia Paez *La ciudad romana de Singilia Barba* (Málaga 1988) 74–5

TARRACONENSIS

Clunia

977 Bergius Seranus – aedilis; early 1st century AD

His name appears on a graffito in the sanctuary of Priapus at Clunia.

S.J. Keay *Roman Spain* (London 1988) 150, citing P. Palol and J. Vilella *Koiné* 2 (1986) 15–25 (article inaccessible to me)

Liria

978 L. Cornelius L. f. Gal. Potitus – honore aedilicio functus, primus pilus in bello Maurico; 2nd century AD; parents L. Cornelius Valerianus, Fulvia Zosime
AE 1985, 622

Roura (location unknown; probably conv. Cluniensis)

979 Ureibos – probable magistrate, named on a token of hospitality with Uxama; second half of 1st century BC
His indigenous name has no close parallels.
C. García-Merino and M.L. Albertos *Emerita* 49 (1981) 179–89 = *AE* 1985, 599

Segobriga

980 M. Valerius M. f. Gal. Reburrus – IIIIvir
Alföldy has recently argued persuasively for the authenticity of this lost inscription, earlier suspected of being a forgery.
CIL II 381* = G. Alföldy *Römisches Städtewesen auf der neukastilischen Hochebene* (Heidelberg 1987) 78–80

Uxama (conv. Cluniensis)

981 Saieos – legate or equivalent, named on a token of hospitality with Roura; second half of 1st century BC
Several other indigenous names in 'Sai-' are attested in central Spain (cf Albertos *OPP* 195–6).
See **979**.

982 Baisaios – colleague of **981**
Several indigenous names in 'Bais-' or 'Baes-' are attested in Spain (cf Albertos *OPP* 47–8), including a Baeso from Uxama.
See **979**.

983 Caldaiecos – colleague of **981**
His name contains the common Celtic element 'Cal-.'
See **979**.

Valeria

984 L. Ca[ecilius?] Gal. ... – IIIIvir; early Empire
Alföldy (see **980**) 87

5

Spurious or Doubtful Magistrates

1 BAETICA

Asta Regia

1* [B]aebi[us] Ser[gia] and T. [...ius f. Ser.]
Hübner believed that these men, stated to have undertaken some project at their own expense (which he conjectured to be restoration of walls and towers), were magistrates. Possibly Baebius is related to A. Baebius, a Roman knight from Asta (*BHisp.* 26.2); however, the inscription is too fragmentary to permit a secure interpretation.
CIL II 5405

Carmo

2* M. Ulpius M. f. L. n. M. pron. Quir. Strabo – IIIIvir, augur, pontifex; fake inscription
CIL II 128*

3* P. Val[erius] San... – aedilis, censor bis, IIIIvir; fake inscription
CIL II 129*

4* C. Sisinn[ius] C. f. Pomptina Balbus – augur, aedilis, IIIvir; fake inscription
CIL II 130*

5* P. Valerius P. f. P. n. L. pron. Quir. Santr... – IIIIvir quater, aedilis, censor ter, d[eae] Cer[eris] sac[erdos], augur, pontifex, principalis curiae, omnibus honoribus in re publica sua functus; perhaps the same as 3*; fake inscription
CIL II 131*

6* P. Volumnius P. f. M. n. Quir. Senecio – IIIIvir; fake inscription
CIL II 502c*

7* Q. Fannius Q. f. Q. n. Tuber – IIIIvir; fake inscription
CIL II 502d*

8* C. Fonteius C. f. Calp. Nothus – aug[ur], IIIIvir; fake inscription
CIL II 502*i**

Corduba

9* Cn. Atrius Flaccus and Cn. Pomp. Flaccus – IIvir quinc.; fake inscription
CIL II 199*

10* [M. Sem]pro[nius M. f. B]ibu[lus] – [IIvir] is restored by the editor but is
wholly conjectural.
F. Fita *BRAH* 56 (1910) 142; *PB* 288

Hispalis

11* Sex. Iulius Sex. f. Quir. Possessor – praef. coh. III Gallor., praepositus
numeri Syrorum sagittariorum, item alae I Hispanorum, curator civitatis
Romulensium m[un.] Arvensium, tribunus militum leg. XII Fulminatae,
curator coloniae Arcensium, adlectus in decurias ab imp. Antonino et Vero
Augg., adiutor Ulpii Saturnini praef[ecti] annon[ae]
Hübner, Dessau, Vives, Thouvenot, and Ganghoffer all thought this text
referred to a curator of Hispalis (Romula) and Arva. *AE* 1965 corrects the
reading to 'curatori civitatis Romulensium Malvensium,' i.e., Romula
Malva in Dacia, where this same curator is attested as a cavalry
commander. Although a genuine curator, he is not a magistrate in Spain.
CIL II 1180 = *ILS* 1403 = *ILER* 1294 = *AE* 1965, 237; Thouvenot *Essai*² 221 n
2; R. Ganghoffer *L'évolution des institutions municipales en Occident et
en Orient* (Paris 1963) 157 n 11

Iliberris

12* M. Valerius L. f. Dexter – IIIIvir quinquen[nalis]; fake inscription
CIL II 183*

Illiturgi

13* M. Valerius Flaccus – IIvir; fake inscription
CIL II 194*

Ilurco

14* P. Aelius Falanus – aedile, IIvir, praefectus C. Caesaris, pontifex sacrorum,
flamen divi Augusti; fake inscription
IL Granada 115

Marchena (ancient name unknown)

15* T. Marcellinus T. f. – ex ordine decurion[um] Marciae coloniae, omnibus
honoribus in re publica sua functus; fake inscription
   CIL II 135*

Osset

16* M. Tullius M. f. Spurina – e[ques] R[omanus], IIvir atque pontifex; fake
inscription
   CIL II 113*

Sacili

17* Anonymus – IIvir
   In this inscription, 'IIvir' is a false reading for 'terr[itoriorum]'; therefore
   no magistrate is involved.
   CIL II 2349 = *ILER* 6344

Sanlúcar la Mayor (ancient name unknown)

18* L. Furin[ius] L. f. Pesulan[us] – IIvir; fake inscription
   CIL II 120*
19* ... Crispini f. Aelianus – IIvir Sing[iliae Barbae?]; fake inscription
   CIL II 501*

2 LUSITANIA

Ebora

20* ... Voconius L. f. Quir. Paullus – aed., q., IIvir sexiens, flam. Romae
divorum et Augg., praef. coh. I Lusit. et coh. I Vettonum, centurio leg. III
Italic.
   This text has been claimed as genuine by Birley and Galsterer. However,
   Hübner has good reason to suspect this inscription to be one of numerous
   forgeries perpetrated by the notorious André de Resende as a means of
   magnifying the importance of ancient Ebora (cf P.O. Spann *TAPA* 111
   [1981] 229–32), and there is for the moment no good reason to question
   Hübner's verdict. The *cursus* appears to have been copied from *CIL* II 4192
   and 4201 (Tarraco), thus presenting a verisimilitude which duped Birley
   and Galsterer into accepting it as genuine.
   CIL II 18*; E. Birley *Roman Britain and the Roman Army* (Kendal 1953)
   152 n 34; Galsterer *Untersuchungen* 56 n 58

Eburobrittium

21* Anonymi – decuriones; fake inscription
CIL II 38*

Emerita Augusta

22* [... Terenti]us L. f. Pap. [Rufinus? ...] Ter.
In this inscription, Hübner suggested reading '[IIvir] ter,' but later
recanted. Other proposals include Mommsen's '[pa]ter' and Hirschfeld's
'[Em]er[itensis]' or '[In]ter[amniensis],' none of which is entirely
convincing. Kubitschek somehow confused this inscription with *CIL* II 515,
thinking that 'Ter.' in that inscription required emendation. But the
reading there is secure, and 'Ter.' is patently 'Ter[etina tribu].' Forni has
lately revived the '[IIvir] ter' suggestion, having apparently failed to notice
Hübner's subsequent retraction.
CIL II 512 and p 820 = *ILER* 5220 = G. Forni in *Augusta Emerita* (Madrid
1976) 34 no. 16; W. Kubitschek *Zur Geschichte von Städten des römische
Kaiserreiches* (Wien 1916) 6–7

Ossonoba

23* L. Quintilius Galio – IIvir viarum curandarum; fake inscription
CIL II 1*

Turgalium

24* L. Fabius C. f. Terullus – IIvir; faked from *CIL* II 741
CIL II 69*
25* Iunius – aed[ilis], IIvir c.i.; found at Turgalium
Whether the initials stand for 'clarissimus iuvenis' or 'coloniae Iuliae,' the
inscription is very suspect. Hübner (in *CIL*) comments, 'Titulum loco
indicato extitisse non nego, textum vero totum fictum esse apparet.' The
inscription should therefore have been relegated to Hübner's section of
forgeries.
CIL II 5276 = *ILER* 764 = *CPIL* 555

3 TARRACONENSIS

Asturica Augusta

26* C. Pacatus and Flavius Proculus – mag[istri]
Hübner, followed by Reid, sees these men as magistrates, presumably
because they act on behalf of the *res publica*. However, it is more

probable, in view of their lack of specific magistracies and the fact that they are making a dedication to the indigenous god Vagodonnaegus, that these are officials of a local religious college.

CIL II 2636 = ILER 947 = F. Diego Santos *Inscripciones romanas de la provincia de León* (León 1986) 63; J.B. Reid *The Municipalities of the Roman Empire* (Cambridge 1913) 236; Pastor *Los Astures* 172

Barcino

27* C. Pub[licius] Mellius – IIIIvir; fake inscription, perhaps influenced by CIL II 4497 and 4527 which name C. Publicius Melissus, sevir at the same city.
CIL II 415*

28* Anonymus – aedil[is]. Hübner reads ' ...MAXIM. AEDIL. APV...' Mariner shows that the correct reading is 'MAXIMAE DILABV[NTUR]'; therefore an aedile is not involved.
CIL II 4533; S. Mariner Bigorra *Ampurias* 28 (1966) 126 = IRB 72

Bilbilis

29* M. Sempronius Tiber[ianus] C. f. – IIvir; fake inscription
CIL II 261*

Calagurris

30* M. Antonius – IIvir
This supposed name is actually a misreading for Q. Antonius (512)
A. Delgado *Nuevo método de clasificación de las medallas autónomas de España* III (Sevilla 1876) 59 and pl CVI no. 22 = Heiss *Monnaies* 165 and pl xv no. 14; cf VM vol I p CXXXVIII

31* L. Feni[us] – IIvir; probably a misreading for 'L. Fabi[us]' (513)
Heiss *Monnaies* pl XVI, 20 = VM 158:1

Castulo

32* Q. Cornelius Q. Vetulus – IIvir bis, flamen Romae et Aug.; faked from CIL II 3350
CIL II 338*

33* Cn. Atinius Cn. f. Palatina Varro – IIvir et flamen Aug.; fake inscription
CIL II 342*

34* M. Atrius M. f. Gal. Chrestinus – omnibus honoribus functus; fake inscription
CIL II 340*

35* L. Atinius Cn. f. Cn. n. Caius – IIvir q.; fake inscription
CIL II 343*

Cieza (ancient name unknown)

36 L. Barb. and M. Clarus – IIvir of the Catinenses; fake inscription
CIL II 357*

Clunia

37* C. Arr[ius], T. Cael[ius], P[ompeius] Rest[itutus], C. Cael[ius] Caud[inus] –
IIIIvir
This supposed coin legend is a misreading of VM 163:3 = Gil 1841
A. Delgado *Nuevo método de clasificación de las medallas autónomas de
España* III (Sevilla 1876) 96 no. 8 = Heiss *Monnaies* 230 no. 6a = VM vol
IV p 111, cf VM vol I p XL

Ercavica

38* Aelius ...ctalis and anonymous – IIviri
A recent rereading by Alföldy suggests that this inscription mentions no
magistrates.
CIL II 3167 = *ILER* 6036 = A. Rodríguez Colmenero *Lucentum* I (1982) 231
no. 79; *CIC* 112; G. Alföldy *Römisches Städtewesen auf der
neukastilischen Hochebene* (Heidelberg 1987) 70–4

Laminium

39* L. Terentius Cn. Pomp. f. Pap. Bassinus – quaestor quinquennalis, aedilis
primus, flamen perpetuus, patronus; fake inscription
CIL II 310*

Libisosa

40* L. Mitidius L. f. Pal. Capito – eques publicus Romanus, curator, adlectus in
ordinem decurionum, VIvir Aug., IIvir iuredicundo, patronus; fake
inscription
CIL II 313a*

Mentesa Bastitanorum

41* Anonymus – IIIIvir
His title should be restored as [II]IIIIvir, (i.e., *sevir*), since the inscription
is a dedication by Imperial freedmen and is unlikely to involve a
magistrate.
CIL II 3380; Galsterer *Untersuchungen* 71

Saguntum

42* C. Gavius C. f. Tullus – IIvir; fake inscription
CIL II 375*

43* L. Laelius L. f. Vopiscus – praefectus fabrum, IIIIvir quinquennalis; fake inscription
CIL II 379*

Tarraco

44* Anonymus – IIIVI... [vixit a]nn. xv...
García y Bellido proposed that this was a duovir (reading 'IIvi[r]'), but this proposal seems unlikely in view of the man's young age at death (maximum 'xv[IIII]'). There are rare instances of teenagers becoming decurions or even aediles (**266, 442, 446**), but never duovirs.
CIL II 4086 = *RIT* 44; A. García y Bellido *Religions orientales dans l'Espagne romaine* (Leiden 1967) no. 21

Tobarra (ancient name unknown)

45* P. Iunius Cassius and C. Valerius Felix – IIviri; fake inscription
CIL II 359*

Toletum

46* Q. Celtisius Q. f. Ambustus – IIvir, Endobell[ici] sacerdos; fake inscription, perhaps inspired by **926**
CIL II **286***

47* A. Mumio Q. Cinii f. – IIvir quinquennalis; fake inscription
CIL II 288*

48* C. Pontius Ael. Ponti f. Furi Asclepiodotus – q[uaestor], aedilis, cos., flamen provinciae Carpetanorum perpetuus; patron of a *res publica* Montensis or Mentensis; fake inscription, found near Toledo
CIL II 292*

Triunchenses

49* C. Lucillius and T. Manlius Cotta – IIviri; fake inscription
CIL II 300*

Vicus Ausetanorum (name uncertain)

50* Sex. Numisius Sex. f. – decurio; fake inscription
CIL II 423*

Vivatia

51* P. Manlius P. [vel Q.] M[i]nuci[ani f.?] Torquatus [vel For(tun)atus] – IIvir; fake inscription

CIL II 349* = C.M. del Rivero *El lapidario del Museo Arqueológico Nacional* (Madrid 1933) no. 342

Indexes

Maps

INDEX OF NAMES

Magistrates' names are arranged alphabetically by *nomen gentilicium* (where known), then by *cognomen*, then (if necessary) by *praenomen* and filiation. Names with fragmentary beginnings will be found at the end. Numbers refer to entries in the Catalogue.

INDEX OF MAGISTRACIES

All numbers refer to Catalogue entries. A question mark after the number indicates a doubtful mention of the magistracy. A letter 'c' after the number indicates a collective citation, e.g., legati.

aedilicia ornamenta **900**
aedilicia potestas **81, 98, 103**
aedilicii honores **434, 445, 677, 678, 899, 916, 919**
aedilicium ius **676**
aedilicius **443**C, **799**
aedilicius honor **978**
aedilis **5, 11, 22, 23, 25?, 26?, 27, 28, 52, 53, 54, 72, 80, 100, 105, 107, 109?, 111, 136, 147, 148?, 155, 158, 171, 172, 174?, 211, 212, 217, 218, 219, 220, 221, 232, 247, 253, 258, 260, 261, 263, 272, 275, 278, 279, 283, 306, 307, 316, 322, 332, 336?, 340, 343?, 344, 345?, 357, 362, 363, 366, 373, 375, 376, 377, 382, 395, 396, 405, 409, 410, 419, 421, 422, 423, 424, 425, 426, 427, 428, 429?, 430, 431, 432, 433, 435, 437, 442, 446, 504, 509, 510, 537, 538, 553, 571, 578, 580, 581, 582, 614, 615, 616, 617, 626, 627, 628, 629, 632, 633, 650, 651, 652, 653, 654, 655,**
684, 721, 722, 723, 725, 726, 727, 737, 742, 743, 744, 745, 759, 760, 762, 763?, 765, 766, 771, 796, 797, 798, 800, 801, 827, 828, 829, 836, 844, 845, 846, 855, 856, 857, 858, 859, 860, 862, 863, 865, 866, 867, 868, 869, 870, 871, 872, 873, 874, 882, 887, 896, 897, 898, 903, 904, 905, 907, 909, 910, 912, 943, 944, 945, 946, 947, 948, 956, 957, 977
aedilis designatus **264?, 374**

censor **55, 56, 57**
curator **91?, 110, 143, 262, 295, 298**
curator annonae **280, 973?, 974?**
curator Baetis **218?**
curator Capitoli **910**
curator rei publicae **151, 152, 153, 267, 320, 349, 921**
curator templi **906**

decemvir **71, 776?**
decemvir maximus **234, 271**

GENERAL INDEX

This index is confined to names and topics discussed in the introductory chapters. Persons, magistracies, places, and concepts discussed in the Catalogue can be found by consulting, respectively, the Index of Names, the Index of Magistracies, the alphabetical listing of cities within the Catalogue, and the boldface Catalogue references provided in the introductory chapters, tables, and notes.

For ease of identification, Spanish city-names are followed in parentheses by the letter B, L, or T, signifying Baetica, Lusitania, or Tarraconensis.

Key to Map 1

Conventus Astigitanus
Anticaria 1
Astigi 2
Aurgi 3
Batora (unidentified)
Cisimbrium 4
Igabrum 5
Iliberris 6
Ilipula Laus (unidentified)
Iliturgicola 7
Ilurco 8
Ipolcobulcola 9
Ipsca 10
Itucci (unidentified)
Osqua 11
Ostippo 12
Sabora 13
Singilia Barba 14
Tucci 15
Ucubi 16
Ulia 17
Ulisi 18
Urgavo 19
Urso 20

Conventus Cordubensis
Arsa (unidentified)
Baxo (unidentified)
Bujalance 21
Corduba 22
Epora 23
Isturgi 24
Iulipa 25
Mellaria 26
Obulco 27
Onuba (unidentified)
Sacili 28
Torre de Albolafia 29
Ugia (unidentified)

Conventus Gaditanus
Abdera 30

Arcilacis 31
Asido 32
Baelo 33
Barbesula 34
Carissa Aurelia 35
Carteia 36
Cartima 37
Ceret 38
Gades 39
Iluro 40
Iptuci 41
Lacilbula 42
Lacippo 43
Lascuta 44
Malaca 45
Oba 46
Saepo 47
Vesci (unidentified)

Conventus Hispalensis
Acinipo 48
Arunda 49
Arva 50
Axati 51
Callenses Aeneanici 52
Canan[i]a 53
Carmo 54
Hispalis 55
Ilipa 56
Ilipula 57
Italica 58
Lucurgentum 59
Montemolín 60
Munigua 61
Naeva 62
Osset 63
Salpensa 64
Sanlúcar la Mayor 65
Segida (unidentified)
Siarum 66
Ugultuniacum 67
Villafranca de los Barros 68

MAP 1 Baetica

Key to Map 2

Conventus Emeritensis
Caesarobriga 1
Capera 2
Caurium 3
Emerita Augusta 4
Metellinum 5
Norba 6

Conventus Pacensis
Ammaia 7
Aritium Vetus 8
Baesuri 9
Balsa 10
Mirobriga 11
Myrtilis 12
Ossonoba 13
Pax Iulia 14
Salacia 15

Conventus Scallabitanus
Bretiande 16
Brutobriga (unidentified)

Collippo 17
Conimbriga 18
Eburobrittium 19
Igaeditani 20
Olisipo 21

Conventus Asturum
Asturica Augusta 22
Bergidum Flavium 23
Brigaecium 24
Lancia 25
Zoelae 26

Conventus Bracaraugustanus
Aquae Flaviae 27
Avobriga (unidentified)
Bracara Augusta 28
Coelerni 29
Limici 30

Conventus Lucensis
Lougei (unidentified; possibly same as 31)
Lucus Augusti 31

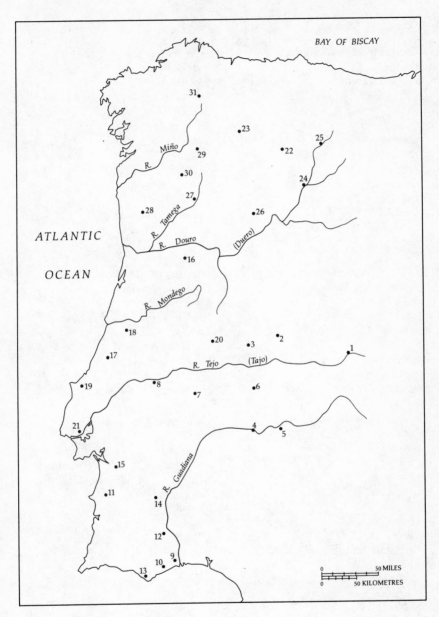

MAP 2 Lusitania and Northwestern Tarraconensis

Key to Map 3

Conventus Caesaraugustanus
Bilbilis 1
Caesaraugusta 2
Calagurris 3
Celsa 4
Complutum 5
Contrebia Balaisca 6
Damania (unidentified)
Ercavica 7
Grallia (unidentified)
Iacca 8
Ilerda 9
Labitolosa 10
Luzaga 11
Osca 12
Osicerda (unidentified)
Pompaelo 13
Sofuentes 14
Tritium Magallum 15
Turiaso 16

Conventus Carthaginiensis
Alaba (unidentified)
Alcalá 17
Archena 18
Attaccum (unidentified)
Baria 19
Bocchoris 20
Carthago Nova 21
Castulo 22
Consabura 23
Dianium 24
Ebusus 25
Gandía 26
Guiuntum (unidentified)
Ilici 27
Libisosa 28
Lucentum 29
Mago 30
Murcia 31
Palma 32
Peñalba de Villastar 33

Pollentia 34
Rubielos 35
Saetabis 36
Salaria 37
Segobriga 38
Toletum 39
Tutugi 40
Valeria 41
Vergilia 42
Villajoyosa 43

Conventus Cluniensis
Amallobriga (unidentified)
Cauca 44
Clunia 45
Intercatia (unidentified)
Lara de los Infantes 46
Maggava (unidentified)
Numantia 47
Palantia 48
Roura (unidentified)
Segontia 49
Termes 50
Uxama 51

Conventus Tarraconensis
Aeso 52
Alcora 53
Aquae Calidae? (Caldes de Montbui) 54
Aquae Calidae (Caldes de Malavella) 55
Baetulo 56
Barcino 57
Dertosa 58
Egara 59
Emporiae 60
Gerunda 61
Iluro 62
Liria 63
Mascarell 64
Saguntum 65
Sigarra 66
Tarraco 67
Valentia 68

BAY OF BISCAY

BALEARIC ISLANDS

MEDITERRANEAN

SEA

0   50   100 MILES

0   50   100 KILOMETRES

MAP 3 Eastern Tarraconensis

Phoenix Supplementary Volumes Series